Detroit Monographs in Musicology/Studies in Music, No. 17

Editor
J. *Bunker Clark*
University of Kansas

AMY FAY

America's Notable
Woman of Music

by

Margaret William McCarthy

HARMONIE PARK PRESS • *MICHIGAN* • *1995*

Frontispiece:

Amy Fay, ca. 1879.
Courtesy of Peirce Edition Project.
Indiana University-Purdue University at Indianapolis.

Copyright 1995 by Harmonie Park Press

Printed and bound in the United States of America
Published by
Harmonie Park Press
23630 Pinewood
Warren, Michigan 48091

Editor, J. Bunker Clark
Typographer, Colleen McRorie

Library of Congress Cataloging-in-Publication Data

McCarthy, Margaret William, 1931-
    Amy Fay : America's notable woman of music / by Margaret William
McCarthy.
        p.   cm. — (Detroit monographs in musicology/Studies in music
; no. 17)
    Includes bibliographical references (p.   ) and index.
    ISBN 0-89990-074-7
    1. Fay, Amy, 1844-1928.   2. Pianists—United States—Biography.
I. Series.
ML417.F286M43   1995
786.2'092—dc20
[B]

95-10196

*The music stops, and yet it echoes on
in sweet refrains . . .
For every joy that passes,
something beautiful remains.*

In loving memory of

*S. Viterbo McCarthy
(1920-94)*

*Clare McCarthy Fenton
(1957-94)*

*William J. McCarthy
(1969-95)*

Contents

PART 1

Scenes from Childhood

PART 2

Music Study in Germany

PART 3

Celebrity

PART 4

The Windy City

PART 5

New York City

APPENDICES

Illustrations

Preface

To bring forth the truth of a person's life is a demanding task, not unlike that of the composer who, while in the process of shaping and developing a musical theme, presents it under varying conditions which in turn will bring to the sonic surface differing aspects of its character. As the theme flows toward the final cadence, the listener experiences a sense of surprise and wonder at having been allowed to observe its various transformations and to explore the depths and richness of its character.

Writing this story has required decisions similar to those facing the composer. As one of America's notable women, Amy Fay helped shape the budding cultural life of the nation at the close of the nineteenth century and the beginning of the twentieth. A performer, educator, lecturer, writer, and clubwoman, she loomed as an important presence in the musical life of the nation in one of its formative stages. At age twenty-five she went to Europe for music study and remained there for six years, during which time she studied with the leading musical figures of the day, including the reigning idol of the musical world, Franz Liszt. Having vowed at age twenty-seven never to marry or even do housework if she could help it, she achieved renown upon her return home as the author of the popular musical memoir *Music-Study in Germany*, which gained a reputation as "the book of the age." In addition she achieved national acclaim as a musical activist in the three cities where she lived and worked: Cambridge, Chicago, and New York. By the end of her life she had evolved into a progressive woman consumed with a desire to advance women in the world of music and in the larger society.

Themes of success and failure, sickness and health, continuity and discontinuity played throughout her life. As they unfolded they passed through changing psychological landscapes that suggest shifting tonal contexts of a musical score comprised of various motives that develop, overlap, and interweave. Amy Fay's unconventional life arouses the interest of those searching for insight and understanding about women's lives. How did her family influence and contact shape her life? What were her ambitions as a woman in an overwhelmingly male profession, and how did she work to achieve them? What, if any, emotional pain did she suffer as a consequence of her choices? Did she regret any of these? If so, how did she cope? What values sustained her? What inner music she was hearing?

Fortunately, Amy Fay's voluminous correspondence, professional writings, and programs, as well as testimony of contemporaries and scholars, make it possible to answer many of these questions. Yet in tracking the development of her thought regarding such important issues as marriage or career, discrimination in the workplace, and equal pay for equal work, much remains speculative. I have had to make decisions about the utilization of these sources to offer, in the best way possible, insight into the person of Amy Fay and her position and influence on American musical life.

Since Amy Fay's life gives credence to much present-day thinking about women's lives, it seems natural to tell her story within the framework of twentieth-century methodology concerning women and their experiences. Three aspects of contemporary feminist thought offer appropriate investigative tools for exploring Amy Fay's life: the theory of affiliation, the theory of the clubwoman as feminist, and the theory of women's illnesses in the nineteenth century. Hence, these become underlaying currents in Amy Fay's story, providing the avenues of inquiry through which her life is approached.

Twentieth-century writers such as Jean Baker Miller and Ruthellen Josselsen have noted the prominence of affiliation in women's development—that is, how, as Miller notes, they "stay with, build on and develop in a context of attachment and affiliation with others," often to the point of destruction of their own identity.[1] In 1980 musicologist Elizabeth Wood pointed out the applicability of the theory of affiliation to the lives of musical women, noting that affiliation has been central in their lives, and that musical women of achievement typically have enjoyed advantages of birth into an educated musical family and a degree of financial security—conditions which have helped them acquire technical training and prepared them to enter professional networks that might otherwise not have been possible. Wood notes that female support systems, especially affiliations with kin, friends, and mentors, have been crucial not merely for emotional interaction but also for formal mentoring and career shaping.[2]

As a member of a prominent New England family, Amy Fay had the advantage of strong family ties, which provided her with relatively easy access to opportunities denied other women. Although her family was thrown into temporary consternation as a consequence of her mother's death when Amy was only twelve, throughout her life she knew what it was like to experience the support of a family with extended lineage, whether in the form of an older sister who would become her surrogate mother or an uncle who would help underwrite most of the expenses for her music study in Germany.

Without question, the relationship Amy Fay forged with her older sister Melusina (Zina) was the most significant relationship of her life. It resembled the counterpoint in a musical score: at varying times Zina was in turn sister, mother, friend, and mentor to Amy. With the passage of time their interaction, interdependency, and emotional bonding intensified. The psychic union between the two sisters sang gently and quietly throughout their lives.

Amy Fay's most important musical alliance was the one forged with Franz Liszt, an association made possible to a great extent through family connections. It brought her international acclaim, especially following the publication in 1881 of *Music-Study in*

---

[1] Jean Baker Miller, "Toward a New Psychology of Women," in *Women's Spirituality: Resources for Christian Development*, ed. Joann Wolski Conn (New York: Paulist Press, 1986), 107.

[2] Elizabeth Wood, "Women in Music: A Review Essay," *Signs* 6, no. 2 (winter 1980): 293.

Germany, in which Liszt figured so prominently. Liszt remained devoted to his famous American student until his death in 1886. Yet as Amy Fay's life played itself out in the public arena, the advantages of her earlier affiliations reached their limits and were not always helpful in seeing her through the professional phase of her life.

Amy Fay's activities as a clubwoman represent a second way in which her life typifies the late nineteenth-century bourgeois new woman. Like her contemporaries, she found in clubs an appropriate outlet for her gifts, talents, and energies, as well as a forum for establishing bonds of sisterhood with other like-minded women. In league with her sisters Rose Fay Thomas and Melusina Fay Peirce, she was at the forefront of the nation's music club activity, and these involvements led her to assume and articulate a more feminist posture in her later years. While living in Chicago she helped found an important organization for women, the Amateur Club, and while living in New York she held the presidency of the Women's Philharmonic Society of New York for over a decade. Both literally and metaphorically, music clubs became replacement affiliations for Amy Fay, providing her with a sisterhood of genetic and non-family members and affiliative support that enabled her to function as a professional. Amy Fay's life also exemplifies the theory of women and nervous disease articulated by such scholars as Jean Baker Miller, Carroll Smith-Rosenberg, and Jean Strouse. Like so many nineteenth-century women of intelligence and sensitivity, Amy Fay was vulnerable to "nerves" or "nervousness." The condition which in some circumstances led to nervous illness in her contemporaries—namely, the severing of affiliative ties—was present in her own life.

In 1870-71 Amy Fay experienced two losses—the death of a former suitor, Benjamin Mills Peirce, and the death of her major professor, Carl Tausig. These two events, in bringing to closure both a romantic and a professional affiliation, triggered a nervousness that threatened to undo all the progress she had made in Europe under her renowned teachers. Because her difficulties with nerves cast such a shadow over her student years abroad and her early professional years, they comprise the third major theme of this biography.

In many ways the symphonic poem provides a useful metaphor for Amy Fay's life. As a new and innovative musical form invented by her illustrious teacher Franz Liszt, it was considered an ideal representation of the Romantic impulse to break away from conventional ways of doing things and to search out new means of artistic expression more in keeping with the revolutionary temper of the time. In its merging of the abstract and the representational, it fused the two distinct artistic modes of music and poetry and broke through existing musical barriers.

Amy Fay, too, defied tradition to challenge existing social barriers. As a performer and teacher, as an organizer on behalf of musical women, and as a writer about music and musicians of her time, she made significant contributions to American musical life.

The biography is a follow-up to five other publications I have written on my favorite subject: "Amy Fay: The American Years" (*American Music*, 1985), *More Letters of Amy Fay: The American Years, 1879-1916* (this publisher, 1986), "Amy Fay" (*New Grove Dictionary of American Music*, 1986), "Amy Fay's Reunions with Franz Liszt" (*Journal of the American Liszt Society*, 1988), and "Feminist Theory in Practice in the Life of Amy Fay" (*International League of Women Composers Journal*, 1991). The idea for the title comes from the acclaimed biographical dictionary *Notable American Women: A Biographical Dictionary*, published in 1971 under the editorial direction of Janice James and Paul Boyers. Since this book attempts to develop and expand upon much of the scholarly information about Amy Fay first presented in that distinguished publication, it seemed appropriate to draw upon its title for the title of this book.

To be sure, Amy Fay has received mention in earlier histories of music in the United States and in histories of piano pedagogy. Such works as H. Wiley Hitchcock's *Music in the United States: A Historical Introduction* (1988), Harold Schonberg's *The Great Pianists* (1987), Robert Gerig's *Famous Pianists and Their Technique* (1974), and Robert Andres's master's thesis and doctoral dissertation on the life and career of Frederic Horace Clark (1992, 1993) mention Fay, either in connection with her relationship with and her observations of Liszt, as an exponent and advocate of the Deppe method of piano playing, or as an accurate observer of musical life in Germany in the latter part of the nineteenth century. (*Living with Liszt: From the Diary of Carl Lachmund, an American Pupil of Liszt, 1882-1884* appeared too late for my use.) In their book *Women Making Music* (1986), Jane Bowers and Judith Tick view Amy Fay principally as a renowned pianist and teacher. In her treatise *Unsung: A History of Women in American Music* (1980), Christine Ammer, while acknowledging Amy Fay's role as a pianist, teacher, and clubwoman, claims that she was important principally because of *Music-Study in Germany*. The present book is the first full-length study of Amy Fay, attempting to place her life and career in the context of feminist theory. Its publication, along with Walter S. Jenkins's *The Remarkable Mrs. Beach, American Composer* (this series, no. 13, 1994) and Adrienne Fried Block's forthcoming biographical study of Fay's contemporary and compatriot Amy Cheney Beach (Oxford University Press), should help to fill the gaps in biographies of earlier American musical women.

Acknowledgments

There are many persons who have assisted in the completion of this book. The staff of libraries at home and abroad have been of important assistance to me as I have gone about my research. I extend special thanks to Elizabeth Keenan and the staff of the Regis College Library—past and present—especially Lily Farkas, William Gallup, Joanna O'Keefe, Sister Eleanor Deady, Armine Bagdasarian, Renate Olsen, Susan Harris, Mary Behrle, Andrea Shaw, and Ellen Smith. I am grateful to Eva Mosely and the staff of the Schlesinger Library at Radcliffe College for their cooperation and helpful advice. I appreciate as well the kindness and helpfulness of the staffs of the St. Albans Public Library in St. Albans, Vermont, the Music Library of the Boston Public Library, the New York Public Library at Lincoln Center, the Chicago Public Library, the Vermont Historical Society, and the Chicago Historical Society. I am grateful to Diana Haskell of the Newberry Library Manuscript Division for her enthusiastic support of the Fay project, to Kenneth Ketner of the Institute of Pragmaticism at Texas Tech University for his unfailing cooperation in my search for Fay family materials, to the staff of the Peirce Edition Project, Indiana University-Purdue University at Indianapolis, and to Gillian Anderson of the Music Division of the Library of Congress for her helpfulness during my 1986 visit to Washington, D.C. I appreciate the assistance of William C. Parsons (Music Division, Library of Congress), James Heintze (American University), and of Martin J. Manning (Library of Commerce). I owe a debt of gratitude to Christa Petrak of the public relations division of the Central Offices of the Stadtbibliothek in Weimar for giving me a wonderful taste of Liszt's years in that city and for extending gestures of friendship and interest since our meeting in 1986. I am thankful to the friendly staff of the Goethe-Schiller Archives at Weimar, to Rudolph Elvers of the Staatsbibliothek in Berlin, and to Genevieve Geoffray of the Mozarteum in Salzburg.

I wish to acknowledge the Music Critics Association Fellowships granted me in the summers of 1973 and 1974, the NEH Summer Seminar grant awarded me in 1975 and the assistance of its director, William S. Newman, whose example as a scholar remains an inspiration. I appreciate the NEH Travel-to-Collections Grant awarded me in the summer of 1987 and the Radcliffe Research Support Awards of 1983 and 1987.

I treasure the assistance and interest of my former research assistant Carole-Terese Naser for transcribing the Fay correspondence and for sharing her invaluable insights with me. I am grateful to Nancy Reich, Floyd Barbour, Adrienne Fried Block, Carol Neuls-Bates, Dorothy Bales, and to Sisters Marian Batho, Ann Ryan, and Camella Gambale for their moral support of my work through the years. My appreciation also goes to others who have read my manuscript in its various stages: Herb Burtis, Sister Dorothy McKenzie, Jeannie Pool, Dr. Camille Roman, Harold C. Schonberg, Jean Walden, Nancy Williams, and Elizabeth Wood. I am thankful to my colleague Steven Belcher of the Regis College art department, to Yolanda Rivas, to Claire Ferguson, to my former student assistant Megan McCarthy and to my present student assistant Amy K. Clines, to Fine Arts staff member Brenda Quinn and faculty secretaries Claire Gorman and Janice Lattuca, each of whom assisted me immeasurably in the preparation of the final document. I also acknowledge with gratitude the help of Rosemary Noon, director of the Regis College Fine Arts Center, for facilitating the creation of a supportive work environment where one can remain focused and concentrated. A special note of thanks goes to my Chicago cousin Betty McCarthy O'Conor, her late husband John, and three of their wonderful children, Tara, Tim, and Ann, who opened their hearts and home to me during my 1986 visit to the research libraries of Chicago. I appreciate the sharing of private family papers of Gregory S. Harris, Amy Fay's great-grand-nephew, and Paul Mitarachi, her grand-nephew-in-law. I value the suggestions given me in 1986 by Richard Dyer to publish some of the fugitive writings of Amy Fay, some of which appear in the Appendix.

I am grateful to the members of my writer's group at Regis College: Drs. Joan Hallissey, Pamela Menke, Jane Roman, Susan Nessen, and especially Sister Catherine Meade, who served as animator for a group whose insights and recommendations proved invaluable to me. Conversations with colleagues at Regis College were constructive, and I should like to thank Sisters Marie de Sales Dinneen, Rosenda Gill, Juan Mahan, Cecilia Agnes Mulrennan, Mary Oates, and Jeanne d'Arc O'Hare, as well as Sara Hoff, Wanda Paik, Anne Walsh, and Dr. Sheila Prichard. I am grateful to Elaine Gorzelski of Harmonie Park Press for her encouragement in the publication of the book and to typesetter Colleen McRorie for her careful work and helpful directives. I extend special thanks to J. Bunker Clark, who has edited the manuscript with care and precision and has given valuable suggestions and recommendations throughout the long process from the first reading to the final edition. I offer appreciation also to the former president of Regis College, Sister Therese Higgins, for her ongoing support and encouragement of my work on Amy Fay. Finally, I extend my gratitude to Sister Sheila Megley, president of Regis College, for her backing of this project.

S. MARGARET WILLIAM MCCARTHY

Regis College
Weston, Massachusetts
May 1995

PART 1

Scenes from Childhood

Family Ties

As a member of the prominent Fay family of New England, one had certain privileges of class. Whether in the sphere of education, religion, or work, one was accustomed to "the best" that life could offer as measured by refined late nineteenth-century New England bourgeois standards. One's ancestors inevitably comprised persons who were among the first to arrive in this country. Most likely the men in the family claimed Harvard as their alma mater, while the females married cultured and influential men who founded orchestras, wrote books, became bishops, headed corporations, and made other singular contributions to the world in which they lived. The long line of family extended to national and international arenas; consequently, one could enjoy access to the primary players of the day. The clan might not always have immense financial assets, but it would always be rich in contacts that could make connections to the movers and shakers of the time.

In addition, the family would generate family histories and genealogical studies that would recall the accomplishments of its ancestors and accustom one to expect to achieve, to develop talents, and to make a difference in the world. As Amy Fay's younger brother Norman once put it, "heredity is the stock-in-trade of ruling families, and they take good care to keep straight records of their generations."[1] One of those records states that the story of the Fays is the "story of but one of those long lines of everyday kind of people of whom Lincoln once said 'God must have loved them, for he made so many of them,'" and goes on to declare that "the Fay family members have been among the reliable, faithful people who in every crisis of our history have proven the backbone of our nation's stability and who in everyday life have helped to make life worth living."[2] Membership in the Fay family carried with it certain privileges as well as certain expectations.

So it was with Amy Fay, born 21 May 1844 in Bayou Goula, Louisiana, the third daughter of Emily and Charles Fay. Family documents reveal that on both maternal and paternal sides her relatives were of distinguished background. Her mother, Emily Hopkins, was the eldest daughter of the Right Reverend John H. Hopkins, the first

---

[1] Charles Norman Fay, "Memoirs of Rose Fay Thomas" (unpublished paper, Library of Congress).

[2] George H. Johnson, *One Branch of the Family Tree* (Columbus, Ohio: Champlin Press, 1913), 24.

Episcopal bishop of Vermont, dubbed "the Bish" by family descendants. Bishop Hopkins was a strong male figure for his daughter Emily and was handsome, versatile, and successful, although not financially.[3] He was, in the words of a great grandniece, "as close to God as you could get in America at the time, even if only by apostolic succession, and so his family considered him."[4] The Bishop intended his sons would be clergymen, and his daughters the wives of clergymen.[5] The Bishop's wife, Melusina, appreciated her brilliant, versatile, industrious, and for some time debt-ridden husband and helped with the education of their ten surviving children in the home. Two of their sons became well known musicians—Charles Jerome Hopkins, composer and keyboard performer and John Hopkins as the composer of the famous Christmas carol "We Three Kings of Orient Are."

Amy's father, the Reverend Charles Fay, was the son of Judge Samuel Prescott Phillips Fay of Cambridge, Massachusetts, an overseer of Harvard University and a mainstay of Christ Church in Cambridge. Judge Fay's Cambridge home, now an administration building at Radcliffe College, was the site where the Harvard alma mater "Fair Harvard" was written in 1836 by Dr. Samuel Gilman, Judge Fay's brother-in-law. Judge Fay's wife was Harriet Howard, daughter of Samuel Howard, a Boston shipwright and a participant in the famous Boston Tea Party, whose ancestry reputedly ran to Anne Hutchinson, one of Boston's first women of independent intellect.

Offspring of families living in such a close-knit society eventually met. When in 1831 Emily's father, the Reverend John H. Hopkins, moved to Cambridge from Vermont in order to take up his new assignment as assistant rector of Trinity Church in Boston, he surely already had heard of Charles Fay, the dashing young Cambridge lawyer whose good looks, intelligence, and social graces had earned him popularity in Boston and Cambridge social circles. Charles Fay had graduated from Harvard in 1829, where he ranked second in an illustrious class that included the poet Oliver Wendell Holmes and the mathematician Benjamin Peirce. Reverend Hopkins lost no time in inviting the young man to his home. Hopkins himself had been a lawyer prior to his ordination into the ministry, and he sensed that he would identify in a particular way with the young Cambridge lawyer. He speculated as well that with some encouragement Fay, too, might be drawn to the ministry. Hopkins, whose favorite pastime was teaching divinity, offered to tutor Charles in the subject. Before long, Charles was a regular visitor to the Hopkins home, where in addition to advancing in his study of theology he met Hopkins's eldest daughter, the fourteen-year-old Charlotte Emily.

---

[3] Sylvia Wright Mitarachi, "Melusina Fay Peirce: Biography of a Feminist" (unpublished paper delivered at Radcliffe Institute, 20 March 1978), 6. In Fay Family Papers (hereafter referred to as FFP), Schlesinger Library, Radcliffe College. This collection includes 2.5 linear feet arranged in three series: 1. Amy Fay; 2. Amy Fay Stone; 3. Margaret Garrad (Stone) and Austin Tappan Wright. Part 1 consists of letters of Amy Fay to her family, especially her sister Melusina Fay Peirce. Included are most of the German letters collected and published by her sister Melusina as *Music-Study in Germany* (1881) as well as descriptions of concerts from this period and later. Part 2 comprises Sylvia Wright Mitarachi's material on her grand-aunt Melusina Fay Peirce, her notes for a book, and miscellaneous family papers. Part 3 contains photos and papers pertaining to the life and career of Amy Fay's actress niece Amy Faystone.

[4] Ibid., 2.

[5] Ibid., 3.

REVEREND CHARLES FAY (1808–88)

*Amy's father and son of Judge Samuel Prescott
Phillips Fay and Harriet Howard of Cambridge.
Practiced law and later entered
Episcopalian ministry, serving parishes in
Bayou Goula and New Orleans, Louisiana;
St. Albans, Vermont; and Marquette, Michigan.*

Courtesy of Peirce Edition Project.
Indiana University-Purdue University at Indianapolis.

SAMUEL FAY (1778–1856)

*Amy's grandfather, a prominent Cambridge judge
whose Cambridge home, Fay House, is now
the Admissions Building at Radcliffe College.*

Courtesy of Peirce Edition Project.
Indiana University-Purdue University at Indianapolis.

Even at a young age, Emily, as she was called, already gave the appearance of considerable maturity. She was intelligent, talented in art, music, and writing. She played the piano, organ, guitar, flute, and harp. Extremely religious like her father, she wrote homilies and poems. When her father sensed how drawn she was to the handsome Charles Fay, he decided to press for a match. Although he realized how unusually talented and devout his daughter was,[6] upon noting Emily's interest in Charles Fay he told her that she already knew enough for a woman and must discontinue her schooling.[7] At the same time, he assured Charles of his daughter's deep attachment to him. Consequently, Charles, though probably not in love with Emily, agreed to become engaged to her. On 5 September 1833, when only sixteen, she and the twenty-five-year-old Charles were married. Meanwhile, Charles, under the persuasive influence of Hopkins, left the law and entered the Episcopalian ministry.

Although Judge Fay objected vigorously to his son's decision to abandon the law, he and other family members did what they could to support the newlyweds. In time, such backing proved indispensable to the young couple. From the outset of their marriage life was arduous, especially for the fragile Emily who, in the course of her brief life of thirty-nine years, bore nine children and assisted her husband in his ministry. The couple's first three years of marriage were spent in Highgate, Vermont, where Charles ministered in the village church. Their first-born child, Alfred, died at the age of five months. In 1836 a daughter, Melusina (Zina), was born. That same year Charles Fay was called to serve as principal of a church school in Montpelier, Georgia. There, two more children were born: Herman in 1837 and Laura in 1841. Shortly thereafter, as Fay received a series of transfers in conjunction with his many ministerial assignments, the young family found it necessary to move from place to place in quick succession.

By the time Amy, the third of the surviving children, was born in 1844, the family had moved to Bayou Goula, Louisiana, where her father was sent to educate the daughters of the sugar plantation owners and minister to the poor planters' families. Amy was baptized Amelia, but called herself "Ammy," the name by which she came to be known.[8] When she was only three months old, her brother Herman died. Early in 1846, when Amy was two, the Fays, including ten-year-old Zina and five-year-old Laura, found themselves in transit once again, this time to New Orleans, where Charles had received an assignment to take charge of an Episcopalian parish. There, on 6 July 1846, Amy's sister Kate was born.

In New Orleans, Emily experienced two of the happiest years of her life. The warm climate, tropical flowers, and southern hospitality of the people proved a welcome contrast to the frigid reserve she had been accustomed to in Vermont society. Despite its other assets, however, New Orleans proved to be a disease-ridden city, and in turn the Fays were seriously affected by bouts with yellow fever, scarlet fever, measles, mumps, and whooping cough. As a consequence, Reverend Fay moved his growing family north to St. Albans, Vermont, where he became rector of St. Luke's Church. There three more children were born: Norman in 1848, Rose in 1852, and Lily in 1855.

---

[6] John H. Hopkins, *Autobiography in Verse, Dedicated to My Children* (Cambridge: Riverside Press, 1866).

[7] Mitarachi, 7.

[8] Madeline Smith, "Portraits of My Aunts," FFP.

Childhood

Back in the harsh Vermont climate, life was difficult, especially for Emily, who, with the birth of each new child, grew ever more fragile. The family home was a large brick house surrounded by eleven acres of land including an orchard, gardens, and a pasture. It was not large enough, however, and the Fays made yet another move to a new and larger property known as "Maple Shade," purchased for them by Judge Fay. A brook separated this house from a little red schoolhouse, where, to add to his modest church salary of eight hundred dollars per year, Charles Fay opened a private school. The students, for the most part children of friends or acquaintances of the Fays, lived in the Fay home. Most were boys of ten to fifteen years of age, but a few were girls. Each day upwards of twelve youngsters trooped to the little red schoolhouse, coming home for mid-day meal and supper, both prepared by Emily. Their days ended with study time followed by bed at nine o'clock.

This busy schedule left Emily and Charles Fay little time for each other or for their children, either as companions or as playmates. For Emily, life was especially difficult. She was caught up in a cycle of work and childbearing that would have exhausted a person far stronger than she. In addition to assisting her husband in running the school, administering the affairs of the parish church, and helping to write the weekly sermon to be delivered by her husband, she taught their children art, English, and music. Meanwhile, Charles ran the church services, the charity society, the Sunday school, and supervised the parish visiting; when he went to neighboring villages without churches, Emily filled in for him. Emily taught Sunday school, trained the choir, played the organ for all the services, organized work for the women's sewing circle of the town, and, since she was a successful practitioner of homeopathic medicine, provided medical services for her children and for anyone else in the neighborhood who called on her for care. As Norman later recalled:

> . . . she set up a case of Homeopathic medicine, pills and tinctures; and we children were brought up on them, dosed and nursed by her exclusively, through measles, scarlet fever, croup, whooping cough, and mumps; all of which I can recall in our childhood. Small pox was then prevalent, and vaccination very new; but she vaccinated us all, so that we all got off with a little chicken pox.[9]

The burden of such a demanding life took its toll on Emily and she grew increasingly more frail.

She and Charles could carry out their "parenting" duties only in conjunction with obligations in the school, the church, and the home. Seldom did the children see the

---

[9] Letter of Charles Norman Fay to Cousin Emily, 3 May 1930, FFP.

affable, fun-loving side of their father displayed in his earlier years of bachelorhood in Cambridge. Nor were they able to perceive their mother as anyone other than a stern disciplinarian who always had work in her hands but seldom a glance or a smile for them.

It is little wonder that in later life the Fay children had few tender memories of their parents. Kate once remarked that she had "no pleasant memories" of her mother,[10] while Norman once recalled poignantly that he "often envied children whose parents, in affluence and leisure, would share their joys and sorrows as ours could not."[11] He recorded only two warm memories of his mother—one of her going out horseback riding with his father, who loved horses and always had one or two in the barn. Norman recalled:

> I can see them still, riding away down the drive to the road, straight
> and slim, and at home in the saddle.[12]

Norman's other tender memory of his mother concerned his music lessons:

> . . . once, small sinner that I was, I was supposed to be practicing at the
> piano, but was really idling somewhere away from it, when suddenly
> I heard her coming. Knowing that she would have noticed the silence
> of my scales, and fearing a knitting needle across my knuckles—the
> standard punishment inaugurated by Aunt Amelia. . . . I hurried to
> the piano and put my head down on my arm on the keyboard, and
> made believe I had fallen asleep. When she came in, she raised me
> softly in her arms, kissed me very gently, laid me on a sofa, and went
> out, leaving me badly conscience bitten.[13]

Perhaps because she saw Zina as her mother figure, Amy's sole reference to her mother comes in a letter to Zina written 24 December 1859 from Rock Point, Vermont, where she and her sisters were visiting their Hopkins relatives. In describing the play periods of the four-year-old Lily (whom the family had begun to call Vallie) and her cousins Belle and Nellie Hopkins, Amy described the following incident:

> Belle said to Lily yesterday, "Vallie, did you know that your mother
> was my papa's sister?" Vallie replied in a decisive tone "But I *tell you*
> I haven't got any mother. . . ." "*No*" said Vallie; she evidently has not
> the remotest idea what the others mean by her Mama, and she seems
> annoyed when they ask questions about her. She is too young to
> understand as yet, but she will know when she grows older.[14]

---

10 Mitarachi, "Family About Family," FFP.

11 Letter of Charles Norman Fay to Cousin Emily, 3 May 1930, FFP.

12 Ibid.

13 Ibid.

14 Letter of Amy Fay to Zina, 24 December 1859, FFP.

KATE FAY STONE
(1846-1928)

Amy's younger sister at the age of
approximately 23.

ROSE FAY THOMAS
(1852-1929)

Amy's youngest sister who, at the age of 38,
married the famous conductor Theodore Thomas.

MELUSINA FAY PEIRCE
(1836-1923)

Amy's older feminist sister, who became Amy's
surrogate mother following the death of their
mother when Amy was twelve.

Courtesy of Peirce Edition Project.
Indiana University-Purdue University at Indianapolis.

Unlike her younger sister, at least Amy had clear memories of her mother, especially of music lessons under her instruction. Early in her music study, Amy had begun to show promise of excellence. Given all her studies, music most absorbed her. She did well in the study of Latin, Greek, German, French, and mathematics, but music was by far her favorite subject and the piano her preferred instrument. When her mother's health weakened—as it did with the birth of each new child—she frequently had to take to her bed, thus being required to monitor Amy's lesson from her couch. Often, when Amy was practicing on the piano, Emily, who was said to have perfect pitch, could be heard to call down from upstairs, "Amy, put your finger on 'G.'"[15] Eventually the sickly Emily enlisted the assistance of her older daughters Laura and Zina in teaching music to Amy and Kate.

When in 1856, at age thirty-nine, Emily Fay died of consumption, her children, especially the older ones, responded with emotional detachment. Emily's life of endless sickness, unrelieved toil, and years of childbearing had depleted her emotionally and made her too forbidding and distant to have been ardently loved by her children. Laura later wrote on the subject of her mother:

> [U]nending battle with poverty and ill health warped her spirit and made her more austere and arbitrary than she would naturally have been. And moreover, the strange, monastic discipline of her early education so moulded her views of life that it unfitted her for the common pleasures of society and shut her up in a bitter loneliness that only those who are more highly endowed and more sensitively constituted than their fellows could appreciate. No wonder that in the little book of poems she left behind, there should have been a little set of verses called, "Death is the One Bright Spot!"[16]

Emily's death, however, was no "bright spot" for Charles Fay who, in the wake of his wife's death, had to reorganize his life and that of his daughters and son. He placed his two youngest children, Rose and Lily, with family friends in Rochester while he assigned Zina the responsibility of running the household for Laura, Amy, Kate, Norman, and the other children registered in the school. Under Zina's watchful eye, Amy continued her study of music, sight-singing, and piano while her father supervised her other studies.

Cambridge

For the next few years, the entire family gathered only during holidays and vacations, when they visited Fay relatives in Cambridge, Massachusetts or Hopkins relatives in Rock Point, Vermont. The visits to Cambridge were especially joyous, however, for there at

---

[15] Madeline Smith, "Portraits of My Aunts," FFP.

[16] Laura Fay Smith, "Charlotte Hopkins," 1914, FFP.

Judge Fay's home the Fay children could meet interesting personalities such as Henry Wadsworth Longfellow and Ralph Waldo Emerson. These acquaintances provided diversion and enrichment for those young lives so wearied by austerity, separation, and loss.

The death of Emily, having caused considerable difficulty for all seven children, affected Zina the most. In the words of one grandniece, "it haunted her, causing a searching, an unease, an atmosphere of questioning about the difficult expectations placed on women in society."[17] For the young Zina, her mother became the legend that accused, challenged, and discouraged.[18] How could she live up to it? Two weeks after Emily's funeral, Zina began a correspondence with her friend Ralph Waldo Emerson in which she wrote:

> My mother died two weeks ago, and left seven children, of whom I am the eldest, and I am twenty. We have besides in the house twelve pupils—boys and girls of different ages, so you may suppose that my time is so much taken up that I have very little leisure for reading and study, so I am very ignorant, I frankly confess, to what I should like to be. To converse about Christianity, however, and human nature, requires but little besides constant reading of the Bible and observation of those about us who are human nature—therefore it is that I have presumed to write to you—though so insignificant and unlearned and nothing more than a woman. If I have said anything impertinent or self-conceited, I beg your pardon most humble, since next after Religion I bow to Intellect.[19]

Following the receipt of this letter, Emerson remained in communication with Zina, even counseling her to enroll at the Agassiz School in Cambridge, where his daughters were also students. The Agassiz school had been established in 1855 by Mrs. Louis Agassiz, the future founder of Radcliffe College, and it boasted a progressive curriculum that included such traditional "masculine" subjects as natural history, mathematics, geography, and botany.[20] Occasionally the school hosted such guest lecturers as Harvard luminaries Professors Louis Agassiz, Darwin's notable opponent, and Benjamin Peirce, the university's famous mathematician. In 1859, at age twenty-three, Zina enrolled at the Quincy Street school, and remained there for two years, during which time she made many friends among her schoolmates. The students, drawn mostly from Boston, Brookline, Cambridge, and Concord, often invited one another as weekend house guests. Zina, who developed a friendship with Emerson's daughters Ellen and Edith, often stayed with the Emersons in Concord.

Meanwhile, in Vermont, Laura had succeeded Zina as head of the household and as Amy's music instructor. Amy corresponded on a regular basis with Zina, keeping her abreast of her life and updating her on her musical progress under Laura's tutelage. Amy's letters chronicled such events as visits to relatives in Burlington, recreational skating

---

[17] Mitarachi, "Family About Family."

[18] Ibid.

[19] Mitarachi, "Melusina Fay Peirce," 21.

[20] Jean Strouse, *Alice James: A Biography* (Boston: Houghton Mifflin, 1980), 67.

with Kate and the young boys of their acquaintance, playing the organ at church services and school. A letter dated 13 December 1859 gives a flavor of life in Vermont during winter vacation:

> My vacation has been spent so far in sewing, practicing, reading, and playing backgammon, besides drawing which occupies two afternoons of the week, and writing letters. I enjoy my leisure intensely and find the freedom from study and responsibility refreshing. One thing I can't account for, I keep wanting to go to sleep, and am in bed very early, for instance I was obliged to retire at half past seven on Sunday evening, being overpowered by Morpheus; you know it was vice-versa before school was out.[21]

Of her life as a student Amy wrote:

> School is desparate hard work, and we have to study in earnest. Charly Farrar comes every day, and is Papa's pupil in seven studies. He teaches our Arithmetic class and has set us back to "Vulgar Fractions." I have determined to understand Arithmetic, so now I do all the examples by myself out of school, before we come to class, by dint of hard labor. It is perfectly plain to me so far, and I mean to work at all the rules we do until I have mastered them completely.[22]

Little could Amy realize that the pattern of letter writing begun in St. Albans would develop into a refined art which eventually would win her international acclaim.

Cambridge Social Life

Amy's experiences in Vermont provided an enormous contrast to her sister Zina's new life in Cambridge. At the "Fay House," her grandfather's home, Zina had the opportunity to meet and interact with distinguished representatives of the Cambridge intelligentsia who were regular guests there. Among those who came to visit were author and teacher James Russell Lowell and E. A. Sophocles, a Harvard professor of Greek and one of the more picturesque figures in American education. Others who routinely stopped by included Harvard Professor of Natural Science Louis Agassiz, the poet Henry Wadsworth Longfellow, Harvard music professor John Knowles Paine, and authors William and

---

[21] Letter of Amy Fay to Zina Fay Peirce, 13 December 1859, FFP.

[22] Letter of Amy Fay to Zina Fay Peirce, 12 February 1860, FFP.

Henry James. The presence of such luminaries living and working in the shadow of Harvard University created a stimulating atmosphere in which Zina and other young people were moulded.[23] Attendance at the theater, a pastime that would have been frowned upon by her mother, became an approved social activity for Zina, as did celebrations and parties hosted by the Fays and others.

During holidays and vacation times Amy, with her sisters and brother Norman, came to visit Zina and their other fun-loving Fay relatives. She enjoyed being a part of the happy environment provided by Grandpa Fay and his unmarried daughter Maria, who was "devout, kindly to nieces and nephews, a good musician, an intellectual, and in a totally proper way, also a lover of fun and games."[24] The spirited Fays hosted evening parties for their relatives and friends. This was Cambridge "at its heady best; a place where learning existed side by side with pleasure."[25] For Amy, these Cambridge interludes were joyous times when she could be free of the more rigorous strictures that prevailed at home in St. Albans. She and her siblings relished the pleasures of friendships with such children of the Cambridge aristocracy as Charlie, Alice, Annie, and Edith Longfellow.

While enrolled at the Agassiz School, Zina met Charles Sanders Peirce, the brilliant son of the eminent Harvard Professor Benjamin Peirce and a blossoming intellect in his own right. In January of 1861 Peirce called on Zina for the first time and within the next week he had invited her out. A whirlwind courtship ensued. The following summer Peirce visited Zina in St. Albans, and in the winter of 1862 the two became engaged. On 16 October 1862, less than two years after their first outing, Charles and the twenty-six-year-old Zina were married by Reverend Fay at St. Luke's Church in St. Albans, Vermont.

The couple's decision to marry disappointed Peirce's parents, Benjamin and Sarah Mills Peirce, and six months after the wedding Benjamin confided as much to his friend Arthur Bache:

> Charlie has gone to be married and I expect him in a week or ten days. We thought that he and Zina had yielded to the evident reasonableness of the delay until spring, but Charlie got into a very nervous state about her health and last Friday we yielded to his wishes and the irrepressible youth started at once for his bride. He understands, distinctly, that although we do not object neither do we approve and that the responsibility for the affair must rest wholly upon him and Zina.[26]

The senior Peirces realized that the newlyweds, though each intellectually gifted, were hardly prepared emotionally for the responsibilities of marriage. Both Zina and Charles were high-strung. From the outset of the marriage Charles would spend twenty hours or more of each day in uninterrupted work of original thinking in a variety of subjects

---

[23] Thomas W. Higginson, *Old Cambridge* (New York: Macmillan, 1890), 17.

[24] Mitarachi, "Melusina Fay Peirce," 14.

[25] Ibid., 15.

[26] Letter from Benjamin Peirce to friend Arthur Bache, 10 October 1862, Max Fisch Papers, hereafter referred to as MFP. Courtesy of Peirce Edition Project, Indiana University-Purdue University at Indianapolis.

such as logic, mathematics, psychology, semiotics, philosophy, literature, and science. During these times of intense concentration, Charles frequently seemed not to hear Zina when she spoke to him. While his activities eventually earned him a reputation as "one of the most original and versatile thinkers ever produced in the Americas,"[27] they prevented his relating in an emotionally satisfying way to his new bride.

At first, Zina accepted Charles's behavior and was sympathetic toward him and his intellectual pursuits, even joining him in his early scientific work. Soon after the wedding she wrote to her brother-in-law, the younger Benjamin Mills Peirce, assuring him that she and Charles were very happy:

> Charley and I enjoy life greatly in our new rooms. For the money we spent I think they could hardly be prettier. We seldom see anybody but our two selves which I think is highly delightful and most pleasant a thing to living alone.[28]

She described their custom of saying morning and evening prayers together, commenting that:

> I think there is nothing like them for beginning and ending the day. Since we came over here Charley and I find them a great comfort as well as a help. A day rendered to Old Time without them is like a piece of knitting ravelling at both ends.[29]

Zina Fay Peirce:
Emerging Role Model for Amy

As Peirce's work of thinking and theorizing increasingly absorbed his attention, Zina sought her own fulfillment by turning her energies to her preferred social causes, one of which was the improvement of women's place in society. For some time she had dreamed of a cooperative housekeeping plan that would free women from the burdens of domestic responsibilities so that they could participate in the paid labor force and thereby use their broader talents. According to her scheme, women would organize associations to perform domestic work collectively and charge their husbands for their services. Zina and her enlightened friends explored ways to bring women together around this and other social causes.

---

[27] Irving Shenker, "A Thinker's Thinker Is Honored Belatedly," *New York Times*, 12 October 1976, 37.

[28] Letter of Zina Fay Peirce to Benjamin Mills Peirce, 10 March 1863, PFP.

[29] Ibid.

While Zina was theorizing in Cambridge with her women friends, several of her Fay and Hopkins relatives in Vermont were "getting on" with their own lives. Her father had begun to court Mrs. Sophronia White, a widow from Grand Isle, Vermont, while Laura was keeping company with Francis Wyman Smith, a clergyman from Eden, Vermont. On the maternal side of the family, grandfather Hopkins was steadily advancing in the ranks of the Episcopal Church in Vermont.

In May of 1864 Charles Fay and Sophronia White were married. In January of the next year Rev. Hopkins was inaugurated as the first Episcopal Bishop of Vermont. The following September, Laura and Francis Smith were wed. These new beginnings among relatives in Vermont convinced Zina that the time was right for her unmarried siblings to experience some new life directions as well. Accordingly, she invited her sisters and brother to come and make their home in Cambridge with her and Charles Peirce.

Amy was the first to accept her sister's invitation, and by early 1866 she moved to Cambridge, remaining with Zina and Charles for three years, and working intermittently as a governess for the children of family friends. She was nearly twenty-two years of age at the time of her arrival, a rich time of life in which to absorb the stimulating Cambridge environment. By this time she had grown into an attractive young woman, memorable for her beautiful blonde, curly hair, her forthright blue eyes, her perfect nose, and her beautiful complexion. She was tall and carried herself gracefully. In addition she was intelligent and entertaining, a good conversationalist, and intellectually curious.

At the Peirce's home Amy met many of the Cambridge aristocracy who were Zina's friends. In June 1867 Alice James wrote a letter to her brother William James describing a visit she and her brother Henry made to the Peirces, one that inaugurated a friendship between Alice and Amy,[30] as evidenced by Alice's gesture of friendship in sending Amy a photograph of herself while Amy was in Europe.[31]

Another frequent visitor to the house was Charles Peirce's younger brother, Benjamin Mills Peirce. Amy had met the younger Peirce during her childhood visits to Zina in Cambridge, and as the years passed she found him increasingly appealing. When she was nineteen she wrote him a letter from Vermont, which hints at the attraction she felt for him:

> I wish so much you were here, Ben; I should enjoy it so much better. I hope that you will be able to come up to St. Alban's for I shall be very sorry if you cannot. . . . I'm learning that splendid sonata of Mozart's that your father gave Zina. It is perfectly exquisite. Since I have been here I have been converted into a sort of hand organ, for they make me play morning, noon, and night until I am completely worn out. It is very good practice, however.[32]

---

[30] In a 6 August 1867 letter to William James, Alice James wrote: "the younger sister seemed an amiable maid but had rather a Philistine way of talking, for instance she told me that a friend of hers who was just married had the 'cheek' to sit down and write to her that she should instantly marry, etc. Mrs. Peirce tried to suppress her anguish of anxiety while her sister was talking but only succeeded in part. Mrs. P. is a nice woman, she seems very intelligent and energetic, if she would only refrain from throwing up her head and glaring at me like a wild horse on the prairies." MFP.

[31] MFP.

[32] Letter from Amy Fay to Benjamin Mills Peirce, 16 July 1863, FFP.

After she had moved to Cambridge, Amy became so smitten with Benjamin that she considered herself in love with him and, at least in the beginning, Ben reciprocated. But after a time something happened that caused Benjamin to distance himself from her. Amy's grandniece Madeline Smith had the impression from some relative that Peirce was an amoral man rather than an immoral one and that "there had been something about men as well as other women."[33] Whatever the case, Amy remained infatuated with Ben Peirce.

She also remained devoted to Zina, whose involvements as a writer and organizer of women made a deep impression on her. As she observed Zina mobilizing the Cambridge women, writing articles on cooperative housekeeping in *Atlantic Monthly*, and convening the first meeting of the Cambridge Co-Operative Housekeeping Society at her father-in-law's home, Amy's admiration for her sister grew and the affection between the two sisters steadily deepened.[34] In fact, many of Amy's later ideas about women's work and place in the world and in American life date from these early years of observing at close hand her sister's activism in Cambridge.

The senior Peirces, on the other hand, viewed the outside interests of their daughter-in-law with disdain. The mother, Sarah, even wrote to her younger son Bejamin lamenting Zina's priorities: "As for Zina we hardly know what she does but she seems always too busy to come to see us. The Fays are not a warm-hearted race."[35]

This purported lack of warmth on the part of the Fays concerned Sarah Peirce, and rightly so. She had become aware that not only Amy Fay but also her younger sister Kate were attracted to her son Benjamin; she did not relish the thought of a second Fay becoming entangled with another of her sons, even though in truth Benjamin Peirce was merely a passing fancy for the flirtatious Kate. Sarah Peirce had come to resent Zina's apparent favoring of her siblings over her husband, and she was pleased that as a consequence of Ben's breakup with Amy there now seemed to be less of a chance that Benjamin would become caught up with Kate. Still, she wrote him the following words of caution:

---

[33] Madeline Smith once wrote to a family member that she felt that "Peirce was not immoral but amoral. She says she understood from somewhere that there had been something about men, as well as other women. But she is not sure where she got this impression. Her mother, she says, would never have discussed this sort of thing with her. But she might have heard it from my aunt Amy Stone, who was a great crony of her mother's (My mother also was very impressed by beauty). I find this improbable since I never heard this from Aunt Amy, who liked to retail gossip, and I don't believe would have been chary of discussing this sort of thing with me. My hunch is that Cousin Madeline heard something like this from one of the other aunts." Sylvia Wright Mitarachi, "Family About Family," FFP.

[34] In 1864, Zina published a long article in the *New York World*, 11 June 1864, urging that women work in food-preparing and dress-making establishments run by themselves. In January 1866 she organized assistance for the destitute women and children of Columbia among the Cambridge ladies and also organized a benefit concert for the Freedmen at Lyceum Hall. In 1868 she published articles on cooperative housekeeping in the *Atlantic Monthly*, and in 1869 organized the Cambridge Co-Operative Housekeeping Society at the home of Professor Benjamin Peirce. Later that year she went to New York to assist in the organization of the Women's Council of New York City, as part of the First Women's Parliament, participated in a Peace Festival at Lyceum Hall, and delivered an address on cooperative housekeeping in Cambridge to an audience of one hundred women. She also was involved with organizations like the Cambridge Women's Union and Women's Educational Association of Boston, with attempts to reform the Episcopal Church by permitting women deacons, and with political activities.

[35] Letter from Sarah Mills Peirce to Benjamin Mills Peirce, 8 January 1867, MFP.

How about the Fays? I should like to give you a word of caution about
Miss K, for I distrust the race and should be very sorry to see the old
role of Amy reenacted.[36]

In the eyes of Sarah Peirce, the Fay women were undesirable as daughters-in-law. It
was enough to contend with Zina, whose passion for getting each of her siblings educated
seemed at times to exceed her passion for her husband.

In truth, Zina was consumed by her ambition to get her sisters and brother educated.
She was particularly interested in helping Amy advance in her music study. In the
summer of 1865, before Amy had even settled in Cambridge, Zina had arranged for her
to have an intense period of study in Geneseo, New York with the Polish pianist Jan
Pychowski. After Amy's arrival in Cambridge, Zina encouraged her to register for regular
lessons at the New England Conservatory of Music with the composer and pianist Otto
Dressel, who had immigrated from Prussia in mid-century and was no doubt an influential
factor in her later decision to go to Germany. Her crowning achievement, however, was
the enlistment of the renowned composer John Knowles Paine, a long time friend of the
Fay family, as musical mentor for her sister.

In 1862 Paine had become Harvard University's first instructor in music, and from
that time on his career had become closely bound up with artistic life in Cambridge.[37]
His earliest course offerings at Harvard included one in musical form and another in
counterpoint and fugue. If Amy were to make progress in the study of music she would
need to have a grasp of such subjects. Yet her gender prohibited her from registering
at Harvard, as formal higher education opportunities for women had yet to become
an integral part of the nation's higher education establishment. The enterprising Zina
prevailed upon Paine to teach Amy privately, thus anticipating a trend which would grow
in the 1870s, whereby many wives, sisters, and daughters of Harvard faculty and alumni
would demand and achieve a Harvard education on a private, tutorial basis. This common
practice, which enabled moonlighting faculty to instruct young women related to the
Harvard community, became known as the "Harvard Annex."[38]

During Amy's tutorial sessions with Paine, the eminent teacher frequently would
allude to the opportunities for music study that abounded in Germany. He himself had
recently returned from three years of study there and had delighted Amy with accounts of
the pianist Carl Tausig, who, he declared, played like "forty thousand devils."[39] Paine's
enthusiastic descriptions of German musical life so excited Amy that she began to fantasize
about going there herself. Such a move would enable her to study with the musical giants
of her day. It also would remove her from the Peirce household, where the atmosphere
had become increasingly strained due to the emotional incompatibility between Zina and

---

[36] Letter from Sarah Mills Peirce to Benjamin Mills Peirce, 15 March 1869, MFP.

[37] Walter A. Spalding, *Music at Harvard* (New York: Coward McAnn, 1935; reprint, New York: Da Capo,
1977), 152.

[38] Barbara Solomon, *In the Company of Educated Women* (New Haven: Yale University Press, 1985), 54.

[39] William S. B. Mathews, *A Hundred Years of Music in America* (Chicago: G. L. Howe, 1889), 138.

Charles. By 1866 the impulse to move away from the ill-matched couple had become
so strong that Amy approached her uncle Charles Jerome Hopkins, only eight years her
senior, about the possibility of setting up housekeeping with him. He wrote in a journal
entry, dated 4 February 1866:

> Spent the evening with my adored niece Amy. The child still begs me
> to take lodging with her somewhere, just as if I could afford it, but it goes
> straight to my heart's marrow to be forced to refuse her constantly. [40]

When a few days later, on 14 February 1866, the subject came up again, Hopkins
wrote once more on the subject:

> Took sweet Amy to hear me play this evening and she told me that
> she dreamed lately that I was keeping bachelor's hall in a little house
> and that she was my housekeeper. She said she thought that we had
> Gottschalk for a guest at tea and it was so nice, she remarked. Alas!
> it is like a stab at my heart when she said this for I am so poor that
> such a Paradise is not to be thought of for me, and this dear child has
> yet to be left to the tender mercies of a boarding house. [41]

Amy's restlessness affected her young siblings as well. As they matured, they too
began to entertain thoughts of leaving the nest Zina had provided, a reality which did
not escape Zina's notice. Her own marriage, already on shaky ground, had been made
bearable only by the proximity of her siblings, and she had once confided to Amy that
"marriage is a brutal thing."[42] Though her own life was at a crossroads, Zina determined to get Amy's future settled before moving on with her own.

She intervened on Amy's behalf with their uncle Storey Fay and successfully elicited
his financial help in subsidizing Amy's study abroad. In putting into motion the events
that would lead Amy to music study in Germany, Zina was readying her younger sister
to take a step that would give her and other ambitious musical women who would follow
a new stature in the world of music. Furthermore, by encouraging Amy to take the study
of music more seriously than most women of her time, Zina was helping her to bring
about a shift in the public's attitude toward music as more than a social accomplishment
for women. Lastly, by sending Amy abroad Zina also was helping to put some distance
between Benjamin Mills Peirce and her younger sister. Fay family gossip was beginning
to hint that Peirce was promiscuous. [43] Zina wished to prevent a renewed relationship
between Ben and Amy. She did not wish to see Amy become trapped in marriage with
such an unpromising partner.

---

[40] Diary of Amy's uncle Jerome Hopkins, 4 February 1866, Ms. Am. 1993(20), by permission of the Houghton
Library, Harvard University.

[41] Ibid.

[42] Mitarachi, "Family About Family," FFP.

[43] Private conversations with Sylvia Mitarachi, summer 1975, revealed the family gossip about Benjamin
Peirce's promiscuity.

On the other hand, by encouraging Amy's study in Europe, Zina was depriving both sisters of a cherished source of emotional support. Since there was little emotional compatibility remaining between her husband and herself, Zina must have asked herself what compensation there could be for the keen sense of affective deprivation that she would feel following Amy's departure for Germany.

In searching out the answer to her question, she concluded that a larger affiliative network with women whose intellectual and literary persuasions were similar to her own would help fill her need for connectedness. Accordingly, she initiated a correspondence with the writer George Eliot (pseud. for Mary Ann Evans), in which she revealed the particulars of a demanding domestic life that sapped her physical strength and prevented her from fulfilling herself as a writer. Eliot empathized with her, assuring Zina that she understood her conflicted feelings and advised her that she should have patience and proceed slowly with her personal goal of being a writer. In a letter dated 14 September 1866, Eliot wrote:

> I am so deeply touched by your words of tenderness and by the details you tell me about yourself, that I cannot keep total silence towards you. . . . The only problem for us, the only hope, is to try and unite the utmost activity with the utmost resignation. Does this seem melancholy? I think it is less melancholy than any form of self-flattery. . . . I want to tell you not to fancy yourself old because you are thirty, or to regret that you have not yet written anything. It is a misfortune to many that they begin to write when they are young and give out all that is genuine and peculiar in them when it can be no better than trashy, unripe fruit. There is nothing more dreary than the life of a writer who has exhausted himself. I enter into those young struggles of yours to get knowledge, into the longing you feel to do something more than domestic duties while yet you are held fast by womanly necessities for neatness and household perfection as well as by lack of bodily strength. Something of all that I have gone through myself. I have never known perfect health, and I have known what it was to have close ties making me feel wants of others as my own and to have little money by which these wants could be met. [44]

Prior to Amy's sailing, Zina wrote another letter to Eliot, dated 2 August 1869, in which she stated:

> I am always waiting for a more convenient season. My sisters are flitting from me now, sweet things; one is going to Berlin to study the piano, another elsewhere, so that I might have long stretches of time; but the ladies here are organizing a cooperative housekeeping society, and as I originated the idea, they look to me to function through. So study and writing must again go to the wall for an indefinite period. [45]

---

[44] Letter from M. E. Lewes (George Eliot) to Mrs. Charles Sanders Peirce, quoted in *Selections from George Eliot's Letters*, ed. G. S. Haight (New Haven: Yale University Press, 1985), 320-21.

[45] Letter from Mrs. Charles Sanders Peirce to George Eliot, 2 August 1869, MFP.

By October 17, Amy had left for New York in high spirits and with good courage.[46]
On October 20, with a party of other Boston people, she set sail from New York for Europe.
Before her departure her friends gave her a benefit concert at Lyceum Hall.   The proceeds,
about two hundred dollars, helped her build up her wardrobe for her German sojourn.[47]
On the day of Amy's sailing, Zina, who was in New York to open a "Women's Parliament,"
was able to wish her beloved sister "bon voyage."   It was a bittersweet farewell.   Although
now Zina would have even more time to continue her organizing, writing, and studying,
she would be deprived of the presence of her beloved younger sister.   As Amy began
her musical adventure abroad, she would use the mails to keep her sister Zina and other
family members abreast of her activities.   Never could she have suspected that her letters
home would become immortalized in the celebrated book which brought her international
renown, *Music-Study in Germany.*

---

[46] Letter of Sarah Mills Peirce to Benjamin Mills Peirce, 13 October 1869, MFP. The letter, though written
before Amy's departure, mentions Zina's being in New York and Amy's plans to sail with a party of other
Boston people.

[47] Ibid.

PART 2

Music Study in Germany

Beginnings in Germany

Awaiting Amy Fay on her arrival in Berlin was an extended and influential network of Fay family friends living and working abroad as part of the American consular delegation. These highly placed individuals helped her settle into a boarding house at 26 Bernberger Strasse and extended themselves to her in other ways as well. As part of their commitment to welcoming her in her temporarily adopted country, they introduced her to prospective friends and familiarized her with German customs and habits. As Amy immersed herself in her new milieu, she experienced once more the privileges of membership in the well-connected Fay family.

Principal among family friends in the diplomatic corps was the United States Minister to the Prussian Court, George Bancroft, also a distinguished historian. Bancroft and his wife smoothed a path for Amy, helping her to gain proximity to major political and cultural figures in Chancellor Bismarck's Germany, including Bismarck himself. In the days and years ahead, Bancroft would see to it that Amy moved comfortably among emperors, dukes, ambassadors, foreign ministers, and ranking officers of the American, British, and German armed forces. At Bancroft's invitation, Amy attended dinner parties, tea parties, and dances, and went to concerts, museums, and beer gardens. As she moved from ballroom to ballroom in the company of the Bancrofts, eligible young men vied to fill out the dance card of this attractive and fashionable young woman from the United States. As Amy wrote home:

> No one could be kinder than Mr. Bancroft. . . . I am very proud of our minister. His reputation as our national historian, together with his German culture and early German associations, all combine to make him an admirable representative of our country to this haughty kingdom, and I hear that he is very popular with its self-satisfied citizens. . . . Mr. Bancroft is passionately fond of music . . . which is of course an additional title to *my* high opinion. [1]

Just two months after her arrival in Berlin she wrote a letter about a party she had attended at the Bancrofts—one of six parties that week—at which the American Minister to China was present:

---

[1] Amy Fay, *Music-Study in Germany* (hereafter referred to as MSG), 48. The 2nd ed. (Chicago: Jansen, McClurg & Co., 1881) was used for these quotes.

On Monday I went to a party at the Bancroft's, which I enjoyed extremely. It was a very brilliant affair, and the toilettes were superb. At the entrance I was ushered in by a very fine servant dressed in livery. A second man showed me the dressing-room, where my bewildered sight first rested on a lot of Chinamen in festive attire. I could not make out for a second what they were, and I thought to myself, "is it possible I have mistaken the invitation, and this is a masquerade?" Another glance showed me that they were Chinese, and it turned out that Mr. Burlingame, the Chinese Minister, was there, and these men were part of his suite. The ladies and gentlemen had the same dressing-room, which was a new feature in parties to me, and as we took off our things the servant took them and gave us a ticket for them, as they do at the opera. I should think that there were about a hundred persons present. There were a great many handsome women, and they were beautifully dressed and much be-diamonded and pearled. Corn-colour seemed to be the fashion, and there were more silks of that colour than any other.[2]

This vivid letter would be followed by many other equally colorful ones which would one day make her famous when they became published under the title of *Music-Study in Germany*. Her correspondence reveals an atmosphere pulsating with artistic activity. Concerts, opera, and ballet flourished, as did theaters and museums. In the wake of the successful launching of the Paris Conservatoire in 1795, a network of conservatories had sprung up throughout Europe, contributing greatly to the vitality of musical life there. After Mendelssohn established the first major conservatory in the German system in Leipzig in 1843, conservatories soon became the standard institutions for professional music education in Germany and in the English-speaking countries. By the end of the century other urban centers such as Berlin, Cologne, Stuttgart, Dresden, Sonnerhausen, and Munich boasted excellent music education institutions; these included highly respected schools established by individual musicians such as Carl Tausig and Theodor Kullak. As the reputation of the German conservatories grew, so too did their appeal to music students throughout the world. Consequently, large numbers of aspiring musicians, convinced that their education would not be complete if they did not enroll in one of the European conservatories, flocked to Germany and Austria for music study.

Piano in Musical Life

At first, American music students were slow to join the pool of international music scholars who streamed toward one or other of the European countries in the nineteenth century. To be sure, the early part of the century had seen more than one American in Europe

---

[2] MSG, 28-29.

in pursuit of music study. In the 1830s Boston pianist Gabrielle de la Motte apparently studied in Paris with Chopin.[3] In 1835-37 the New York violinist and conductor Ureli Corelli Hill studied with Ludwig Spohr in Kassel.[4] In the 1840s pianist James Monroe Deems studied abroad,[5] and in 1849 the Harvard-educated musician and painter Charles Callahan Perkins studied in both Paris and Italy.[6] Still, when William Mason went to Europe in 1849 for music study with such teachers as Franz Liszt, he was considered "a rare specimen of his kind."[7]

Even as late as 1869, the year of Amy Fay's departure for Germany, the number of American music students bound for Europe had not become conspicuously large. It was Amy Fay who led the new wave of late nineteenth-century American musicians who made a European sojourn a *sine qua non* for establishing musical credentials.[8] Her pioneering move placed her at the head of a long line of women musicians who, in going abroad for study, dramatically announced to the world that they had the courage to pursue music as a profession rather than as a genteel, female accomplishment that kept idle hands busy. This contingency was prestigious, and included Cincinnati pianist Julie Rivé-King (1854-1937), who in 1872 set out for Germany for studies with Carl Reinecke at Leipzig, Carl Blassman at Dresden, and Liszt at Weimar.[9] Chicago pianist Fannie Bloomfield (later, Bloomfield-Zeisler, 1863-1927) went to Vienna in 1878 for a five-year period, during which time she worked with Paderewski's last teacher, Theodor Leschetizky.[10]

In the 1880s and 90s the flow of American students to Europe accelerated. Pianists comprised the majority of women seeking study abroad. Among the more renowned was Anna Mayhew-Simonds of Boston, who went to Berlin in 1880 for piano study with Theodor Kullak and organ study with John Knowles Paine's teacher, Karl Haupt. Mayhew-Simonds's sparkling letters from Germany appeared in the nation's newsy arts magazine *Folio.*[11]

Women violinists and composers were represented among nineteenth-century music students abroad as well. In 1881 violinist Geraldine Morgan (1867-1918) went to Berlin for study with the great Joseph Joachim and later to Leipzig for work with Henry Schradieck.[12] Violinist Maude Powell (1867-1920) had two periods of study in Germany,

---

[3] According to H. Earle Johnson, September 1981. See also Richard Randall, "Boston, Dwight, and Pianists of Nineteenth Century America: The European Connection" (D.M.A. diss., University of Colorado, 1984), 85.

[4] *New Grove Dictionary of American Music in America* (1986), s.v. "Hill, Ureli Corelli," by Robert Stevenson and Betty Bandel.

[5] Oscar Thompson, *International Cyclopedia of Music and Musicians*, 9th ed., ed. Nicolas Slonimsky (1964), s.v. "Deems, James Monroe."

[6] *Baker's Biographical Dictionary of Musicians*, 7th ed. (1986), s.v. "Perkins, Charles Callahan."

[7] Arthur Loesser, *Men, Women, and Pianos* (New York: Simon and Schuster, 1954), 538.

[8] Christine Ammer, *Unsung: A History of Women in American Music* (Westport, Conn.: Greenwood, 1980), 51.

[9] Ibid., 52.

[10] Ibid., 55.

[11] Anna Mayhew-Simonds, "Letter from Germany," *Folio* 19, nos. 2 (February 1880), 4 (April 1880), 5 (May 1880), 10 (October 1880).

[12] Ammer, 35.

one at the Leipzig Conservatory in 1881-82 and the other at the Berlin Hochschule in 1884-85.[13] By the fall of 1888 a correspondent of the *New York Sun* was astonished at the hundreds of earnest American "ladies" working at music in Berlin.[14] Later such composer luminaries as Mabel Wheeler Daniels (1878-1971), Margaret Ruthven Lang (1867-1972) and Helen Hood (1863-1949) joined their ranks as music students in Europe, where they hoped to make a name for themselves. Several of them became Fay's lifelong friends.

The steady increase in the numbers of women pianists going to Europe for serious music study signaled the partial demise in the United States of the "piano girl," that arch-symbol of the dilettante who, whether she had talent for music or not, devoted herself to the keyboard as a socially laudable female accomplishment.[15] Conversely, the swelling numbers of women pianists bound for European study announced the emergence of the "new girl"—that is, "the young woman who was too busy to play the piano unless she had the gift and then played it with consuming interest."[16] Amy was a "new girl."

Tausig's Conservatory

Ever since her student days in Cambridge, when Harvard Professor John Knowles Paine had suggested that she should consider taking lessons from this genius who played "like forty thousand devils," Amy had yearned to become one of Carl Tausig's students. Tausig was "the phenomenon who was considered Liszt's peer, whom Rubinstein called the infallible, who had mastered the entire literature as it was then known."[17] He was known to rouse audiences to hysteria by the excitement of his playing and when, on occasion, he played the prestissimo unison at the end of the Chopin E-minor Piano Concerto in broken octaves, musicians themselves applauded madly, and the conductor would rap the podium with his baton until it broke.[18]

But upon registering at the Conservatory, Amy discovered that gaining lessons with Tausig would not be a simple matter. Since his rigorous tour schedule necessitated frequent and prolonged absences from his institution, his presence in Berlin was an exception rather than a rule. Amy had crossed an ocean and travelled to Berlin only to find that the object of her quest was elsewhere most of the time.

---

[13] Ibid., 31-32.

[14] Loesser, 538.

[15] Jane Bowers and Judith Tick, *Women Making Music* (Urbana: University of Illinois Press, 1986), 35.

[16] Adrienne Fried Block and Carol Neuls-Bates, *Women in American Music* (Westport, Conn.: Greenwood, 1979), xx.

[17] Harold C. Schonberg, *The Great Pianists*, 2nd ed. (New York: Simon and Schuster, 1987), 256.

[18] Ibid., 261-62.

She determined to make the best of the situation by auditioning for lessons with Tausig's associate Louis Ehlert, who was well known abroad as composer, conductor, and critic and whose impeccable credentials included study at the Leipzig Conservatory with Mendelssohn and Schumann. After hearing Amy play, Ehlert "said some encouraging words,"[19] and took her into one of his advanced piano classes.

Ehlert indoctrinated Amy into the strict methodology of the time. He used the Cramer *Studies*, insisting that she play them both fast and loud; scales were to be played the same way. Amy found the approach taxing and wrote home:

> You have no idea how hard they make Cramer's Studies here. Ehlert makes me play them tremendously *forte,* and as fast as I can go. My hand gets so tired that it is ready to break, and then I say that I cannot go on. "But you *must* go on," he will say. It is the same with the scales. It seems to me that I play them so loud that I make the welkin ring, and he will say, "But you always play *piano.*" And with all this rapidity he does not allow a note to be missed, and if you happen to strike a wrong one he looks so shocked that you feel ready to sink into the floor.[20]

Clearly Amy felt technically outdistanced by her three (unnamed) classmates, each of whom she perceived as meeting Ehlert's expectations with apparent ease. She thought she would never "catch up with them," and wrote home of her feelings of musical inferiority:

> I know that Ehlert thinks I have talent, but, after all, talent must go to the wall before such *practice* as these people had had, for most of them have studied a long time, and have been at the piano four or five hours a day.[21]

Amy welcomed the opportunity of studying with many of Berlin's most thorough and well-known musicians. One of the more eminent was Carl Friedrich Weitzmann, theorist and former concertmaster in Riga, Reval, and St. Petersburg. Others included pianist-critic Otto Lessman and Oscar Beringer, the pianist, pedagogue, and Tausig protégé. In addition, she found it stimulating to be in classes with the talented student body at the conservatory, who came from all over the world, France excepted.[22]

Like most German conservatories of the time, the school year at the Tausig Conservatory consisted of two semesters, the first running from mid-October to February or mid-March, the second from Easter to mid-July.[23] Classes generally met two or three

---

[19] MSG, 16.

[20] MSG, 21-22.

[21] MSG, 21.

[22] The lingering political tensions between Germany and France culminating in the Franco-Prussian War of 1870-71 accounted for the absence of French students in German conservatories at the time of Fay's enrollment at Tausig's Conservatory.

[23] E. Douglas Bomberger, "American Music Students in Germany, 1850-1900: An Overview," paper delivered at the national meeting of the American Musicological Society, Chicago, 7 November 1990.

times weekly, Saturdays included. In addition to her piano studies, Amy's program of study at the Tausig Conservatory included group piano, in tandem with a core curriculum comprising courses in ear training, sight reading, harmony, and ensemble performance. Piano classes consisted of three to six students. In keeping with German custom of the time, men and women were taught separately in all classes (except choir), a custom which Amy found curious, as she wrote home:

> Young people of different sexes can never see anything of each other. I regard it as a shocking system, as the Germans manage it. Young ladies and gentlemen only see each other at parties, and a young man can never call on a girl, but must always see her in the presence of the whole family. I only wonder how marriages are managed at all, for the sexes seem to live quite isolated from each other. The consequence is, the girls get a lot of rubbish in their heads, and as for the men, I know not what they think, for I have not seen any to speak of since I have been here. [24]

Piano teaching methods at Tausig's Conservatory reflected the current German musical practice, which concentrated more on finger development than on efficient muscular coordination. [25] In the German system student pianists, under their strict teachers, were encouraged to work diligently to strengthen their fingers, which took over much of the work of the arms in the more sonorous piano literature of the Romantic era. [26] In many instances the emphasis on finger development was carried to the extreme of using gadgets and contraptions that allowed exercise away from the piano. Frequently, student pianists experienced muscle fatigue, tension, and pain in their arms and hands, and at the Stuttgart Conservatory several students reportedly lost the use of the third finger through overstraining. [27]

The advantages of group instruction in piano were two-fold. First, students gained much needed confidence in playing before others. Secondly, the student artists gained exposure to emerging piano repertory. Since the piano was popularized in the nineteenth century, the majority of important composers, attracted by the range of sound production made possible by improvements in piano building, were in the process of generating important contributions to piano music. As students listened to their peers play unfamiliar or recently composed works, they gained a more comprehensive knowledge of the music heard. Such information could be put to good use later when planning for concert programs or when searching out suitable repertory for the students who they in turn would one day teach.

---

[24] Ibid.

[25] Ibid.

[26] Reginald Gerig, *Famous Pianists and Their Technique* (New York: Robert B. Luce, 1974), 229-30, 235.

[27] Ibid.

One of the most memorable of all her professors was her harmony instructor, the charming and humorous Professor Weitzmann. Since he did not understand English, and Amy at the time was hardly an accomplished German conversationalist, Weitzmann's efforts to have the young American understand the rules of harmony led to many amusing scenes between the two, as Amy described in a letter home:

> As he does not understand a word of English, I cannot say anything
> to him unless I can say it in German, and as he is determined to make
> me learn Harmony, it would be of no use to explain that I did not know
> what he was talking about, for he would begin all over again, and go
> on *ad infinitum*. [28]

One Sunday each month she attended "Music Reading" classes, in which all the scholars of the more advanced classes played. Amy was impressed by the magnificent playing of many of the female performers, especially with their technique and artistry when performing the most difficult pieces. Although for the most part she could acknowledge that her studies were beneficial to her musical growth, she still regretted at not having attained her *real* goal of meeting and studying with Tausig.

Not until 10 January 1870, four months after her arrival in Germany, did Amy even succeed in meeting the Maestro. Following his return from one of his extensive tours, Tausig paid a visit to Ehlert's class, in order to hear his colleague's students play. Amy described the visitation:

> He came in, and, scarcely looking at us, and without taking the trouble
> to bow even, he turned on me and said, imperiously, "*Spielen Sie
> mir Etwas vor.* (Play something for me.)" I got up and played first an
> *Etude*, and then he asked for the scales, and after I had played a few
> he told me I "had talent," and to come to his lessons, and I would
> learn much. [29]

The very next afternoon Amy went to Tausig's class, after which she wrote home:

> It is not surprising that he is so celebrated, and I long to hear him in
> concert, where he will do full justice to his powers. He thrills you to
> the very marrow of your bones. He is divorced from his wife, and I
> think it not improbable that she could not live with him, for he looks
> as haughty and despotic as Lucifer, though he has a very winning way
> with him when he likes. His playing is spoken of as *sans pareil*. [30]

---

[28] MSG, 24.

[29] MSG, 35-36.

[30] MSG, 36.

Tausig's difficult personality eventually drove Ehlert from the Conservatory.   In April 1870, following a quarrel between the two, Ehlert left in mid-term.   Despite his hasty departure, he took the time to write an evaluation of Amy's work and mail it to her family in Cambridge:

> I promised to write you about Miss Fay's progress after she had been here six months, and keep my word in saying that we are satisfied with the abilities of the young lady, and with the progress she had made in the highest degree.   Miss Fay is very talented, energetic and clever, and has besides an unfailing memory, and there is no doubt that if she is not broken off too early from her studies that she will take an excellent position in her art. [31]

After informing the Fays that he would soon leave the Conservatory, Ehlert acknowledged that in Amy Fay he lost his "favorite pupil." [32]

Still, Ehlert's departure did little to pave the way for Amy's lessons with Tausig, and instead she was assigned to the piano class taught by Oscar Beringer with the understanding that at least she would be allowed to observe Tausig's classes.   Following her first visit to one of Tausig's classes she wrote home of the tyrannical manner in which he conducted his classes:

> Tausig is so hasty and impatient that to be in his classes must be a fearful ordeal.   He will not bear the slightest fault.   The last time I went into his class to hear him teach he was dreadful. . . .   Tausig has a charming face, full of expression and very sensitive.   He is extremely sharp-sighted, and has eyes in the back of his head, I believe.   He is far too small and too despotic to be fascinating, however, though he has a sort of captivating way when he is in a good humor. [33]

While enrolled at the Conservatory, Amy practiced six hours daily.   Remaining free time was spent absorbing as much German culture as she could, all the while keeping up her home correspondence with accounts of her life abroad.   She found time to attend a Washington's birthday party at which Chancellor Bismarck was present, [34] and continued to go to museums, opera, symphony, and ballet.   She heard the violinist Joseph Joachim and pianists Clara Schumann, Anton Rubinstein, and finally Tausig himself.   To her surprise, she concluded that as an interpreter Clara Schumann was on the whole superior to either Tausig or Rubinstein. [35]

---

[31] Letter of Ehlert to Fay family, n.d., FFP.

[32] Ibid.

[33] MSG, 40, 42.

[34] MSG, 47-48.

[35] MSG, 39.

Two Personal Crises

In May 1870 Amy received a telegram from home with calamitous news pertaining to her estranged love, Benjamin Mills Peirce. A letter from Zina informed her that the thirty-year-old Peirce was dangerously ill and on the verge of death. Her reply home reveals the utter desolation she felt upon learning of Peirce's failing health:

> I can do nothing but cry all the time, and if the news of his death actually comes, I think I shall go crazy. I can't bear it, so it is no use to talk to me about religion and resignation, and all that sort of stuff. It is too great a blow, and I cannot feel God has any mercy or love for me if He condemns me to it. Your letter was dated over three weeks ago and the thought that Ben may have died in the meanwhile makes me frantic. I can't believe those beautiful eyes are closed forever, or that his soul could have passed away without my feeling the least presentiment of it. It is too unnatural, too horrible. But I fully expect your next letter will confirm my worst fears. I thought if I came to Europe something dreadful would happen while I was gone, and that everything would be changed. So it has happened and I shall never want to go home again. The very sight of Cambridge would be hateful to me. I am very sorry for Mrs. Peirce and for the whole family. It must be a terrible blow for them but it is still worse for me, and nobody can feel it as I shall, out of whose mind Ben has never been for one moment, since I first knew him . . . can't write anything while I am in this state, and I sent a letter to Laura a week ago, with all my news in it. The words of that dreadful telegram ring in my ears continually, and I shan't know an easy moment until your next letter arrives, though when it comes it will be long before I shall dare to open it. [36]

Clearly, Amy was more emotionally invested in Peirce than he was in her. Yet her letter shows that she had been unable to accept Benjamin's lack of emotional reciprocity and that she had deluded herself into believing that, despite his actions, Benjamin really cared for her.

When Zina's next letter did arrive, it confirmed Amy's worst fears. Benjamin, who had become a mining engineer following his graduation from Harvard University and had accepted employment under her uncle Joseph Storey Fay at the Champion Iron Company in Marquette, Wisconsin, had died of unnamed causes in the wilderness of Wisconsin. This news nearly totally effaced Amy and she poured out her grief in a touching letter home:

---

[36] Letter of Amy Fay to Zina Fay Peirce, 10 May 1870, FFP.

> Oh! if I could have married him and taken care of him I believe he would be alive and well this day, or at least if he had died he would have had a good nurse until his last breath, for I know by instinct how to manage sick persons. The worst of it is that we were so estranged from each other for the last two years and that everyone has known more of him than I, who loved him most. You say that perhaps he is nearer to me now and knows me as I am. No, I don't believe it. He did know me as I am, on earth, for he was very penetrating, and I don't believe he ever misunderstood me in his life and I believe that in his secret heart he cared for me still. Why he should have separated himself from me or have allowed circumstances to separate us is one of those inexplicable nightmares that I can't fathom. [37]

The poignancy of the moment was heightened and intensified by the painful reminder of her estrangement from the young man whom she claimed to have loved "the most." Her world seemed to have come to an end.

Yet in the midst of her grief, while still wondering how she could go on living, she received the good news that Tausig would give her a hearing. Throughout the first six months of 1870, she had waited for that day to come. Finally Tausig had consented to audition her. Thankful for the distraction that preparation for the audition might facilitate, she set the audition date for June. For the occasion she played a Scarlatti sonata, and on its merits she was accepted into Tausig's classes. The mood of her letter home, if not exactly optimistic, presented a striking contrast to the emotional tone of her correspondence following news of Ben's death:

> . . . I got into Tausig's classes finally, so I had to practice very hard. He was as amiable to me as he ever can be to anybody, but he is the most trying and exasperating master you can possibly imagine. It is his principle to rough you and snub you as much as he can, even when there is no occasion for it, and you think yourself fortunate if he does not hold you up to the ridicule of the whole class. [38]

But the lesson following her audition resembled a nightmare rather than a dream come true. Tausig asked her to play the scale of F major. He instructed her to:

> "Put the fifth finger on the top note of the scale, instead of turning the thumb under and ending on the second," which was what I had been doing. He also said, "Curve your fingers," and, indeed, he made me curve them so much that it seemed to me I was playing upon my finger nails. Not a word more did I get out of him, who could play scales with a velvety smoothness and velocity which seemed like a zephyr

---

[37] Letter of Amy Fay to Zina Fay Peirce, 16 May 1870, FFP.

[38] MSG, 82.

plowing over the keys. I know well by subsequent experience that I must have played the scale of F sharp Major with a stiff wrist, and there must have been wholly absent from it either smoothness or velocity. All that I did was to play the notes correctly, nothing more.

Now, why did not Tausig take that scale through with me, note by note, and show me how to practice it with one hand! Why did he not at least play the scale through before me as he practiced it himself? Then I could have got an idea. I knew nothing of the legato or wrist movement. All I knew was that a scale ought to sound like a string of pearls, and that I couldn't do it. That was one of the things I had crossed the ocean to learn, and I had come to Tausig as the man who could teach me.

"You must practice the scales every day," he said, and he never heard me play another one, though I did practice them religiously every day.[39]

Next Tausig had her play a Chopin scherzo, but as she did so he stood over her shouting such epithets as "Terrible! Shocking! O, Gott! O Gott!" As Amy described it:

I was really playing it well, too, and I kept on in spite of him, but my nerves were all rasped and excited to the highest point, and when I got through and he gave me my music and said, "Not at all bad" (very complimentary for him), I rushed out of the room and burst out crying. He followed me immediately, and cooly said, "What are you crying for, child? Your playing was not at all bad." I told him that it was "impossible for me to help it when he talked in such a way," but he did not seem to be aware that he had said anything.[40]

During her next lesson with Tausig, evidently somewhat remorseful over his previous comportment,

he entirely changed his tone, and was extremely sweet to me. I think he regretted having made me cry at the previous lesson, for just as I had sat down to play, he turned to the class and made some little joke about these "empfindliche Amerikanerinnen (sensitive Americans)." Then he came and stood by me, and nothing could have been kinder than his manner. After I had finished, he sat down and played the whole piece for me, a thing he rarely does, introducing a magnificent trill in double thirds, and ending up with some peculiar turn in which he allowed his virtuosity to peep out at me for a moment.[41]

---

[39] Amy Fay, "How to Practice," *Etude* 2, no. 19 (November 1884): 205.

[40] MSG, 83.

[41] MSG, 103-04.

Amy's optimism was short-lived, however, for shortly after this rewarding lesson Tausig stunned all his students by announcing that "he was *not going to give another lesson to anyone*" and that within a few weeks he would close his conservatory.[42] Amy was stunned. How could such a thing happen? First she had lost Ben Peirce. Now she was losing Tausig. She was furious! She went to Tausig, telling him that she thought it most unreasonable that having come such a distance and at such expense to have lessons with him, she should have to go back without them, but her pleadings fell on deaf ears. Tausig dismissed her quickly, reminding her that most of his scholars came from great distances and that he could not show any "special favor" to her. The enraged Amy wrote home a peppery evaluation of the mercurial Tausig, calling him:

> a capricious genius, entirely spoiled and unregulated, and the conser-
> vatory is merely a plaything to him. He amused himself with it for
> awhile, and now he is tired of it, and doesn't like to be bound to it,
> and so he throws it up. Money is no consideration to him.[43]

Within a period of four months, Amy had suffered two forms of loss—personal and professional. The death of Ben Peirce ended forever the possibility of marriage to the greatest romantic love of her life. The passing of Tausig brought to closure any hopes for a valued potential professional affiliation.

How would these losses affect Amy? Extant letters written home in the months immediately following Peirce's death and Tausig's leave-taking of his conservatory fail to mention these incidents again. Yet it is almost certain that Amy continued to correspond with family members about her feelings of loss, and that because of the personal nature of their content, these letters were suppressed by the principal recipient, Zina. It is most likely too, that although Amy seemed to be coping with her feelings of loss, in reality she was not, and that the buoyancy and resilience permeating her correspondence as she reclaimed her role as music student in Germany was achieved at the cost of unresolved grief. Time would show that the termination of two such emotion-laden affiliations would have a long-term imprint on her life.

In the months and years ahead, Amy became victimized by bouts with illness of the nineteenth-century variety: "nerves." A letter written home in 1871 describes her condition: "I am such a nervous creature . . . that the least thing gives me a violent headache, or robs me of sleep; even a call upsets me, if the person is animated or excited."[44] This vulnerability to nervousness became more pronounced during her time in Germany, and precipitated one particular behavior pattern: backing down from professional opportunities which would have opened doors for her in the musical world. Often, for example, she would "fall apart" before a planned concert or other significant musical opportunity, claiming "sickness" as the reason for her inability to play before one public or another. During her formative and early professional years, such behavior became an entrenched

---

[42] MSG, 83.

[43] MSG, 84.

[44] Letter of Amy Fay to Zina Fay Peirce, 8 September 1871, FFP.

part of her *modus operandi*. These struggles with "nerves" became so problematic that they threatened to bring about her undoing as a concert artist.

For the next decade or so, nervousness would plague Amy. At pivotal moments inviting professional advancement she seemed to "choose" illness. This tendency placed her in the company of other nineteenth-century women of similar class and background who typically resorted to illness as a response to long-term, unsatisfying life situations. For such American women of intelligence and sensitivity, nervous illness was a classic way in which to express—in most cases unconsciously—dissatisfaction with aspects of their lives. Literature of the day on child rearing, genteel women's magazines, and children's books all reinforced the expectation that women, in order to be respected in society, must become loving wives and mothers.[45] While some women negotiated those assigned roles gracefully, for others fitting the mold was painful. Thus a certain percentage of women, faced with stress developing out of their own peculiar personality needs or because of situational anxieties, set up defense mechanisms in the form of hysteria.

Amy's pattern of succumbing to nerves while retreating from success was not unlike the reaction of contemporary women who, after experiencing success, often withdraw from the arena in which they achieved it. Psychiatrist Jean Baker Miller writes of such a predisposition to "nerves" as follows:

> It has long been recognized that people sometimes have what are called "negative therapeutic reactions." This means that they make a major gain and then seem to get worse after it. Bonime has suggested that many of these reactions are in fact depressions and that they occur when a person has made a major step toward taking on responsibility and direction in his/her own life. The person has seen that she/he can move out of a position of inability and can exert effective action in her/his own behalf, but then becomes frightened of the implications of that new vision; for example, it would mean the person really doesn't need the old dependent relationships. She/he then pulls back and refuses to follow through on the new course. Such retreats occur in men as well as women, but for women this situation is an old story, very similar to what goes on in life.[46]

For such women "the threat of disruption of an affiliation is perceived not as just a loss of a relationship but as something closer to total loss of self."[47] The death of Benjamin Peirce and the loss of lessons with Tausig affected Fay's emotional stability and precipitated frequent occurrences of psychological paralysis that, at pivotal moments in her professional development, prevented her progress. Her self-proclaimed nervousness proved particularly troublesome during the next phase of her music study in Germany, when she was under the instruction of Theodor Kullak, but that chapter in her life was preceded by visits from home in the persons, first of her brother-in-law Charles and later of Zina.

---

[45] Carroll Smith-Rosenberg, *Disorderly Conduct* (New York: Oxford University Press, 1985), 213.

[46] Jean Baker Miller, "Toward a New Psychology of Women," in *Women's Spirituality*, ed. Joann Wolski Conn (New York: Paulist Press, 1976), 116.

[47] Ibid., 107.

Interlude

As it happened, Charles, an employee of the United States Coastal Survey, had come to Europe in June 1870 in conjunction with his work of setting up possible sites for observation parties for the December eclipse of the sun. [48] Since his travels took him through Berlin, he visited Amy there, and from August 10 to 15 he and his sister-in-law enjoyed a "poetic" five days sight-seeing, enjoying the beauties of the Elbe river, visiting art galleries, and catching up on news from home. [49]

When Zina arrived the following January, she and Charles travelled together toward Leipzig via Florence, Milan, Turin, Geneva, and Nurenburg before meeting Amy in Leipzig on January 23. [50] Her favorite sister provided an emotional balm for her. More than anyone, Zina truly understood Amy's enormous sense of loss at the death of Ben and the departure of Tausig. Zina brought Amy up to date on such family news as their younger sister Kate's plans to marry William Stone of Walpole, Massachusetts on 22 June 1871 in Cambridge. In addition, the sisters took in some cultural events together, on one evening attending a concert, on another, the opera. Finally, on the morning of January 26, Amy played for Zina, [51] before heading back to Berlin to continue her lessons.

With Kullak

In the fall of 1870, just one year after her arrival abroad, Amy transferred to another conservatory, the Neue Akademie der Tonkunst, so that she could study with its director, the famed Theodor Kullak. Like Tausig, Kullak was one of the most prominent teachers of the nineteenth century. A pupil of Czerny, he had begun his career as a virtuoso, but he later retired from concert work to establish, with Julius Stern and Adolph Bernhard Marx, the Berliner Musikschule. Five years later, in 1855, he broke away to found his own school, the Neue Akademie der Tonkunst, which flourished and became known as Kullak's Academy. In its first year the school enrolled 141 students, but by 1880, when Anna Mayhew-Simonds studied there, it had increased its enrollment to over one thousand. [52]

---

[48] Max Fisch, "Peirce as Scientist, Mathematician, Historian, Logician, and Philosopher," MFP.

[49] MSG, 86.

[50] Charles Sanders Peirce diary, 23 January 1871, MFP.

[51] Ibid., 26 January 1871.

[52] Anna Mayhew-Simonds, "Letter from Germany," *Folio* 19, no. 10 (October 1880): 377.

Upon auditioning Amy, Kullak accepted her immediately as his student, arranging for her to have one private lesson per week. In Amy's estimation his reputation as a very strict and thorough teacher was well-earned.[53] She recalled her first lesson very well:

> In a moment Kullak stood before me. His personality was extremely interesting and artistic. His deep-set eyes looked penetratingly at me through his spectacles, and his strong and passionate mouth at once impressed me. I said to myself: "Here is an artist, and no mere pedagogue." Kullak did not ask me to play a scale, nor did he say anything about technique, whatever. He probably thought that as I had been in Tausig's conservatory a year I must know how to practice. He asked me what pieces I had been studying last. I said Tausig had just given me Liszt's "Au bord d'une source." "Play it," said he, taking the music and setting it up on his own piano, at which he seated himself. . . . Kullak gave me some additional beautiful ideas about the first half. "Those skipping notes in the left hand were stray drops of water sparkling through the air," he said, and certainly, as he played them, they were. I was inspired and helped by his playing, and I imitated him as well as I could. When I had finished he exclaimed, enthusiastically, "Fraulein, Sie sind eine geboren Kunstlerin! (You are a born artist!)."[54]

Kullak proved much less intimidating than Tausig, however. In his studio there were two pianos, side by side, and during the lessons he sometimes played along with her or before her, a procedure that she found helpful as she tackled such demanding works as the Beethoven G-major Concerto, the Rubinstein Concerto in D minor, and the Beethoven Sonata in A-flat major, op. 110. Amy admired Kullak's finished, elegant style and his octave playing. She described her first impressions in a letter home:

> He looks about fifty, and is charming. I am enchanted with him. He plays magnificently, and is a splendid teacher, but he gives me immensely much to do, and I feel as if a mountain of music were all the time pressing on my head. He is so occupied that I have to take my lesson from seven to eight in the evening.[55]

After working with her new teacher for about a year she wrote home:

> I am entirely absorbed by my Music, and am working very hard at it. Oh! I am getting to play so beautifully. If you could only hear me play that Fantasia of Schumann's in E-flat major, you would open your little

---

[53] Schonberg, 255.

[54] Amy Fay, "How to Practice," *Etude* 2, no. 9 (November 1884): 205. The title of Liszt's "Au bord d'une source" is erroneously misprinted as "Au bord d'nue sonne."

[55] MSG, 100.

eyes and ears! Kullak was enchanted the other day, and says I am a
born artist, and I think I am myself. My touch is getting so delicious,
and as I get more power I am also acquiring that pianissimo, which
make such an effect.[56]

Yet despite Kullak's words of praise, Amy still lacked confidence. Although by her
own account she was playing beautifully, and although she admitted that she needed
experience appearing before audiences if she were to become a successful performing
artist, she kept putting off this ultimate test. The reason she inevitably gave was that
she needed more study, more time. On one occasion she wrote home:

> I want to finish my artistic education completely, before I come home,
> and it often seems to me that to accomplish my object, not one year,
> but two or more are necessary! This is a most dismal thought, but one
> of perpetual recurrence, and that is the reason why I am so often
> miserable. I am continually distracted by my desire to go home, and
> my equally intense one to be an artist. I don't think I shall play in
> concert this winter. I don't feel fitted for it yet. I haven't got to the
> point where I can sit down and play a thing perfectly, and I don't care
> to appear in a concert hall till I am entirely sure of myself. In Music
> one must resign oneself to gradual growth, and it's no use trying to
> hurry up matters.[57]

In the privacy of her practice room, Amy continued her daily routine, taking an
occasional respite from her labors in the evenings, when she attended concerts by prominent
artists. She followed Wagner's growing reputation with great interest, and took special
note of the progress of women musicians. She admired the playing of Sophie Menter,
and when she heard a symphony concert conducted by Alicia Hund she considered the
event "quite a step for women in the musical line."[58]

Yet the psychological trauma that engulfed Amy at the time of Ben's death and
Tausig's departure continued to take its toll, making her diffident about playing before
people, even in intimate settings. When, in February of 1872, Clara Schumann's half-
sister Marie Wieck invited her to her home to meet her father, the renowned pedagogue
Frederich Wieck, Amy was delighted to accept the offer. But when Wieck asked Amy
to perform for the guests, she refused repeatedly. He was perplexed by her reticence,
as she noted in a letter describing the incident:

> . . . on my continued refusal he finally said that he found it very strange
> that a young lady who had studied more than two years in Tausig's
> and Kullak's conservatories shouldn't have *one* piece that she could play
> before people.[59]

---

[56] Letter of Amy Fay to Zina Fay Peirce, 8 September 1871, FFP.

[57] Letter of Amy Fay to Zina Fay Peirce, 23 November 1871, FFP.

[58] MSG, 117.

[59] MSG, 167.

As Wieck perhaps intended, that remark provoked Amy; she marched to the piano and played the fugue at the end of Beethoven's A-flat sonata, op. 110. Once again, she described her state of mind while playing:

> . . . you cannot imagine how dreadfully nervous I was. I thought fifty times I would have to stop, for, like all fugues, it is such a piece that if you once get out you never can get in again, and Bülow himself got mixed up on the last part of it the other night in his concert. But I got well through, notwithstanding, and the old master was good enough to commend me warmly. He told me I must have studied a great deal, and asked me if I hadn't played a great many *Etuden*. I informed him in polite German "He'd better believe I had!"[60]

In December 1872, after playing at a large reception hosted by a member of the diplomatic corps, she wrote home "I'm picking up my courage again by degrees. I'm getting more confidence, which is the thing I need. I wouldn't be afraid to play before anybody if I could only do abroad as I do at home, but that is just the difficulty. I compose little preludes to all my pieces now, and modulate from one to the other."[61] After more than two years under Kullak's supervision, she still wrestled with feelings of inadequacy and discouragement over her self-perceived lack of progress as a concert artist. She wrote home "my life seems to be a succession of beginnings, which never result in anything."[62]

While she complained about not getting concert practice and about Kullak's reluctance to bring her forward, when he finally did invite her to play, she declined, writing home: "with my nervousness, I thought I better not attempt such a thing, until I had some experience in public playing."[63] But how was she to gain such "experience" if she declined opportunities to play? On two separate occasions early in 1873 she withdrew from scheduled public appearances, claiming nervous illness as her reason for not following through on what had been billed as her first "Kunstreise." She wrote home:

> . . . on Saturday evening to my surprise, von Brenner came to see me. He said that Kullak had spoken to him of me and that I was fitted to play in concerts, and that from all he had heard of me he was sure that I could get this concerto up by Wednesday. I said I knew I couldn't. He said I must try. . . . You have tomorrow and Monday evening. I'll come again and you must play it for me. Tuesday we have rehearsal with the orchestra, and Wednesday you play it in concert. . . . He was here again day before yesterday and I had to tell him how my illness had arrested matters. . . . But was there ever anything so provoking as my illness. Mr. Dievel had got all the programs printed with my name on them, and we called it my first "Kunstreise."[64]

---

[60] MSG, 167-68.

[61] Letter of Amy Fay to Zina Fay Peirce, 18 December 1872, FFP.

[62] Letter of Amy Fay to Zina Fay Peirce, 16 February 1873, FFP.

[63] Ibid.

[64] Letter of Amy Fay to Zina Fay Peirce, 16 March 1873, FFP.

It appeared that Amy feared the very success for which she longed. Despite the adulation of teachers, she continued to retreat from opportunities to perform in public. Her mentors and those who observed her felt that she was ready for the concert hall. Her repertory included the more challenging works of Beethoven, Chopin, and Schumann. Yet she could not free herself from the inner insecurities and paralyzing mind-sets that prevented her breaking new professional and personal ground.

What more could she do? To whom could she turn? She decided to pursue one more avenue that promised ultimate success—namely, instruction with a greater, even more renowned master than Kullak. She would seek out lessons from the greatest musician of the day and the rage of Europe, Franz Liszt.

Liszt

By 1873, like thousands of music students throughout the world, Amy, too, was caught up in the Liszt fever that had spread like wildfire throughout the musical world of the late nineteenth century. As conductor and teacher, Liszt was the most influential figure of the new German school dedicated to progress in music. The greatest piano virtuoso of his time, Liszt was revered throughout the Western world. From 1869 until his death eighteen years later, his summer villa in Weimar had become a mecca for flocks of students who came each summer anxious to be admitted to his classes.

In 1871 the American pianist James Madison Tracy described Liszt's Weimar salon for the readership of *Folio* magazine:

> His so-called lessons consisted of weekly matinees given at his home, at which times those who had his permission were present. This number never exceeded a dozen persons, being composed largely of celebrated players and singers; for artists in both departments frequently sought his advice. At such times, the few young ladies and gentlemen (mostly the latter) present, were expected to be prepared to play, if called upon, whatever piece had been previously selected by Liszt. Liszt often played one or two pieces himself, and if there was any other artist present, he was called upon, and expected to contribute something toward making up the program. The criticisms of Liszt at these matinees were musically severe, scathing in nature, amounting sometimes to positive harshness and despotic sarcasm; but as soon as the experiences were over he would take the performer to one side and shake him warmly by the hand, telling him that his extreme severity was only intended for the player's good.[65]

---

[65] James Tracy, "Personal Recollections of Liszt" (part 1 of two-part article), *Folio* 4, no. 3 (February 1871): 31.

Amy longed to be among Liszt's students. With the assistance of Dievel, the musician acquaintance whom she had met at a social gathering when she first arrived in Germany, she contacted Liszt's agent, who in turn agreed to present her to the maestro and to find her a boarding place. On 30 April 1873 she arrived in Weimar, where she found herself in the company of many other "hopefuls" aspiring to work with Liszt. Among them were the American pianists John Orth and Kathi Gaul, the young French composer Vincent d'Indy, and a charming French-speaking Belgian musician named Camille Gurickx. Amy wrote home that she was "wild to see" Liszt. She had heard that "everything depends upon the humour he happens to be in when you come to him," and hoped that when her moment came she would "hit upon one of his indulgent moments."[66] Having observed Liszt at the theater, she noted "his wonderful variety of expression and play of feature."[67] A few days later she met the maestro in person at a private party given for him and his scholars. She described her meeting in a letter home to Zina:

> We were . . . having a merry time, when the door suddenly opened
> and Liszt appeared. We all rose to our feet, and he shook hands with
> everybody without waiting to be introduced. Liszt looks as if he had
> been through everything, and has a face *seamed* with experience. He
> is rather tall and narrow, and wears a long abbé's coat reaching nearly
> down to his feet. He made me think of an old time magician more than
> anything, and I felt that with a touch of his wand he could transform
> us all. After he had finished his greetings, he passed into the next room
> and sat down. . . . After he had finished his cigar, Liszt got up and
> said, "America is now to have the floor. . . ." This was a dreadful ordeal
> for us new arrivals, for we had not expected to be called upon. . . . I
> slipped off into the back room, hoping Liszt would forget all about me,
> but he followed me almost immediately, like a cat with a mouse, took
> both my hands in his, and said in the most winning way imaginable,
> "*Mademoiselle, vous jouerez quelque-chose, n'est-ce-pas?*" I can't give you
> any idea of his *persuasiveness,* when he chooses. It is enough to decoy
> you into anything. . . . I sat down and plunged into the A flat major
> Ballade of Chopin, as if I were possessed. The piano had a splendid
> touch, luckily. Liszt kept calling out "Bravo" every minute or two, to
> encourage me, and somehow, I got through. When I had finished, he
> clapped his hands and said, "Bravely played." He asked with whom
> I had studied, and made one or two little criticisms. I hoped he would
> shove me aside and play it himself, but he didn't.[68]

Amy impressed Liszt favorably, and on the following day he asked one of the other students if she knew "Miss Fy" (*sic*), and requested her to tell Amy to come and see him.[69] Upon learning of Liszt's request, Amy went immediately to his salon. As she

---

[66] MSG, 197-98.

[67] MSG, 206.

[68] MSG, 207-09.

[69] MSG, 210.

entered the room he came forward and greeted her cordially, and although he did not invite her to play on that occasion, she knew that one day soon the maestro would ask her to do so. Accordingly she returned to her rooms to practice the piece she would play when her turn came to play in Liszt's classes, the Chopin B-minor Sonata.

Three afternoons a week Amy went to Liszt's class, which usually was comprised of four or five students. On the day of her playing debut in his class, three gentlemen students were also present in the teaching salon. Liszt left the room for a moment, at which time Amy tried to persuade them to leave the room also, so that when Liszt returned she could play for him in private. But when he returned they merely laughed and said they would not move one inch. When Liszt learned from them of Fay's request that they withdraw so that she would not have to play before such artists, he responded with a smile "Oh, that is healthy for you," and added "you will have a very choice audience, now."[70]

Amy played her piece "pretty successfully," and according to her own estimation:

> Nothing could exceed Liszt's amiability, or the trouble he gave himself, and instead of frightening me, he inspired me. Never was there such a delightful teacher! and he is the first sympathetic one I've had. You feel so *free* with him, and he develops the very spirit of music in you. He doesn't keep nagging at you all the time, but he leaves you your own conception. Now and then he will make a criticism, or play a passage, and with a few words give you enough to think of all the rest of your life. There is a delicate *point* to everything he says, as subtle as he is himself. He doesn't tell you anything about technique. That you must work out for yourself.[71]

Amy's lessons with Liszt exacted an emotional toll nonetheless, and she described this in a 21 May 1873 letter to Zina:

> I cannot tell you what it has cost me everytime I have ascended his stairs. I can scarcely summon up courage to go there, and generally stand on the steps awhile before I can make up my mind to open the door and go in![72]

Her awe of the Master excited yet exhausted her. As she later (15 July 1873) wrote home:

> When I come home from the lessons I fling myself on the sofa, and feel as if I never wanted to get up again. It is a fearful day's work every time I go to him. First, four hours' practice in the morning. Then a nervous, anxious feeling that takes away my appetite, and prevents me from eating my dinner. And then several hours at Liszt's, where

---

[70] MSG, 212.

[71] MSG, 212-13.

[72] MSG, 211.

one succession of concertos, fantasias, and all sorts of tremendous things
are played. You never know before whom you must play there, for
it is the musical headquarters of the world. Directors of conservatories,
composers, artists, aristocrats, all come in, and you have to bear the
brunt of it as best you can.[73]

In the studio Liszt was very strict. He walked up and down as students played,
frequently stopping and pointing out passages that were not being played satisfactorily.
On occasion, when a particular student couldn't play a certain passage acceptably after
several attempts, Liszt made every one in the class sit down and try it.

In other less formal settings Liszt demonstrated many of the effects he had invented.
On one occasion "he began playing the double roll of octaves in chromatics in the bass
of the piano. It was very grand, and made the room reverberate."[74] In Amy's mind,
the secret of Liszt's fascination was "this power of intense and wild emotion that you
feel he possesses, together with the most perfect control over it."[75] Even when he made
mistakes, he displayed an amazing talent for covering them up. Amy gained an entirely
new idea of piano playing from Liszt. The maestro praised her work and whenever she
did anything well he would call out "*charmant.*"[76]

Liszt continually distinguished Amy by marks of interest. He even included her on
his list of "principal scholars."[77] On one occasion he paid her a visit and played on her
piano. At the same time he told her of a matinée he would be giving the following Sunday
for a countess of distinction. As Amy explained:

> None of the other scholars were asked, and when I entered the room
> there were only three persons in it besides Liszt. . . . After the company
> was all assembled, it numbered eighteen persons, nearly all of whom
> were titled. . . . Liszt was so sweet. He kept coming over to where I sat
> and talking to me, and promised me a ticket for a private concert where
> only his compositions were to be performed. He seemed determined
> to make me feel at home.[78]

Liszt liked Amy. In trying to explain his fondness for her, Amy wrote "Liszt felt that
I comprehended him, and that was the secret of his preference for me."[79]

Liszt was not the only one who considered Amy to be "special." In 1873 Alexander
Wilhelm Gottschalg, a correspondent for the prestigious *Neue Zeitschrift für Musik*, praised
Fay's playing at Liszt's 29 June 1873 matinée in these terms:

---

[73] MSG, 231-32.

[74] MSG, 241.

[75] MSG, 242.

[76] MSG, 232.

[77] Louis Nohl, *Life of Liszt*, transl. George P. Upton (Chicago: Jansen, McClurg & Co., 1884), 198.

[78] MSG, 214-15.

[79] Letter to Amy Fay to Laura Smith, 12 July 1874, FFP.

Franz Liszt and former students. This 1883 photo reveals the loyalty and strong bonds Liszt evoked from his students. Given the hundreds who boasted of having Liszt as their teacher and who flocked to Weimar for annual summer reunions with him, it is to be noted that although Amy Fay is not pictured in the photo, Liszt included Amy Fay among his principal scholars.

Foto Louis Held.

Above: *Liszt house in Weimar, where in the spring and early summer of 1873 Amy Fay studied.*
Below: *Liszt house interior where Amy had her piano lessons.* Fotos Louis Held.

> Frl. Ami Fai (aus Nordamerika, welches letzere in der siejahrigen Saison ziemlich stark vertreten ist) spielte Tausig's geistreiche, aber sehr knauplige und gepfefferte *Soirees de Vienne* recht brave.

> Miss Amy Fay (of North America, which nation has been pretty strongly represented here this season) played Tausig's ingenious but very highly seasoned *Evenings in Vienna* right bravely.[80]

Liszt occasionally spent leisure time with his favored students, inviting them to his home after his day's sessions, or having an occasional picnic for them. It was at one of Liszt's student picnics that Amy met Camille Gurickx, the young student pianist from Brussels. The two got on well from the beginning, and before long their friendship blossomed into a full-fledged romance. Gurickx became increasingly demonstrative in his affection, frequently caressing Amy's beautiful hair and saying lovingly in his native language, "Oui, tu a une charismante-petite-tête."[81] When he gave Amy a locket with his initials monogrammed on it, she cherished it throughout her life.[82]

In September 1873, before Liszt returned to his Roman villa following his season in Weimar, Amy had her final lesson with him. It was an ordeal for her, as Liszt was tired and out of sorts from his engagements and his busy schedule. At this, her last lesson, Liszt accompanied her performance of the Rubinstein concerto:

> Liszt's splendid accompaniment and his beautiful face to look over to—it was enough to bring out everything there was in one. If he had only been himself I should have had nothing more to desire, but he was in one of his bitter, sarcastic moods. However, I went rushing on to the end—like a torrent plunging into darkness, I might say—for it was the end, too, of my lessons with Liszt![83]

It was not, however, the last time that she would see Liszt, for she would have the opportunity to say one more good-bye, and on that occasion Liszt would be in better spirits. Amy described that leave-taking:

> Liszt was kindness itself when the time came to say good-bye, but I could scarcely get out a word, nor could I even thank him for all he had done for me. I did not wish to break down and make a scene, as I felt I should if I tried to say anything. So I fear he thought me rather ungrateful and matter-of-course, for he couldn't know that I was feeling an excess of emotion which kept me silent.[84]

---

[80] Quoted in Robert Stevenson, "Liszt's 'Favorite' California Pupil: Hugo Mansfeldt (1844-1932)," *Inter-American Music Review* 7, no. 2 (spring-summer 1986): 33.

[81] Letter of Amy Fay to Zina Fay Peirce, 6 October 1874, FFP.

[82] Madeline Smith, "Portrait of My Aunts," FFP.

[83] MSG, 264.

[84] MSG, 269.

Reluctantly she returned to Berlin in order to resume her instruction with Kullak. But in the after-glow of her experience with Liszt in Weimar and her romantic interlude with Gurickx, Kullak could no longer satisfy. She missed both Liszt and Gurickx. Her letters home make frequent references to her dear Belgian friend and reveal how fond she was of him. On one occasion she reported how Gurickx longed for her to wear flowers in her hair. She even expressed her eagerness to have one of her nieces or nephews named after him.

In the autumn of her discontent she once again decided to cast about for a new teacher. Upon recommendation from her American pianist friend William Sherwood, she chose Ludwig Deppe, a prominent teacher, pianist, and conductor from Hamburg.

With Deppe

At the time Deppe enjoyed a reputation as a leading musical pedagogue. He believed that most keyboard instruction focused too much attention on finger strength development. He instead emphasized the use of the upper arm, shoulder, and back muscles to control arm weight. He consistently followed the rule that "Your elbow must be *lead* and your wrist a *feather*." This "feather-light" hand was to be carried about and supported by the large upper arm and shoulder muscles, which in turn were to be strengthened by isometric exercises apart from the keyboard, such as on horizontal bars. [85]

Deppe had formulated a series of ten exercises requiring twenty minutes of playing, ten minutes for each hand. Each exercise had a definite object, such as trills done slowly in single notes, then in double thirds, scales, and raising and lowering the fingers while maintaining a loose wrist. According to Amy, the most important exercise required the raising of the forearm and letting the fingers drop on the black keys from above, sinking with the wrist but holding the first joint of the finger very firm.

At her first session Deppe explained to Amy that her principal difficulties were mechanical. He praised her conception and style, but noted that her execution was uneven and hurried. Additionally her wrist was stiff, her third and fourth fingers very weak, her tone not round and full enough, and her pedalling unsatisfactory. Finally, Deppe told her that she was "too nervous and flurried," [86] but that he could help her, insisting that she must get over her agitation. Amy wrote home to Zina:

> Ah! if I had only studied with Deppe before I went to Weimar. . . . But if I had known Deppe four years ago, what might I not have been now? [87]

---

[85] Gerig, 256-57.

[86] MSG, 287.

[87] MSG, 302.

THE

DEPPE

FINGER EXERCISES

FOR

Rapidly Developing an Artistic Touch

IN

Piano Forte Playing,

Carefully Arranged, Classified and Explained,

BY

AMY FAY.

75

PUBLISHED BY

S. W. STRAUB & CO.

CHICAGO.

Title-page of the Deppe exercises edited by Amy Fay in 1880.

Amy worked with Deppe through the summer of 1874; on that August 24 she made her official debut at a concert in a fashionable watering place near Hannover, and, in her own words, "it was a complete success."[88] She did not play any solos, however, for Deppe felt unsure of her courage. She wrote home to Zina about the experience:

> But I wasn't the least frightened, and the audience only affected me
> so far as to excite me. They all told me that my cheeks and lips glowed,
> and as to my hands, they burned like coals of fire and were as electric
> and supple as they could be. I was astonished myself at the beauty
> of my scales, trills, and passages. They were so pearly yet so soft.
> My programme was à la Joachim, only three pieces, and all chamber
> music. . . . Suffice it to say they were all exquisite.[89]

After the concert Deppe gave Amy a champagne supper. Amy described the toast Deppe proposed:

> When he poured out the wine he proposed a toast to two ladies. One
> was me of course, and the other was in America, he said, namely the
> sister of Fräulein Fay, "whom I judge to be woman of genius, so truly
> and rightly does she feel about art (I've translated your letter to him)
> and who so nobly sympathizes with and stands by Miss Fay. To Miss
> Peirce, whose acquaintance I long to make."[90]

This time Amy's nerves surfaced after the concert. She wrote: "I scarcely slept at all of course after such excitement, and today I am so nervous and trembly that I can hardly hold a pen."[91] She wrote how happy she felt Liszt would have been if he could have heard the progress she had made:

> I think now though that I could interest him [Liszt] immensely. He will
> be in Weimar late in the autumn or even in the winter. . . . If I were
> going to remain here I should certainly go and see him and play to him.
> I am sure he would be struck by the change in my playing. If I could
> only get a letter of recommendation from him to Steinway or somebody,
> as I believe Mehlig had! But I would never dare ask it, unless I really
> had distinguished myself in his eyes by my playing, nor would he give
> it otherwise, for he is dreadfully careful and conscientious about these
> things, and it is a difficult thing to get a testimonial from him.[92]

---

[88] Letter of Amy Fay to Zina Fay Peirce, 25 August 1874, FFP.

[89] Ibid.

[90] Ibid.

[91] Ibid.

[92] Letter of Amy Fay to Laura Fay Smith, 12 July 1874, FFP.

In the fall of 1874, Amy's father began to pressure her to come home, even going to the trouble of writing Deppe himself of his wishes regarding his daughter. But neither Amy or Deppe thought she was prepared to go home, as Amy wrote to Zina:

> I read your letter and Papa's to Deppe but he declares that I must not think of going home this winter, that he will never give his consent to it. . . . I believe if I stick it out with Deppe this winter I will be a great artist, and return prepared to make engagements. . . . I mean I'll be able to make the tour of the country and accomplish my ambition of being a concert player and making money as such before I settle down to teach. My training with Kullak and all the rest was without aim or method, but Deppe has a plan, an organized gradation in all he does, and he says he doesn't want to send me into the world till I am all armed and equipped![93]

Amy and Deppe prevailed, and for one more year she studied with Deppe, who seemed to understand that Amy could not hold up well under stress. Accordingly, he continued to try to build up her courage by easing her into public performance through collaborative rather than solo experiences. On another occasion he encouraged her to play a Mozart concerto, which he would direct in private. But her nervousness remained problematic. Even in the fall of 1874, after a whole year of study with him, Deppe apparently still questioned Amy's ability to overcome her fear of playing in public.

In May 1875, she accepted an invitation to perform in a Philharmonic concert at Frankfurt in which, besides playing a Beethoven sonata for violin and piano with a violinist named Oertling, she played three solos—Raff's "Capriccio," Hiller's "Zur Guitarre," and Chopin's "Etude in Sixths." She apparently overcame her nervousness, writing home:

> In my first solo I occasionally missed a note, but my second was without slip, and my third—Chopin's Study in Sixths—was encored, though I took the tempo too fast.[94]

She received a highly laudatory review in the 11 May 1875 issue of the *Frankfurter Zeitung und allgemeiner Anzeiger*, which concluded by stating that "we can but congratulate the teacher of the young lady, Herr Ludwig Deppe, of Berlin, upon such a young scholar."[95] Amy did not resent Deppe's insistence that she study so much chamber music, and when she returned home and became a teacher, she was tireless in promoting Deppe's method.

Back in Cambridge, meanwhile, Zina eagerly awaited her sister's letters. From the outset she recognized their exceptional content and style, and she took care to preserve each one carefully. Surely, Zina thought, the letters would have great appeal for a wider audience—especially those letters from Weimar. So Zina carefully selected and arranged the Weimar correspondence for the editor of the *Atlantic Monthly*. It appeared in the October 1874 edition with an accompanying note by Zina, which read:

---

[93] Letter of Amy Fay to Zina Fay Peirce, 22 July 1874, FFP.

[94] MSG, 349.

[95] MSG, 351.

The reader will please to note the dates of the letters which, as well as those from Weimar about Liszt, were written home without a thought of publication. One of Amy's friends wished to print extracts from her letters, and though she would not say "yes," she did not say "no." With this negative permission they were arranged for the *Atlantic* without her supervision, and are given almost *verbatim* as they left her rapid pen.[96]

Her reference to herself as "friend" was not totally misleading, for Zina was a "friend" to Amy. But the phrase "almost *verbatim*" requires a more refined reading, for Zina in fact exercised a heavy editorial hand, deleting many passages which would have thrown considerable light on Amy's personal life and on her relationship to Liszt. Zina felt an obligation to honor the literary conventions of the time which discountenanced women presenting intimate views of themselves or of speaking of themselves in too complimentary a fashion. Why else would Zina omit Fay's letter of 12 July 1874 in which she refers to Liszt's liking her "personally?" The only explanation is that Zina, not wanting to offend the *Atlantic* readership by violating the literary canons of the day, deleted material that revealed a more intimate view of her sister, especially insights about her personal concerns, her insecurity about playing in public, and her relationship with Liszt. As Amy wrote home:

> Thank heaven Zie omitted any of Liszt's commendatory remarks or anything self-laudatory. That looks awful in print, and I would have suppressed still more—for instance "and that was the beginning of my friendship with Liszt." I would have liked to have had the thing entirely impersonal. Though Liszt continually distinguished me by marks of interest, I think though that it was more because he liked me personally, and not on account of my musical talent, which was really not at all remarkable in comparison with the others. In fact I never did myself justice, because I was so overcome with the sense of my own powerlessness. It would have been very different if I could see him again after this year of study.[97]

Amy, thousands of miles away, had returned to Berlin with thoughts of going home. She had become convinced that her teachers had done all they could for her and that she would have to do the rest. After six years spent in striving to move from the status of amateur to that of artist, she had concluded that:

> Masters can put you on the road but they can't make you go. You must do that for yourself. . . . Concert-playing, like everything else, is *routine*, and has got to be learned little by little.[98]

---

[96] *Atlantic Monthly* 34, no. 104 (October 1874): 453-65.

[97] Letter of Amy Fay to Laura Smith, 12 July 1874, FFP.

[98] MSG, 341.

En route home in August of 1875, she and Zina, who had come to join her husband Charles for part of his second and longest European sojourn for the United States Coastal Survey, went to Weimar for a farewell visit to Liszt.[99] No descriptions of this visit with Liszt have surfaced, doubtless because Zina, the one to whom Amy would have written about such an occasion, was at her side. By then the Grand Duke had seen the letters published in the *Atlantic* and no doubt had shown them to Liszt. Amy shared with Laura her concern over their reception:

> I told Zie I knew that someone would get hold of them and send them to Liszt. I don't know as the Grand Duchess will have relished my saying that she "didn't dare ask Liszt to play" etc.! One can't be too careful what one puts into print.[100]

Although no accounts of Liszt's discussion with Amy about the publication have surfaced, time would show that Liszt was delighted with Amy's descriptions of himself. It would also show that Zina's marriage was in serious jeopardy. Following her visit to Weimar with Amy, Zina decided not to rejoin her husband for the trip home to the United States, choosing instead to remain by Amy's side and to accompany her home. The decision displeased the Peirce family, but Charles defended his wife's actions in a letter to his brother James:

> You may have the idea that Zina has done wrong in going home. That would be wronging my darling very much. She was quite right in going and I fully agreed to that, although the very sudden way in which she did leave when I fully expected to see her, was a great blow to me. But she thought that if we met we shouldn't have the strength of mind to separate and therefore acted on impulse. She didn't go home because of Amy, but because her health required it.[101]

Charles desperately wanted to believe that his wife had left without him for health reasons, but clearly Zina's decision to remain with Amy rather than with her husband signalled that something was amiss in her marriage. Once both she and Charles were home, periods of sporadic separation between them increased, coming to a head in 1876, when Zina refused to join him when he was transferred to New York in conjunction with his scientific work. That decision marked the end of their marriage, although a divorce settlement was not reached until eight years later.

At home, meanwhile, the subscribers to the *Atlantic* had proven that Zina's hunch was correct; they had delighted in Amy's account of her studies with Liszt. By the time she

---

[99] Mitarachi's typewritten partial curriculum vitae of Zina (MFP) states that from May to August 1875 Zina was in Berlin and then in Weimar with Amy.

[100] Letter of Amy Fay to Laura Fay Smith, 12 July 1874, FFP.

[101] Letter from Charles Sanders Peirce to James Peirce, 10 December 1875, Ms. CSP L339, by permission of the Houghton Library of Harvard University.

arrived home, her articles had made her a celebrity and had piqued the public's curiosity about this American woman who had undertaken six years of music study in Germany.

The public had other reasons to celebrate Amy Fay. As the first of an extensive line of late nineteenth-century women to go abroad for music study, she was a pioneer who pointed out new musical horizons for many of her women contemporaries and for subsequent generations. Among them was Helen Hopekirk (1865-1945) of Edinburgh, who registered at the Leipzig Conservatory in 1876.

> Two years later the pianist Eugen d'Albert was quoted as estimating that twenty per cent of the concert audiences in any German city consisted of Americans; while New York's *Musical Courier* for November 22, 1891 assessed the American population of Berlin at two thousand, almost all music students. We will state confidently that the females were in the majority among them and that students of the piano outnumbered all other music students several times over. That same volume of the *Musical Courier* carried regular advertisements of German music schools in every issue: the conservatories of Leipzig, Dresden, Hamburg, Weimar, and Sondershausen all considered it profitable to take regular substantial space in this American journal.[102]

Amy's decision to go abroad for serious study typified the "new girl" replacing the "piano girl." It announced the arrival of the nineteenth-century "New Woman" in the arena of music. This New Woman—single, highly educated, and economically autonomous—rejected marriage, sought professional visibility, espoused innovative, often radical economic and social reform, and wielded real political power.[103] Like Amy, she was likely to be "a member of the affluent new bourgeoisie—frequently a child of home-town America; she felt herself part of the grassroots of her country."[104] Her quintessential American identity, her economic resources, and her social standing permitted her to defy conventions, pioneer new roles as Amy had done, and still insist upon a rightful place within the genteel world.[105] For the next half century, men and women would argue and debate the pros and cons of the New Woman, agreeing only on one point: the New Woman challenged existing gender roles and the distribution of power.[106] That Amy was a New Woman, not only in terms of the musical profession but also in light of the changing life style of the late nineteenth century, would become clear when she returned home.

---

[102] Loesser, 538-39.

[103] Smith-Rosenberg, 213.

[104] Ibid., 245.

[105] Ibid.

[106] Ibid.

PART 3

Celebrity

Celebrity

Upon her return home, Amy experienced many changes both within and outside family circles. Several of her family still resided in Cambridge, but they now did so under new familial conditions. Her father was living on Harvard Street with his second wife Sophronia White, while Rose and Lily were sharing quarters at 101 Pinckney Street. Kate and her husband, William E. Stone, were nearby on Exchange Place. Within walking distance on Arrow Street were Zina and Charles, but their marriage was on the brink of failure, and it was only a matter of time before Zina would leave Charles forever. Only Laura, by now married to Nelson Smith and living in Vermont, and Norman, an up-and-coming businessman newly relocated in the midwest, were geographically outside the Cambridge family circle.

Musically, too, there were new developments for Amy to assimilate. The distinctions between the popular and cultivated traditions, which were barely visible at the beginning of the century, had become a reality of the nation's musical life.[1] Conservatories of music were on the rise. Music was firmly entrenched in public school curricula and was on the verge of becoming accepted in colleges and universities as well. Major concert halls were either already constructed or were on the drawing boards in many leading cities. The piano was gaining prominence on the concert stage. Music criticism was establishing its foothold in the musical world and the country's musical life had come under the purview of John Sullivan Dwight, the city's and the nation's most eminent music critic. In sum, the institutional foundations of the cultivated tradition in music were becoming firmly consolidated.[2]

Following her return, Amy went to New York for the first few months rather than moving to Cambridge right away. Why New York? No doubt because Zina was there, preparing for a woman's gathering she was to convene on 20 December 1875, at which she would speak on the duties of women, the importance of occupation, and the advantages of the cooperative system in reducing living costs. Zina had booked Chickering's former rooms on 14th Street in New York City for the occasion. Anticipating that the event might

---

[1] H. Wiley Hitchcock, *Music in the United States: A Historical Introduction*, 3rd ed. (Englewood Cliffs, N.J.: Prentice-Hall, 1988), 44.

[2] Ibid.

be an appropriate setting in which to showcase her concert-pianist sister, she invited Amy to use the women's meeting to present her first professional recital. The notion of playing before an audience affiliated with Zina appealed to Amy, as did the idea of staying with her while she prepared for her performance. After all, Zina had done much to promote her study in Germany, and Amy wanted to make her cherished sister proud of her. To insure a successful performance she selected familiar pieces that she had played in Germany to the approval of her teachers and peers:[3]

Study in Sixths (Etude, op. 25, no. 8)	Chopin
Sonata, op. 27, no. 5	Beethoven
Chant polonais, no. 5	Chopin
Clavierstück	Schubert
Canzonet	Jensen
Märchen	Raff
Gnomen-Reigen	Liszt

Dwight reported that the critic from the *Brooklyn Union* lauded Amy's performance, calling it

> an entertainment of novel and unusual interest. . . . None can hear her play without predicting for her an unusually brilliant career. Her technique is faultless, her touch clear, elastic and sympathetic, and her interpretation of the most varied compositions equally successful. The ease with which she plays the most difficult works is only equalled by her extraordinary memory, and we hope sincerely that the opportunity may soon again be offered the public to listen to music of such an entirely satisfactory character.[4]

After such a promising start, Amy was anxious to make her all-important Cambridge debut; she set the date for 19 January 1876, at Lyceum Hall. For that event family and acquaintances would be on hand, as well as an even larger number of persons who, though unknown to her, were anxious to hear for themselves one of their own who had come so far in the world of music. Amy knew that she had much riding on her performance before the hometown crowd. Dwight would be in the audience and his pronouncements would be important.

> Dwight was the "chief oracle" of his times when the times were in transition, when many new forms of music were first emerging, when orchestras were first beginning, when audiences for serious music were just forming, when the influence of Germany on music was just being discovered.[5]

---

[3] *Dwight's Journal of Music* 35, no. 20 (8 January 1876): 159.

[4] Ibid.

[5] Betty Chmaj, "Fry versus Dwight: American Music's Debate over Nationality," *American Music* 3, no. 1 (spring 1985): 76.

The publication he had founded in 1852, *Dwight's Journal of Music*, had gained a reputation as the finest music periodical in America. Its pages were filled with essays on music history and theory, translations of French and German treatises, biographies, journals, and reviews of concerts. It reflected Dwight's conviction that music had a high moral purpose, and its self-assured pronouncements earned him the title "The Autocrat of Music."[6] Though *Dwight's Journal* never had more than a few hundred subscribers, they were widely scattered and

> included a majority of the most active laborers in the American musical vineyard. Contributors were many and important: Curtis, Lowell Mason, the great Beethoven biographer Alexander Wheelock Thayer, William Foster Apthorp, and others.[7]

Dwight's efforts had helped shape the nation's audiences—especially those in New England—into listeners of great sophistication quite accustomed to hearing performances by musicians of international stature as well as concerts by the best of domestic talents. Dwight was so successful in his attempts at shaping a rich musical climate in the Cambridge-Boston area that frequently he could not keep up with the musical attractions he himself had helped attract to the community. In the days preceding and following Amy's debut, Dwight complained in his *Journal* that other scheduled concerts, though "full of interest," came "too near together."[8] On the week of her debut, Amy Fay's was but one of many concerts from which to choose. Competing for Dwight's attention, for example, were four programs of the renowned pianist Hans von Bülow, a concert by the Theodore Thomas Orchestra, concerts by the Harvard Symphony Orchestra, and programs by the Boston Philharmonic Club. Yet on any other week the situation would have been similar, so rich was the musical life of Cambridge and Boston.

Dwight, however, made it a priority to get to Amy Fay's Lyceum Hall concert, where he heard the following program:

Gigue	[Johann Wilhelm] Haessler
Sonata quasi una fantasia, op. 27, no. 1	Beethoven
Song without Words—Duetto	Mendelssohn
Chant polonais, no. 5	Chopin (arr. Liszt)
Märchen (Fairy Story)	Raff
Gnomen-Reigen (Elfin Dance)	Liszt
Andante spianato and Polonaise, op. 22	Chopin
Canzonet	Jensen
Capriccio	Raff
Des Abends (Evening)	Schumann
Valse caprice, on Strauss's "Nachtfalter"	Tausig

---

[6] Ibid., 70.

[7] Ibid., 64.

[8] *Dwight's Journal of Music* 35, no. 21 (5 February 1876): 174.

The critic found Amy's playing impressive and wrote:

> Her technique was brilliant, her touch is full of vitality and nervous energy, her readings are intelligent, she has remarkable strength, and plays with verve and freedom, as well as with artistic accuracy. [9]

Amy was quick to send Dwight a note thanking him for his positive comments, which she assured him she would send to her teachers abroad, "who would be delighted with it, and feel that their labours over her were not in vain." [10] Furthermore, she reminded Dwight that before her departure for Europe in the summer, she would give another concert on April 1 at Mechanics Hall in Boston in which she would play an almost entirely new program which including two etudes by Chopin, Liszt's *Grand Polonaise* in E major and *Valse Impromptu*, and the Mendelssohn G-minor Concerto arranged for quintet.

Meanwhile, before that April event, Amy moved back to Cambridge into the home on Pinckney Street shared by her sisters Rose and Lily. She found it pleasant to be near old friends like Henry Wadsworth Longfellow and the Jameses once again, and when she needed a reprieve from practicing she would visit these dear friends, all of whom enjoyed her good company. William James, in a letter to his brother Henry, describes such a visit by Amy:

> Miss Ammy [sic] Fay paid me a long visit the other night—Alice, father and mother having gone to hear Mr. Thaxter read a translation of the Agamenron by Fitzgerald (of Omar Khayam notoriety) at the Thayers— she being chaperoned by her brother-in-law Stone, who sat speechless one hour and a half listening to our gabble, and said that you were C. S. Peirce's particular admiration. [11]

As the time for the Mechanics Hall concert approached, however, Amy experienced renewed bouts with nervousness. Working with the high-strung instrumentalists who were to accompany her in the Mendelssohn concerto brought on headaches and emotional exhaustion. As a consequence she withdrew from the normal forms of social discourse in which she usually delighted, and she even put off an engagement with her dear friend Longfellow. Two notes of explanation she wrote him shed considerable light on her emotional state. In the first she stated:

> I have taken ill and am not well, and it is raining hard this morning and I wish to beg you to let me come another day for dinner instead of today. My head has ached badly since yesterday, which makes me feel heavy and stupid, and I am afraid I should not be very entertaining. [12]

---

[9] Ibid., 175.

[10] Letter of Amy Fay to John Sullivan Dwight, 3 March 1876, Boston Public Library, Special Collections.

[11] Letter from William James to Henry James, 12 December 1875, Ms. Am 1092.9(2596), by permission of the Houghton Library, Harvard University.

[12] Letter from Amy Fay to Henry Wadsworth Longfellow, 1876, Ms. Am 1340.1(2647), by permission of the Houghton Library, Harvard University.

In the second, a response to Longfellow thanking him for the get-well gift of a bottle of wine he had sent her to assist her restoration to health, Amy referred once more to strains caused by concert preparation:

> I took a glass . . . this morning when I returned from my rehearsal and felt much refreshed and revived by it. It is very strengthening I think. I slept off a good deal of my fatigue last night, and am quite myself today, as my anxiety about my concert is allayed, and I believe it will go well. The rehearsal yesterday was a little too much for me. But first rehearsals are always trying. Instruments, like people, must learn to agree.[13]

The nervous tension precipitated by the Mendelssohn was difficult enough to bear, but when the double bass player failed to appear at the actual concert, Amy was nearly undone. Placed at a disadvantage, both musically and emotionally, she could not summon the verve and energy noted by Dwight at her Lyceum Hall performance. The critic remarked on the difference in her playing, writing that:

> . . . there was felt a certain hardness and lack of the sympathetic quality in most of her interpretations. Doubtless it was owing in a great measure to embarassment. The somewhat unfortunate accompaniment to the Concerto (the double bass not making an appearance) may well have disconcerted her; it was a correct, but rather a literal, cold rendering. So too in the Schumann pieces there was too much conscious effort; while in the Polonaise and Waltz by Liszt, the brilliant mastery seemed too much the triumph of determined will; she possessed the music (playing all from memory), but the music hardly possessed her.[14]

Yet Dwight could still praise Fay's "free, bold sure hand" and prophesy that "this lady, in whom Liszt had taken so much interest is destined to take a high place among our pianists, we can hardly doubt."[15] Despite such a qualified review, Amy took courage; after all, she would have other chances to prove herself on the concert stage.

Meanwhile there was a wonderful summer ahead. Zina invited Amy to be her travel companion on a European trip, the declared purpose of which was to meet her husband Charles, who was still abroad in conjunction with his project with the United States Coast Guard Survey. In reality, however, Zina had an agenda of her own, which included stopping off in London to gather materials for a projected book on cooperative house-keeping, and arranging a visit to Weimar for meetings with Liszt and Gurickx.

In April 1876 the two sisters, filled with anticipation of impending delights abroad, sailed for Europe. Prior to their departure, the *Boston Daily Advertiser* commissioned Zina to chronicle her travels in a series of pieces for the popular newspaper.[16] Using the

---

[13] Letter from Amy Fay to Henry Wadsworth Longfellow, 1876, Ms. Am 1340.2(1925), by permission of the Houghton Library, Harvard University.

[14] *Dwight's Journal of Music* 36, no. 1 (15 April 1876): 214.

[15] Ibid.

[16] These appeared in the issues of 28 April, 3 June, and 20 July 1876.

pseudonymn "Zero," Zina sent back lively and informative articles to the hometown paper. Of special interest was her report from Weimar, which recounted the meetings with Amy's friends from student days in Germany—the New York pianists William and Mary Sherwood, Baltimore pianist Kathi Gaul, and especially the Belgian pianist Camille Gurickx.

The two sisters stayed at the Russicher Hof, where their friend, the Vermont-born composer Silas Pratt, also was registered. Pratt engaged a drawing room equipped with a new Chickering piano, and over a ten-day period organized "the most charming impromptu soirees imaginable" for visiting Liszt scholars to drop in on any or every evening for informal music making.[17] The joy of these gatherings was exceeded only by the delight in the special time spent with Liszt and Gurickx.

When the sisters first arrived at Liszt's home, the music was already in progress, and Liszt was playing the bass of a four-handed composition with one of his pupils. After the piece drew to a close, the visitors from Cambridge stood, the circle opened, and Liszt saw and greeted the Fay sisters. Zina observed that

> his figure is a little bent, and he begins to show his sixty-five or more years, but there was never a more wonderful head, or a more singular, tragic and changing face, or rather mask, than his.[18]

She also noted that

> It has been said that no one can enter Liszt's salon without being affected by it, and that the assertion has some truth in it I can testify in my own case.[19]

Amy's visit to Liszt's salon brought to mind memories of three years before, when she was among many of the same musicians seeking Liszt's approval and advice:

> Amid these young creatures, with their concert-room triumphs all before them, moved about the colossal virtuoso whose similar triumphs are all behind him. To them the least of his musical honors would be a glory. To him, they are all as vanity, faded and worthless in comparison with the meed [recognition] which the world bestows on creative genius alone, and which has long been his only real aspiration. Liszt rarely plays now, not even to this high-strung and appreciative audience. . . . Like a caged lion he walks up and down restlessly among his pupils, all of whose "eyes wait upon him," and makes here a little jest, there a trivial remark, yonder a sly sarcasm, until we wonder how much of real earnestness there is behind that face with the Voltarian smile, which is at such variance with its powerful, tragic features and square, iron jaw.[20]

---

[17] *Boston Daily Advertiser*, 3 June 1876.

[18] *Boston Daily Advertiser*, 28 April 1876.

[19] Ibid.

[20] Ibid.

Amy observed the close interplay of the Maestro with his students, which Zina described in such detail:

> Liszt always looks at his listeners himself, and of the things he makes his pupils do. "Throw me a look" he will say, as he sees their eye-lids drop too fixedly over the keys. It is not such an easy thing to learn, they say, and requires just a little more "cheek" than most of them at first possess. [21]

When Liszt visited Pratt's quarters at the hotel, Zina noted that

> it was truly exquisite to hear him put his hands on some chord in the piece, and by one of his subtle modulations transform the whole phrase. He teaches just as some master of literature might discourse on poetry, and illustrates any point in hand by snatches from this composer and that throughout the whole range of music. [22]

One afternoon during their stay in Weimar the sisters met Liszt in the street, and he invited them to attend an organ concert to be given by one of his young blind students at the Stadtkirche. Liszt confided to Amy that he dreaded going because blind musicians often came to him but were rarely true artists, the disadvantage against them being too great. After hearing the youth, however, Liszt apparently revised his opinion, for Zina noted that he "sat with closed eyes and a tranquil almost transfigured look, listening as if he really enjoyed it." [23] Another memory of Liszt lingered following the third and last matinée the sisters attended, when Liszt closed the session by playing from manuscript, and with great feeling, the Adagio ("Gretchen" movement) from his *Faust Symphony*. [24]

The meetings with Gurickx were equally unforgettable, particularly for Amy, who cherished the opportunity to be with the young man with whom she had fallen in love during her student days in Weimar. The bonding which had begun there in 1873 had led Amy to think seriously of accepting Gurickx's proposals of marriage. Accordingly, Zina welcomed the opportunity to acquaint herself more fully with the young man who hoped to become her brother-in-law. After observing him at close range she was pleased to note that "he has no affectations, mannerisms or small jealousies, but is the simplest of young men." [25] As a pianist she found him

> simply "colossal," one of those pianists who, as Ferdinand Strakosch said of him, "will one day drive his carriage and horses," and "dictate his own terms." [26]

---

[21] Ibid.

[22] Ibid., 20 July 1876.

[23] Ibid., 28 April 1876.

[24] Ibid., 20 July 1876.

[25] Ibid., 3 June 1876.

[26] Ibid.

She was struck by his physical appearance as well, writing:

> Gurickx is short and firmly built, with a broad hand that knows no
> fatigue and fingers that seem to know no difficulty, though in him the
> clearness of the passage playing is not that to which your attention is
> called any more than to Fräulein Gaul's, but rather, like hers, to the
> vividness with which the "points of the piece start out," and to its effect
> as a whole. His best performances are in Bach, Scarlatti, Schumann
> and Liszt.[27]

Zina described Gurickx's touch as "electric" and felt sure that his exciting way of building
climaxes would "set an American audience crazy."[28] She wrote:

> When Gurickx plays any great work, it is with his whole body, his hair
> falls forward and during his performance his face sharpens and grows
> older with the intense concentration of all his energies which he puts
> into it. . . . Now he may be considered the finished artist, and this
> season Liszt, who previously had not taken much notice of him, as soon
> as he presented himself made an appointment with him, at which he
> kept him playing for two and a half solid hours, and thereafter sent
> for him for study every day of his stay in Weimar.[29]

At the conclusion of their stay in Weimar, Amy, sensing Zina's approval of Gurickx,
apparently consented to become engaged to him quietly. Before any formal public
announcement could be made about the couple's marriage plans, however, Amy's father
and her brother Norman would have to be consulted about the matter. To proceed with
marriage plans without their approval would have been unthinkable in an age in which
men still made major decisions pertaining to their single daughters and sisters.

After their farewells to Liszt and Gurickx, the sisters next went to London, where
they visited the national Trainery School for Cookery, attended museums and the theater,
and observed the quality of life in general. The ideas that Zina formulated would take
shape several years later in her book *Co-Operative Housekeeping*.

In August 1876, Zina and Amy returned home to Cambridge, after which Zina
finalized a step which she had been considering for over a year; namely, abandoning
Charles. When Charles went to New York on a work assignment for the United States
Coast Guard Survey, as explained earlier, Zina refused to join him, thereby formalizing
the separation that had been sporadic since 1875. In deciding to separate from Charles,
she confided to her brother-in-law James her conviction that reconciliation with him
was impossible.

---

[27] Ibid.

[28] Ibid.

[29] Ibid.

Amy could not have been surprised by Zina's decision. Toward the end of her student years abroad she had deduced from Zina's letters that her marriage with Charles had become troubled. As early as 1874 Amy was upset by reports that Charles was insensitive to his wife's "state of feebleness."[30] She resented Charles's apparent lack of consideration for his wife, as she believed that in marriage "both parties ought to respect the tie they have formed and try to get along amicably."[31] She believed "that love was a passion one couldn't command and that the passion of love rarely lasted any way between married people."[32]

As for herself, in 1871 Amy had declared emphatically to Zina "I wouldn't marry for anything and it is the worse thing you can wish on me."[33] Although her subsequent romantic involvement with Gurickx eventually caused her to reconsider her vow to remain single, when she did muse on marriage she was haunted by memories of her mother's hard life and her sister Laura's difficulties with childbearing. She once wrote home "how sad poor Laura's letters always are, aren't they? I suppose she is going to have another baby and it is so hard for her."[34] Other aspects of marriage also repulsed her, in particular housework and the loss freedom. On this latter point she once wrote home to Zina "never will I do it, and if I go home I shall make Mother understand that immediately."[35] She finally advised Zina on the subject of her own marriage, writing:

> You ought to stick to Charlie, or if you find that you can't get along
> with him, you ought to separate from him and combine with me.[36]

Meanwhile, Amy was delighted to accept an invitation from the renowned conductor Theodore Thomas to appear as guest soloist with his orchestra at a Sanders Hall concert in Cambridge scheduled for 21 February 1877. Of all the opportunities an aspiring musician could hope for, none could surpass this chance presented to Amy. Theodore Thomas was, after all, one of the leading conductors in the world who had stimulated the growth and development of sophisticated audiences for symphonic music in the United States. He had conducted for the first time in the nation works by such composers as Tchaikovsky, Dvořák, Rubinstein, Bruckner, Goldmark, and Richard Strauss. His annual concert series in Cambridge was eagerly awaited by New England audiences anxious to hear orchestral music of the highest caliber. In accepting Thomas's invitation to appear with his orchestra, Amy realized what opportunity now lay before her. An impressive performance with the Thomas Orchestra could open important doors in the world of music and do much to further her fledgling career. On the other hand, a disappointing execution could impede the advancement of her career as a soloist.

---

[30] Letter of Amy Fay to Zina Fay Peirce, 21 July 1874, FFP.

[31] Letter of Amy Fay to Zina Fay Peirce, 23 November 1871, FFP.

[32] Letter of Amy Fay to Zina Fay Peirce, 11 November 1874, FFP.

[33] Letter of Amy Fay to Zina Fay Peirce, 30 October 1874, FFP.

[34] Letter of Amy Fay to Zina Fay Peirce, 22 July 1874, FFP.

[35] Ibid.

[36] Ibid.

Knowing that so much was at stake at the forthcoming concert, Amy chose to play from memory a work she had studied thoroughly while abroad and with which she felt secure, the Chopin F-minor Concerto. When the double bill of the internationally famous Thomas and the hometown celebrity was announced, it created an atmosphere of heightened anticipation among the Cambridge crowd.

Would Amy rise to the occasion that had been presented her? Would her nerves stay out of the way of a satisfactory performance? Would her memory hold up under the pressure of performance? Large numbers turned out for the occasion to hear for themselves the answer to such questions. By the time the concert began, every seat in the house was taken. Furthermore, Dwight was there in his role as premiere music critic.

As Amy began to play, Dwight and the audience sensed immediately that she was not at her best. Periodic memory lapses weakened her performance. Dwight did not miss the "long flashes of silence" and "the certain nervousness" that occurred while Amy played. Yet he conceded that

> She gained courage, and with it freedom, however, as she went on; the broad *recitativo* in the *Larghetto* movement was well emphasized, and the rapid finale was played firmly, brilliantly and clearly. Yet it is the brilliant rather than the poetic side of Chopin that she represents. The effort was heartily applauded. Later in the evening she was very successful in a piano solo: "Elfin Dance," a concert study by Liszt, and was compelled to reappear and give another piece. [37]

Still, the hoped-for artistic triumph had eluded her and grudgingly she had to acknowledge that her performance under Thomas's baton would hardly help advance her career.

If musically the event was a disappointment, the occasion proved enormously successful from a social standpoint, in that it inaugurated the beginning of a long friendship between Theodore Thomas and the Fay family. Thirteen years later, in 1890, it would culminate in the marriage of Amy's younger sister Rose to the conductor following the death of his first wife. That marriage would prepare the ground for Amy's brother Norman to join with Thomas in founding and financing the Chicago Symphony Orchestra in 1891.

Amy, in turn, continued to enjoy the artistic and social life of Cambridge, attending concerts and lectures and taking advantage of her proximity to old friends. She especially cherished her friendship with the poet Longfellow, and he in turn valued his association with her. They socialized in a wide range of contexts, from friendly chats over cups of tea to Christmas dinner with the Longfellow family. Correspondence between the two confirms how devoted they were to each other. In a letter dated 28 February 1877, Longfellow wrote a charming invitation to Amy on the occasion of his birthday:

---

[37] *Dwight's Journal of Music* 36, no. 24 (3 March 1877): 399.

Dear Miss Fay,

Will you do me the favor to dine with me on Tuesday the twenty-seventh?

It is my birthday, and I feel as if I were standing on the top of a lofty tower. You have no idea how dizzy it makes one feel to look down from such a height!

Your Septuagenarian friend,
H.W.L.[38]

Such personal affiliations were especially comforting in the wake of disappointments suffered in connection with the Thomas concert.

Amy remained on the concert circuit in 1877 and 1878, playing before audiences in Boston and Cambridge, St. Albans and Burlington, Vermont, and at the Worcester Music Festival. Following an appearance on 7 May 1877 at Lyceum Hall in Cambridge, the *Boston Globe* critic praised her "desirable touch, her grace of conception, and her comprehensive execution."[39] And in September of that year the Vermont press lauded the "beautiful liquid quality of her touch," and, in a manner typifying male critics, remarked on her appearance, stating that Miss Fay was "still young, and we shall be pardoned for saying, attractive."[40]

In the fall of 1877 she gave three concerts at the Union Hall in Boston, each of which was reviewed by Dwight in his journal. For the first, on October 16, she performed the following program:

Prelude and Fugue in F minor	Bach
Bourée in A minor	Bach
Sonata pastorale, op. 28	Beethoven
Country Scenes, op. 28 (Wood-notes, Wayside Flowers, Under the Lindens, Shepherd's Lament, Village Dance)	Paine
Spinning Song (from *Flying Dutchman*)	Wagner-Liszt
Nouvelle melodie	Rubinstein
Midnight Barcarolle, op. 12	Jerome Hopkins
Ballade in G minor, op. 23	Chopin
Ballade in A-flat major, op. 47	Chopin

Dwight wrote on the series:

We thought Miss Fay appeared, upon the whole, to better advantage than she did last year,—strength and firmness of touch, freedom and brilliancy of execution still taking precedence over fineness of feeling

---

[38] Letter from Henry Wadsworth Longfellow to Amy Fay, 28 February 1877, Ms. Am 1340.1(2361), by permission of the Houghton Library, Harvard University.

[39] *Boston Daily Globe*, 8 May 1877.

[40] *Daily Messenger* (St. Albans, Vermont), 19 September 1877.

and conception. Naturally therefore she was most successful in the rendering of the more modern concert pieces. She missed the spirit—a very fine imaginative, poetic spirit—of the Bach Prelude and Fugue, taking liberties with the tempo, and showing small regard to light and shade. The fugue voices were not clearly individualized; and the *Bourrée* sounded altogether vague and undefined. In the Pastoral Sonata of Beethoven, the first movement lacked the serene repose which so beautifully characterizes it, no less its sunny cheerfulness; the reiterated three-four monotone of the bass was over-loud, and the whole movement was urged on at an almost *agitato* speed. The *Andante* was better, more subdued and even; and the Scherzo and Trio were quite nicely rendered. We felt the restlessness again in the *rondo finale*. [41]

Yet Dwight found much to praise in Fay's playing, writing that:

Mr. Paine's little "Country Scenes" are charming little pieces, happily contrasted, and these seemed to be played *con amore*, certainly with grace. Miss Fay's most finished, elegant, and satisfactory performance was of the Lisztian version of the Wagner "Spinning Song"; there all her passages were beautifully smooth and flowing. In the "Melody" of Rubinstein she showed genuine expression. The *Barcarolle* by Mr. Hopkins was rhythmical, but rather commonplace. The G minor *Ballade* of Chopin came out much more fairly than the things of Bach and Beethoven, and indeed there was much to praise in her rendering of both the Ballades. [42]

For her second recital, 30 October 1877, Amy unveiled a completely different program which, according to Dwight, "exhibited her wonderful memory and her brilliant and unflagging execution in a wide range of difficult and interesting pieces."[43] It comprised the following selections:

Gigue	Haessler
Sonata quasi una fantasia, op. 27, no. 1	Beethoven
Song without Words—"Duetto"	Mendelssohn
Chant polonais, no. 5	Chopin-Liszt
Märchen (Fairy Story), op. 102, no. 4	Raff
Gnomen-Reigen (Elfin Dance)	Liszt
Valse Caprice, on Strauss's "Nacht-falter" (Night-Moths)	Tausig
Des Abends (Evening)	Schumann
Capriccio	Raff
Canzonet	Jensen
Andante spianato and Polonaise, op. 22	Chopin

---

[41] *Dwight's Journal of Music* 37, no. 16 (10 November 1877): 127.

[42] Ibid.

[43] Ibid.

Dwight was more impressed than he had been the week before, commenting:

> The *Gigue* by Haessler, a pupil of one of old Sebastian Bach's best
> pupils, . . . was very neatly and intelligently played. The Sonata
> Fantasia of Beethoven was better suited to her than the *Pastorale* of the
> first Recital, and its movements were presented evenly and clearly, the
> *Adagio* quite impressively; the Scherzo (*molto vivace*) so like a clashing,
> flashing sword dance, and the Finale were given with much fire and
> spirit. In the Mendelssohn "Duetto" the two voices were significantly
> individualized. Liszt's transcription of one of Chopin's Polish Songs
> was really a charming piece, and to our ears entirely fresh; nor did it
> seem to suffer in the rendering. Raff's *Märchen*, a pretty thing, full of
> fire-fly sparkles, was gracefully given with a light staccato touch. . . .
> Schumann's "Des Abends" we have heard played with more expression;
> yet we cannot say that it was badly done. The Chopin *Andante* and
> *Polonaise* were highly satisfactory; indeed such seemed to be the verdict
> of the general audience, a larger one, and more responsive, than upon
> the first occasion.[44]

For her third concert, November 27, Amy played:

Prelude and fugue in B minor	Bach
Sonata in C major, op. 53 ("Waldstein")	Beethoven
Nocturne in C minor	Field
Thirty-Two Variations in C minor	Beethoven
Nocturne in F major, op. 15, no. 1	Chopin
Nocturne in F-sharp major, op. 15, no. 2	Chopin
Etude in A minor, op. 25, no. 11 ("Winter Wind")	Chopin
Liebestraum Nocturne	Liszt
Rhapsodie hongroise, no. 14	Liszt

Dwight thought that this concert was the most satisfying of the three. He remarked on
Amy's "evidence of power of will and intellect, as well as physical nerve and muscles,
to carry through such a programme with unflagging certainty."[45]

As the reviews came in, they suggested Amy was improving and that she was becoming
more comfortable before audiences. Her programs reflected an expanding repertory that
championed such American composers as Hopkins and Paine. Her memory was holding
up. Despite the fact that her playing tended to emphasize the brilliant rather than
reflective side, and her tempos often got away from her, her programs were presented
with flair and intelligence. She was the living proof of her own words, uttered before
she left Germany in 1875, that concert playing could only be learned by experience.

---

[44] Ibid.

[45] *Dwight's Journal of Music* 37, no. 18 (8 December 1877): 143.

As her reputation grew, concert managers sought her out and she began to accept students for instruction in the Deppe method, for which she had become an enthusiastic advocate, charging ten dollars for twenty lessons. In September 1878 she became the first person ever to play a complete concerto (Beethoven B-flat major) at the Worcester Music Festival, the nation's oldest music festival. Her appearance marked only the second time that a woman had performed as soloist at the festival, although through the years its organizers came to favor such women pianists as Teresa Carreño, Julie Rivé-King, Adele aus der Ohe, Fannie Bloomfield-Zeisler, and Olga Samaroff.

Although the critic for the *Massachusetts Daily Spy* stated that "she was cordially received and accomplished her difficult task most satisfactorily,"[46] the critic of the Worcester paper was less complimentary. He criticized Fay's uneven tempo, attributing it to possible "nervousness."[47]

By the end of 1878, Amy had known both success and disappointment on the concert stage. For six years she had been a student in a German culture that was heavily masculine and heavily reliant on discipline. She had been forced to make adult decisions while in a subservient student role. Although she had worked long and hard, she had yet to free herself totally from the nervousness that had bedeviled her from her student days in Germany. Whereas other women of her background often had assumed the social pose of nervousness as a strategy for gaining male support, this was not the case with Amy. She sincerely wanted to shake the nervousness that plagued her, causing so many of her successes to be followed by failures. If she were to secure a niche for herself on the concert stages of the nation, she would have to gain control over her nerves. She determined that she would do so, but not in Boston or Cambridge. For the next decade or so she would live and work in Chicago, that thriving capital of the midwest. Before taking leave for the "windy city" she divided up her students between local piano instructors William Sherwood and Warren Locke.[48] She felt ready to take on Chicago. Was Chicago ready for Amy Fay?

---

[46] Quoted in Raymond Morin, *The Worcester Music Festival: Its Background and History, 1858-1946* (Worcester, Mass.: County Musical Association, 1946), 41.

[47] *Worcester Evening Gazette*, 28 September 1878.

[48] Amy Fay, "The Deppe System Vindicated," *Etude* 3, no. 4 (1 April 1885): 79.

PART 4

The Windy City

Fraternal Affiliations

Why Chicago? Why, toward the end of 1878, would Amy Fay leave enlightened Cambridge for a frontier city still in the throes of recovery from the Great Fire of 1871? Did she sense that the soon-to-be reconstructed city was on the verge of becoming one of the world's largest urban centers? Or that it might hold the promise of more career opportunities? Did she hope to ignite a conflagration of another sort and set the musical world of Chicago afire?

As it transpired, Amy's move came about at the request of her brother Norman, who two years before had moved to Chicago, where he had risen to prominence as one of that city's most distinguished businessmen.[1] The thirty-one year old Norman, a confirmed bachelor at the time, requested that his sisters Amy, Zina, Lily, and Rose join him in setting up housekeeping in the new home he was building at 43 Bellevue Place in the affluent downtown area. In calling his sisters to Chicago, Norman anticipated that they would transform his house into a warm and supportive family home. His invitation was also his way of fulfilling an obligation to look after his single sisters. Accordingly, once Norman had invited them to join him in Chicago, they had little choice but to go, as society expected women to follow dictums issued by the family men concerning their places of residence.[2]

For the thirty-five year old Amy, the move to Chicago presented challenges. Surprisingly, at first she was more homesick than she had even been in Germany. A letter to Longfellow, written while she was staying at Kelly's boarding house at 275 East Indiana Street prior to the completion of Norman's home, describes her feelings of nostalgia:

> On the opposite side of the room is a register, and I often sit there warming my feet on the furnace, and as I do I warm my heart by gazing at your portrait. You sit, leaning on your hand, and gazing meditatively at me, till it seems as if you are about to speak. Sometimes I speak

---

[1] Norman Fay was in turn general manager of the Bell Telephone Company of Illinois, vice-president and then general manager of the Chicago Company, and president of Chicago Arc and Light and Power Company.

[2] For a further discussion of the "man's position" in society, see Joan Kelly, *Women, History, and Theory* (Chicago: University of Chicago Press, 1984), 57.

to you, and though you do not reply, you are a good listener! . . . I
have never had such desparate and protracted fits of homesickness as
I have had here.[3]

Nevertheless, before long she adapted to life in the windy city. With the assistance of her
socialite brother she and her sisters quickly gained entrance to the important social circles
of Chicago's north side. The popular Norman was enjoyable company and possessed
great power of *repartée*.[4] He delighted in his bachelor status, glibly reporting in successive
Harvard reunion booklets how he had eluded the nuptial state. In 1887 he wrote "I am not
married, or likely to be, but have built a house and live with my sisters at 43 Bellevue Place,
where I hope to see you or any of the Class who pass through Chicago."[5] Similarly in
1899 he wrote that he had "married no wives," and in June 1919 he still gloated in his
bachelorhood, writing for his Harvard classmates: "I have not succeeded in contracting any
marriages; have made no offers of heart and hand recently."[6] Norman's bachelorhood
facilitated his sisters' immersion into Chicago's high society, and the Fays became popular
newcomers in social and cultural circles of the city.[7]

At Bellevue Street, Norman assumed the position of head of the household, managing
his sisters' finances, distributing to each a monthly allowance of fifty dollars and monitoring
carefully each one's expenses. This arrangement, in promoting his sisters' economic
dependency upon him, reflected the phenomenon of "sex-hierarchy" operative in the late
nineteenth-century family structures.[8]

How did the sisters meet this reality? On the one hand, Rose and Lily remained quite
content to assume the more traditional duties associated with domesticity—running the
household, supervising meal preparation and house cleaning, hostessing guests, handling
correspondence, and pursuing their respective hobbies of singing and dressmaking.[9]
Zina and Amy, on the other hand, were determined to break out of the restricted atmosphere of the domestic arena and work outside the home—Amy as a professional musician
and Zina as a manager of boarding houses. Among the siblings, concessions to Amy's and
Zina's demands no doubt were facilitated in part by the open atmosphere of the midwest,
which tended to enlarge the scope of women's place to include economic ventures, even
in instances where they did not need to work.[10] Such societal acceptance of women's

---

[3] S. Margaret William McCarthy, ed., *More Letters of Amy Fay: The American Years* (Detroit: Information
Coordinators, 1986), 3. Hereafter referred to as MLAF.

[4] Norman's friends were legion and came to include, among others, the famous pianist and eventual Premier
of Poland, Ignace Paderewski.

[5] *Sixth Triennial Report of the Secretary of the Class of 1869 of Harvard College* (Boston: Rockwell and Churchill,
1888), 22.

[6] *Harvard College Class of 1869 50th Anniversary, 11th Report* (Cambridge: Riverside Press, 1919), 89.

[7] Not until 1922, at age seventy-four, did he venture matrimony with Lillian Hale, of an old Newburyport,
Massachusetts family, and set up his own home in Cambridge, where he and his wife lived most happily together
for nearly twenty years!

[8] For more on sex hierarchy in society, see Kelly, 54.

[9] See Kelly, 129, for further descriptions of women's duties in the bourgeois home.

[10] Lucy Eldersveld Murphy, "Business Ladies: Midwestern Women and Enterprise, 1850-1880," *Journal of
Women's History* 3, no. 1 (spring 1991): 81.

economic enterprises was in considerable contrast to the less tolerant attitude in the northeast. Nearly a decade before Amy Fay's arrival in the state of Illinois, the cultural climate of the midwest had become quite receptive to the notion of women undertaking their own professional enterprises. [11] For example, in 1870 the U.S. Census Bureau of Midwestern Businesswomen in Illinois, Indiana, Iowa, Michigan, Minnesota, Ohio, and Wisconsin listed among its businesswomen 1,894 women teachers of music and 1,667 boardinghouse keepers. [12] When Amy and Zina arrived in 1878, they soon entered the mainstream of professional women musicians and boardinghouse keepers.

Chichago

In other ways too, the frontier environment into which Amy Fay moved in 1878 was on the brink of tremendous cultural growth. The Great Fire of 1871 left the city a pile of smoking stone and iron with no concert hall or studio. Yet the burgeoning town soon arose like a phoenix from the ashes. In musical circles, as in all areas of life, Chicago citizens demonstrated a resilience and determination to build anew the musical life that had been so devastated by the burning flames.

During the two decades after the fire, Chicago more than tripled in population and multiplied many times over its various forms of wealth and communications systems. Enterprising musicians were successfully shaping a climate in which diverse musical activity flourished: concert life, instrument manufacturing, education, and publishing. Both public and private concerts prospered, with keyboard music occupying a prominent place. Church organists commonly presented concert series; Harrison M. Wild, S. E. Baldwin, and others appeared frequently in organ recitals. The recognized "dean" of Chicago organists was Clarence Eddy, who arrived in Chicago in 1874 to become the general director of the newly planned Hershey School of Musical Art. Eddy achieved considerable renown when he presented his famous series of one hundred recitals without a single repetition between 1877 and 1879; his wife Madeline, from whom he eventually separated, became a close friend of Amy Fay. [13]

As the piano assumed a new dominance in musical life, it became both a cultural symbol and a source of entertainment. Piano manufacture and sales increased dramatically. Like their counterparts throughout the country, Chicago residents discovered that the instrument provided a pleasant diversion both in the privacy of their homes—where the piano was a status symbol—on the concert stage, and at such music clubs as the Apollo Club, the Mozart Club, the Schubert Club, the Chicago Quintette Club, and the

---

[11] Ibid., 65-83.

[12] Ibid., 66.

[13] In 1902, Fay spent the summer as a guest of Mrs. Eddy at her chateau in France.

Mendelssohn Club. Along with international touring virtuosos, local pianist Charles Liebling regularly drew large audiences to programs which skillfully blended substantial works with lighter compositions.[14]

In its own curious way, the treatment of the piano reflected the social vision that helped shape late nineteenth-century family life. In such settings sexuality was to be concealed and certain topics could not be introduced in genteel company:

> At dinner one asked for "white meat" rather than breast of chicken.
> Even legs of pianos were covered in a "proper" home. All this modesty
> kept sexuality and pleasure in the background, repressed in the interest
> of productive goals.[15]

To study music became synonymous with studying the piano. The popularity of the piano in domestic quarters created a climate conducive to enlarged educational opportunities in music. As public schools began to include music in the curriculum, enterprising musicians saw great possibilities for promoting its study in conservatories and schools of music. In 1875 Sara Hershey founded the Hershey School of Musical Art, with which, besides Clarence Eddy, such musical personalities as Frederic Grant Gleason and Clayton F. Summy were associated.

Musical publications, too, were proliferating. By 1884 a list of Chicago musical publications included *The Indicator*, *Music and Drama*, *Chicago Magazine*, and *Song Friend*. By the time Amy Fay had completed her eleven years in Chicago, the city was ready to welcome in 1891 its most serious music periodical, *Music*, edited by W. S. B. Mathews.

As the music page became a regular feature of the daily press, George P. Upton, one of the reigning music critics, wielded a powerful influence on musical life of the city as he went about his daily activities of judging, chronicling, persuading, and educating. In fact, the presence of Upton as the city's music critic of the powerful *Chicago Daily Tribune* defined in a special way the musical climate of the city. In 1880, a little over a year after Fay's arrival in Chicago, Upton's book *Woman in Music* was published, fanning the flames of what became a long-lasting and incendiary argument about the "proper sphere" for women in music. Even today the book's impact on collective societal expectations about the proper place of women in music lingers on.

Before the book's publication, Amy could write in 1880:

> There is no denying that Chicago is a fascinating sort of place to live in,
> after one gets accustomed to its way. Rose says she is less bored here
> than in any other place she was in. The busy, wide-awake atmosphere
> gives life a hopeful aspect. Life is not less of a struggle here, but one
> has more heart to contend, and the very rapidity with which the city
> has rebuilt itself, is a constant reminder of how much can be done when
> there is a will.[16]

---

[14] Kenneth J. Rehage, "Music in Chicago, 1871-1893" (M.A. thesis, University of Chicago, 1935), 21.

[15] Kelly, 131-32.

[16] MLAF, 7.

After the release of Upton's book, Amy would discover how much "of a struggle" life could be in Chicago, but during her first few months she was quite taken with the city. She saw as one of its greatest symbols of artistic progress its newly built Music Hall (now, Orchestra Hall), which, despite its "shallow stage" and "cheap decorations," had admirable acoustics. Amy wrote to Longfellow in 1880 that she

> was the first person to sound a note of music in the new Hall. What composer do you think I played? Wagner. I had some prickings of conscience, as I thought Beethoven ought to be the presiding genius of the new Hall, but I finally got over it by saying to myself that Wagner is the composer who represents progress, and is therefore better suited to Chicago.[17]

In the 1880s Chicago claimed as one of its more culturally active citizens Mrs. Potter Palmer, a renowned patroness of the arts and "the undisputed queen of Chicago society."[18] The city could not yet boast the presence of a permanent symphony orchestra, but Norman Fay would change that in 1891, when in collaboration with his future brother-in-law Theodore Thomas, he would organize the Chicago Symphony Orchestra.

Amy Fay's Chicago Career Begins

The dynamic, thriving Chicago at the turn of the 1880s was the backdrop against which Amy's day-to-day formation emerged. The city was full of promise as well as disappointment—a testing ground where Amy would come to terms with herself personally and professionally, capitalizing on her strengths and accepting her limitations. There she would create a legacy of professional and personal achievement, earn the respect of colleagues both at home and abroad, and achieve visibility as performer, writer, lecturer, and clubwoman. There, also, her feminist tendencies would become even more pronounced before reaching a new level of intensity later in New York when she would summon the courage to question some of Upton's views about women's musical potential. In Chicago she would conclude that it was better for musicians not to consume their energies "attempting to encompass an impossible ambition," but rather to "do their best to become fine musicians" and "to leave it to the privileged few to set the world on fire."[19] And it was the locale where she made peace with her decision to remain a single, professional woman. As she philosophized in a letter written in 1887:

---

[17] Ibid.

[18] *Notable American Women: A Biographical Dictionary*, ed. Janet and Edward James and Paul Boyer (Cambridge: Belknap Press of Harvard University Press, 1971), 8-10.

[19] Amy Fay, "How to Practice," *Etude* 2, no. 12 (December 1884): 214.

> . . . after thirty-five life is monotonous anyway. The only exciting thing
> about it is falling in love and getting married, and when that important
> question is settled one way or another, there is nothing left of an exciting
> nature. One can be *comfortable*, and that is all.[20]

Amy hoped for a fresh start in Chicago. Whereas in Cambridge she was no longer a bright, new face in the concert world, Chicago offered the hope of a new beginning in her effort to make a name for herself as a performer. She made an impressive start at a concert in which she shared the stage with the great violinist and intimate friend of Brahms, Eduard Reményi. She described the occasion in a 1879 letter to Longfellow:

> I made my first appearance with Orchestra, in a Symphony Concert
> at which Reményi also played and I received a good notice from Upton
> of the "Tribune" who is the grand critic of the Northwest. They tell
> me a smile from him goes a long way out here. Reményi behaved
> handsomely, and came out and sat on stage while I was playing. What
> a wonderful genius he is! Every time I heard him I was impressed.
> His playing is *so* fascinating! It made me long to go back to Liszt more
> than ever.[21]

In the wake of such an auspicious beginning, Amy announced an ambitious project of a concert series at Hershey Hall on May 12, 14, and 16, 1879, when she would be assisted by one Miss Mantey, a professional violinist who also was newly registered among professional musicians of the city. In planning the program, Amy relied on many of the works she had performed back east: the Sonata in D major by Beethoven, the Ballade in G minor and Nocturnes in F major and F-sharp major by Chopin, the Fourteenth Rhapsody by Liszt, and *Country Scenes* by Paine, along with smaller single works by Schubert (Impromptu, op. 142), Bach (Bourée in A minor), Mendelssohn (*Songs without Words*), Schumann (*Des Abends*), Kullak (*Landischer-Reigen*), Haessler (Gigue), Jensen (Canzonet), Raff (Fairy Story), and Gluck ("Gauohe" from *Don Juan*). This familiar repertory was already "in her fingers" and might give her the advantage over her nerves.

The announcement of these recitals attracted the attention of the general public and the Chicago press, not the least of which was the formidable *Tribune* critic, Upton. Since his position in Chicago was similar to that of Dwight in Boston, Amy realized that a good review from him would carry considerable weight in furthering her career. Would such a notice be forthcoming? No. The first coverage was cautious in tone and amounted to a graceful "non-review" avoiding any mention of Amy's playing whatsoever. Upton merely stated that it was not his intention to estimate her position as an artist or her ability as a player. He wrote:

> It will be more grateful to wait until the series is finished, and will be
> more just to the player, as her programmes are sufficiently wide in their

---

[20] MLAF, 11.

[21] Ibid., 4.

sweep to afford a basis for a final opinion. It is sufficient now to note that her reception was a very kindly one and that several of her numbers were enthusiastically recognized.[22]

After the completion of the series, Upton made his final judgment; namely, that Amy

cannot take a high place in the concert room. It is no secret that Miss Fay has been a close student and has been brought up in an atmosphere of music. No one could come away from studies with such men as Tausig, Kullak, Liszt, and Deppe, without gathering from each the materials that go to make up an artist and without enriching themselves musically. As a result of her studies with these masters she has gained true musical feeling, a remarkable memory, and exquisite taste, and thoroughly intelligent grasp of composition and good technique. She is in every respect a highly cultivated musician, well versed in the rules and traditions of the schools. If to these she joined the requisite repose and concentration of a virtuoso, she would achieve great results in the concert room, but in this respect she is deficient. Physical nervousness, when it cannot be controlled, will mar the best efforts, and no one can be more painfully aware of this than the player. We are nonetheless glad to welcome so accomplished a musician in our midst, for we know that she cannot help but exercise a powerful influence in the field of teaching and private playing by those associated with her. To these departments of labor, the most honorable and responsible in music, and the most far-reaching in fixing and educating musical taste, she will bring rare gifts and unquestionable qualifications.[23]

Upton's comments confirmed that Amy continued to struggle with a nervousness in performance and did not yet reveal the grace under pressure to which she aspired. Still, at times, she was very good. She determined to remain on the concert circuit.[24]

Early in 1880 she went on tour with the Thursby Concert Company, appearing with "handsome success" in such places as Des Moines, Rochester, Detroit, Washington, and Louisville, and achieving "a brilliant success" throughout the cities of the northwest and west.[25] She herself was greatly taken by the musicality of the people there, commenting in a letter to Longfellow that the people in Milwaukee were much more musical than in Chicago, and going on to write that:

This particular concert that I played at was given by the Men's Club, and was consequently crowded. There were fully two thousand people

---

[22] *Chicago Tribune*, 13 May 1879, 5.

[23] Ibid., 18 May 1879, 11.

[24] Privately, another critic in Chicago, Frederic Gleason, panned Amy's playing. In a diary entry dated 20 February 1880, he remarked on a recital in which "Miss Fay made quantities of blunders all the way through." Frederic Grant Gleason Collection, Newberry Library, Chicago.

[25] *Chicago Tribune*, 7 March and 28 March 1880.

in the Hall, yet the audience was so absolutely still that it seemed as if I could literally have heard a pin drop. It is a pleasure to play before an audience like that, because one feels as if one were listened to with some understanding.[26]

Her success on tour reinforced her courage.[27] It also helped build up her name in musical circles. She continued to play in public, and she also opened up a private teaching studio at Central Hall, charging the then going rate of three dollars per lesson.

The "Book of the Age"

Zina, meanwhile, had been devising a scheme designed to keep her sister's name before the public. She had not forgotten the popularity of Amy's letters home as published in the *Atlantic Monthly*, and was convinced that the larger correspondence held the potential for a book. Since the letters revealed so much hitherto unchronicled information about Germany and German musical life, Zina mused that the volume might even be entitled *Music-Study in Germany*. She had Amy enlist the advice of Henry Wadsworth Longfellow, who in turn proposed that she

> leave out the portions not strictly musical, and make it wholly a sketch of the divine art, as you found it in Germany. The impatient public like short books and a good many of them. Yours, long or short, I liked so much that I cannot believe that anybody would dislike it.[28]

Accordingly, Zina drafted approximately three quarters of the letters, taking care to emphasize their musical contents. In addition, in accordance with the social conventions of the day, she also omitted any self-laudatory or self-revelatory passages. Then she appointed her brother Norman to deliver the manuscript to the publisher Jansen and McClurg, along with a letter of endorsement from Longfellow, which stated:

> If I know anything about books, that is a good book. It is as good as my favorite novel, *Charles Auchester*. And I hope it will impart to youthful aspirants the indispensable conception that mastery in any Art means long years of study and effort and self-discipline.[29]

---

[26] MLAF, 6.

[27] Even Gleason acknowledged in his diary entry of 22 May 1880 that the "terrible pound" of Amy Fay was for once "alleviated by the fact that she used a Steinway piano."

[28] Letter from Henry Wadsworth Longfellow to Amy Fay, 8 February 1880, Ms. Am 1340.1(2575), by permission of the Houghton Library, Harvard University.

[29] Ibid.

MUSIC-STUDY IN GERMANY.

FROM THE

HOME CORRESPONDENCE

OF

AMY FAY.

EDITED BY THE
AUTHOR OF "CO-OPERATIVE HOUSEKEEPING."

Second Edition,
REVISED AND ENLARGED.

"The light that never was on sea or land."—WORDSWORTH.
"Pour admirer assez it faut admirer trop, et un peu d'illusion est
necessaire au bonheur."—CHERBULIEZ.

CHICAGO:
JANSEN, McCLURG & COMPANY.
1881.

Title-page of Music-Study in Germany *(Chicago: Jansen, McClurg & Company, 1881).*

Impressed by Longfellow's strong endorsement, Jansen and McClurg contracted with Zina to publish the manuscript under the title *Music-Study in Germany*.

Amy now was eager to inform Liszt about the turn of events regarding the German correspondence, in which he himself figured so prominently. On 21 August 1880 she wrote him news of her forthcoming book:

> At Christmas I hope to have a book published. It is entitled *Music Study in Germany* and has been compiled by my sister Mrs. Peirce from my letters. Since she is very clever with a pen, she has put the letters together very skillfully. Mr. Longfellow was very interested in them and did me the great honor of going through the book himself and recommending it to his own publisher. In this book there is much about you, Meister, and if it is finally published I will do myself the honor of sending you a copy. I believe that I have the correct concept of you. I have so often thought that I would like to write your biography! And then I would have to hear everything from your own lips![30]

Following the book's publication in 1881 she wrote to Longfellow of her appreciation for his endorsement of *Music-Study*:

> I am glad you liked the appearance of *my* little book. I thought Jansen and McClurg got it up in very good style. They took a great deal more interest in it after you had seen and talked with General McClurg about it. I was so much obliged to you for what you said to him. . . . They told me at the store that the book is selling rapidly, which I hope is proof of its success. The papers accorded it high praise, and everybody I have seen who has read it is quite enthusiastic over it. So your judgment of it is confirmed, and I cannot help being pleased, as the book was refused by several publishers, and none of them saw anything in it. Zina reduced it fully one quarter in size, and thereby left out several of the best things in it, as she considers. She has been quite inconsolable about it, now that people enjoy the book so much, and wishes she had not yielded to the clamourings of the publishers for condensation. However, I think perhaps it is just as well as it is. At any rate we have erred on the safe side.[31]

Music-Study in Germany includes a preface by Zina, dated Chicago, December 1880, which states:

> In preparing for the public letters which were written only for home, I have hoped that some readers would find in them the charm of style which the writer's friends fancy them to possess; that others would

---

[30] La Mara (pseud. for Ida Maria Lipsius), *Briefe hervorragender Zeitengnossen an Franz Liszt* (Leipzig: Breitkopf und Härtel, 1904), 373.

[31] MLAF, 9.

think the description of her masters amid their pupils, and especially Liszt, worth preserving; and that piano students would be grateful for the information that such an analysis of the piano technique of the greatest artists has been made, that any earnest pupil can with comparative ease and certainty conquer the difficulty of the piano-forte which includes all others—the SCALE.

How much of her Deppe's piano "method" is original with himself, pianists must decide. That he has at least made an invaluable *résumé* of all or most of their secrets, my sister believes that no student of the instrument who fairly and conscientiously examines into the matter will deny.[32]

The book propelled Amy's celebrity status to new heights. The musical press heaped praise upon it, and composer Ethelbert Nevin went so far as to call it *"the book of the age,"*[33] while the *Musical Bulletin* applauded the book, stating that

in the letters are preserved many hints and suggestions upon art (crystallized wisdom and experience) which, dropped from the mouths of illustrious men in daily intercourse are, as it were, embalmed through the medium of such letters and thus preserved for our instruction.[34]

Similarly, the December 1883 issue of *Etude* praised Amy's book, remarking:

A more delightful correspondence upon life in Germany, and music study in particular, we have never opened, and it is with earnest pleasure that we recommend it to teachers and pupils as highly inspiring as well as instructive and entertaining. . . . Miss Fay has handled her subject with the dexterous ability of a thorough connoisseur, and her book deserves a place in every cultivated home.[35]

In 1882, at the suggestion of Liszt himself, *Music-Study* was translated into German and provided with a preface by its publisher, Robert Oppenheim.[36] Its appearance in Germany attracted the attention of the editors of such prestigious German periodicals as *Allgemeine deutsche Musik-Zeitung, Das Magazin für die Literatur des In- und Auslandes,* and *Nord und Sud.*[37] The distinguished German critic Otto Lessmann commented in the first of these reviews that:

---

[32] MSG, [5].

[33] MLAF, 150.

[34] *Music Bulletin* 2, no. 3 (February 1881): 43.

[35] *Etude* 1, no. 12 (December 1883): 24.

[36] *Etude* 4, no. 9 (September 1886): 180.

[37] *Allgemeine deutsche Musik-Zeitung* (Berlin) 9, no. 32 (11 August 1882): 300-01; *Das Magazin für die Literatur des In- und Auslandes,* 13 May 1882, 279; *Nord und Sud,* July 1882, 144-45.

Cannes, Dec 23.
1880.

Dear Amy, [30y]

The book has just reached me, and right glad am I to see it, and in such nice attire. Your binding already my opinion of its merits. I am sure of liking it better than ever; for a book is much... is worth twice in manuscript; which it is the kind in thoughts, glorious and satisfactory.

Binder tells the tale nicely. This is a charming Christmas present. As I sent I hold it, and enjoy it; and as such it amuses it, and Being so... you meant it, and said it. Thanks!

I have more thanks than more to send you, nevergreen...: I kept the dreadful inferior version unchanged, the ... unchanged, nevergreens eglantine: shining, and nothing is left. Her letters.

So when I tell you that Sarah Bernhardt

Salvini; and Ostrolok, or
before, I know not which,
Mr Collier's "Pandora".

This is my "Masque
of Pandora," set to music,
with slight changes.

Tell Rose that she
must, through brief, were
charming. We were all
delighted to see her again.

I venture my grand-
mother on a card, and
am
                    Yours sincerely,
                         H. W. L.

has been here, and is gone,
it is no more. Already
know it.

People strangely hug a wonderful actress, and a fascinating woman. I did not see
her, either in public or in private, and therefore cannot
speak of her histrionic
talent, or her social charms.
I did mark, in the
newspaper, we have the
Midsummer Opera, with
Madam Langton? Then

Longfellow's letter to Amy Fay thanking her for the Christmas gift of Music-Study in Germany which he considered a "charming Christmas present."

> What the book offers is the fresh tone which the writer uses. . . . I knew
> Miss Fay personally from her student days at Tausig's Conservatory
> where I was teaching at the time and even if the memory of the fine
> slender figure with the open expression and the bright blond hair had
> disappeared, the charming conversational tone in her letters would have
> conjured her up for me again. [38]

While Amy's fame as a writer of highly popular musical memoirs was spreading throughout the world, her recognition as a performer did not keep pace. She continued to receive mention in the local press, but reviews of her playing often were reserved. When, on 20 April 1881, she appeared at a Wednesday matinée performance at Hershey Hall with a violinist, a soprano, and one of her pupils, Kate Huff, the *Chicago Tribune* critic, presumably Upton, noted that while Amy's numbers "received a very cordial reception," in his opinion "the most interesting part of the program was the playing of Miss Huff, whose intelligence, expression, and technique all bore testimony to Miss Fay's fine abilities as a teacher."[39] Was Upton's singling out of Amy's student another way of reinforcing his argument that Amy should consign herself to the teaching studio? If so, he made his point even more strongly in a review of Amy's recital of March 1882 in the *Chicago Tribune* in which he reported that Amy's rendition of the Beethoven Sonata, op. 110, was not satisfactory, noting that:

> the use of the pedal was such at times as to seriously interfere with
> a clear delivery of the subject, especially in the second and last move-
> ments. The phrasing, too, was not all that could be desired. But aside
> from those minor defects, we dissent decidedly from the interpretation
> of the Sonata. The lyric part of the first movement, especially the leading
> idea, was by no means cantabile enough. The second movement needs
> to go faster and with more Schumann-like fire, for here we come upon
> one of the places in Beethoven's music where the Schumann culture
> is definitely foretold. The third movement, the delicious and nobly
> pathetic arietta was given too heavily, and with not enough feeling.
> The introduction to it, also was not broad enough. Still it is due Miss
> Fay to say that her playing of this part of the sonata made an evident
> impression upon the audience. This aria is followed by a fugato move-
> ment in which it was the misfortune of the artist to come to grief through
> an unfortunate lapse of memory. However, she bravely began again
> with notes in hand and carried the entire last movement through with
> evident familiarity. As to the effect produced in this part of the Sonata,
> it was by no means satisfactory. [40]

Amy's inability to rid herself of the performance anxiety dating from her German sojourn forced her to try a new solution.

---

[38] *Allgemeine deutsche Musik-Zeitung* 9, no. 32 (11 August 1882): 301.

[39] *Chicago Tribune*, 20 April 1880, 18.

[40] *Chicago Tribune*, 2 March 1882.

"A Good Lead":
The Piano Conversation

In 1883 she decided to experiment with a creative concert format which would enable her to combine her gift with words with her pianistic talents. She called these presentations "Piano Conversations," because at each one she included a brief commentary before each piece played, speaking to her audiences just long enough to impart her own feeling, thought, and information in regard to it.[41]

She had a double purpose in introducing this unique approach to her performances. First, she felt that such a novel strategy would renew the press's interest in her career. More importantly, she sensed that by establishing a personal, direct contact with her listeners she would put both them and herself at ease. She would be operating from one of her strengths, since from her youth she had possessed a remarkable ease with language. Her deepened sense of connectedness with her audience might allay her nerves as well.

Her intuitions proved correct. The "Piano Conversations" attracted large audiences, which enjoyed the conversational style characterizing her letters home from Germany. They also put Amy herself at ease. The Chicago press praised both the concept and contents of the "Piano Conversations." The *Chicago Herald* of 11 March 1883 commented that Amy had struck "a good lead." Other words of praise appeared in the *Chicago Evening Journal* of April 7, the *Chicago Inter-Ocean* of April 7, and the *Chicago Indicator* of April 21. But perhaps the most telling review was given by the critic of the *Chicago Times* who, in an April 8 review, stated that Amy's "playing has gained so decidedly in power that high artistic rank must frankly be conceded her." Only the *Chicago Tribune* review of April 15, presumably by Upton, merely noted that Amy's programs were largely attended by both professional and amateur musicians.

So successful were the "Piano Conversations" that, at the conclusion of the inaugural 1883 series, the Chicago Amusement Bureau Company engaged Amy as a client. With the Bureau's backing, her programs flourished even more and inspired many of her colleagues to emulate her idea. Among the first to do so was her eminent musical confrere and friend from student days in Weimar, William Sherwood. On 16 March 1884, less than a year after Amy's first "Piano Conversations," Sherwood announced a concert in which he would "prelude each selection with some remarks in connection with the interpretation of the composition."[42]

Other associates followed suit. In October 1887 the blind Boston pianist Edward B. Perry circulated announcements of a "Piano Forte Lecture Recital" to be given on October 7 of that year. As late as 1914, *Musical America* announced in its issue of August 22 that

---

[41] In deciding upon this new method of concert giving, she may have reflected the influence of her uncle, Charles Jerome Hopkins, who as early as 1867 gave what he called "concert lectures" in New York.

[42] *Chicago Tribune*, 16 March 1884, 17.

Title-page of Piano Conversation booklet.

Miss Amy Fay's

PIANO CONVERSATIONS.

❧❧❧

PROGRAMME No. 2.

1—Sonata Quasi Fantasia, Op. 27, No. 1,
- - - - - *Beethoven.*
*Andante, Allegro ed Allegro molto vivace,
Adagio, Finale.*

2—Duetto, Song without words, - *Mendelssohn.*

3—Chant Polonais, No. 5, - - *Chopin.*
(Arranged for Piano by Liszt.)

4—Maerchen, (Fairy Story) - - - *Raff.*

5—Gnomenreigen, (Elfin Dance) - - *Liszt.*

6—Valse Caprice on Strauss' Nachtfalter,
(Moths) - - - - *Tausig.*

7—Des Abends, (Evening) - *Schumann.*

8—Capriccio, - - - - *Raff.*

9—Canzonet, - - - - *Jensen.*

10—Andante Spianato and Polonaise, - *Chopin.*

❧❧❧

Chickering Pianos used at all Miss Fay's concerts.

Three programs of Piano Conversations.

Miss Amy Fay's

PIANO CONVERSATIONS.

———

PROGRAMME No. 1.

1—*a.* Prelude and Fugue, F minor, from the Well
Tempered Clavichord.
b. Bouree, A minor, from the English Suites,
- - - - - *Bach.*

2—Sonata Pastorale, Op. 28, - - *Beethoven.*
Allegro, Andante, Scherzo Trio, Rondo.

3—Country Scenes, Op. 28, - *J. K. Paine.*
1. Woodnotes.
2. Wayside Flowers.
3. Under the Lindens.
4. Shepherd's Lament.
5. Village Dance.

4—Spinning Song, from the Flying Dutchman,
- - - - - *Wagner-Liszt.*

5—Nouvelle Melodie, - - *Rubinstein.*

6—Midnight Barcarole, - *Jerome Hopkins.*

7— { *a.* Ballade, G. minor, } - *Chopin.*
{ *b.* Ballade, A Flat major, }

Miss Amy Fay's

PIANO CONVERSATIONS.

❧❧❧

PROGRAMME No. 3.

1—Prelude and Fugue, B minor, from the Well
Tempered Clavichord, - *Bach.*

2—Grand Sonata, C major, Op. 53, *Beethoven.*
Allegro von brio, Adagio molto, Rondo.

3—Nocturne, C minor, - - *Field.*

4—Variations, E Flat major, - *Mendelssohn.*

5—Valse Mignonne, - - *Seeboeck.*

6—Nocturne, F Sharp major - - *Chopin.*

7—The Wind Demon, - *Jerome Hopkins.*

8—Liebes Traum, - - - *Liszt.*

9—Rhapsodie Hongroise, No. 14, - - *Liszt.*

❧❧❧

Chickering Pianos used at all Miss Fay's concerts.

MISS AMY FAY'S

PIANO CONVERSATIONS.

The undersigned take pleasure in announcing themselves as MISS FAY's authorized agents.

AMUSEMENT BUREAU COMPANY,

WEBER MUSIC HALL.   CHICAGO, ILL.

John Orth, another of Amy's student friends from her Weimar years, had given a "lecture recital" at a local church in Denver, Colorado, in which he

> gave many intimate and interesting anecdotes of his life in Weimar, making his auditors feel that they had met the venerable Abbe Liszt and been included in his household life. [43]

Before long, large numbers of performing artists were giving lecture recitals. It was an idea whose time had come. The "Piano Conversations" did more than signal a personal "break-through" for Amy; they helped shape the concert life of the late nineteenth and early twentieth centuries. The "Piano Conversation" became emblematic of how the word, both spoken and written, had continued to assert itself in Amy's life.

In Chicago, Amy's flair for language extended to other arenas as well. As both lecturer and writer she gained considerable popularity. She spoke regularly at both national and state meetings of the Music Teachers National Association, and she wrote music criticism for the nation's leading musical magazines. [44] By 1890 she had successfully negotiated with S. W. Straub & Company to publish her edition of *The Deppe Finger Exercises for Rapidly Developing an Artistic Touch in Piano Forte Playing*, for which she wrote the preface. The book comprised a series of ten exercises arranged, classified, and explained by her. In the preface, she presented the rationale for her book; she explained that Deppe felt that just as there was an acknowledged Italian method of singing there should be a finely developed system for forming fine piano technique, which, if rightly followed, would enhance the pianist's development. Yet in piano playing no particular way of doing things had been decided upon and recognized as the true method. Amy also noted that while most piano teachers advocate proper hand position, Deppe went much further, advising:

> turning out the wrist sufficiently to enable the fourth finger to rise freely, and to press the key squarely down, without playing on the side of the finger, as must be the case, when the wrist is not turned out. The wrist must be so supple that it can turn without throwing out the elbow in a triangular position to the body. The thumb must be so curved so as to enable it to rise freely from the hand, and to press the key down with the side of its first joint. The first joints of the other fingers should be firm and perpendicular to the key. This is most important to tone production, since the strength of the tone must come along from the firmness of the fingers, combined with the looseness of the wrist. [45]

---

[43] *Musical America*, 22 August 1884, 21.

[44] Amy's writings appeared in *Etude*, November and December 1884; April, August, and December 1885; August and December 1887; and in *The Indicator*, 25 October and 1 November 1884, and 15 and 22 February 1890.

[45] Amy Fay, ed., *The Deppe Finger Exercises for Rapidly Developing an Artistic Touch in Piano Forte Playing* (Chicago: S. W. Straub & Co., 1880), n.p.

She became a recognized authority on the Deppe method of playing, and she attracted students from near and far to study the method with her at her studio in room 20 in the Central Hall Block. Upon completion of their study with Amy, many wrote to express their delight with the results in their own and their students' playing.

At least two of her scholars became famous in their own right. One, John Alden Carpenter, became one of the nation's distinguished composers; another, Almon Kincaid Virgil, developed a practice clavier in the form of a small piano having nearly the full compass of the instrument and patented his own piano method which he promoted as the "Virgil Method."[46]

As Zina witnessed her sister's career on the rise, she began to address her own ambitions as a writer. In 1884 her book *Co-Operative Housekeeping: How Not to Do It and How to Do It* was published in Boston by the James R. Osgood Company. Mutual support had enabled the Fay sisters to gain more than a toe-hold in the public sphere.

Amy Fay and the Ladies of the Club

Like so many progressive women of the 1880s, Amy found in club activities an outlet for her emerging feminism. Ever since the establishment in 1868 of the nation's first two major women's clubs, Sorosis and the New England Women's Club, the growth of women's clubs throughout the nation had accelerated. In the course of the next two decades or so, other women's groups emerged, among them the Women's Christian Temperance Union, Young Women's Christian Association (YWCA), the Daughters of the American Revolution (D.A.R.), the Association of Collegiate Alumnae (later to become the A.A.U.W.), the Congress of Mothers (later to become the National Parent-Teachers Association), and the National Council of Women. The burgeoning of so many women's clubs saw the emergence of clubwomen as feminists who, "whether dedicated to social or to self-improvement, had in common their power to afford women a more complete, and therefore more authentic self-expression."[47] As women's associations proliferated, they gave wide exposure to female "influence," invigorated their members, and politicized their leaders. In addition they created a space for women in public life.[48]

The flurry of club activity among the women of the nation, coming as it did among a population already disposed to form associations, gave further validity to the observation, made by social observer Alexis de Tocqueville as early as the 1830s, that

---

[46] Fay, in fact, resented Virgil's advertisements, and felt that he should have announced himself as a promoter of the Deppe method.

[47] Karen Blair, *The Clubwoman as Feminist* (New York: Holmes and Meir, 1980), xii.

[48] Nancy Woloch, *Women and the American Experience* (New York: Alfred A. Knopf, 1984), 287.

Americans of all ages, conditions, and all dispositions constantly form associations. They have not only commercial and manufacturing companies, in which all take part, but associations of other kinds, religious, moral, serious, futile, general or restricted, enormous or diminutive. . . . If it be proposed to inculcate some truth or to foster some feeling by encouragement of a great example, they form a society. Wherever at the head of some new understanding you see the government in France, a man of rank in England, in the United States you will be sure to find an association. [49]

Even Norman Fay could not resist the wry observation that Chicago was "clubbed to death." [50]

With the mushrooming of women's affiliative groups in the latter third of the nineteenth century, the climate was ripe for the emergence of a variety of culture clubs, not the least of which was the music club. Not surprisingly, in the latter third of the century women's music clubs sprang up in countless cities and towns throughout the country. [52] From the outset they became spring boards for feminists. How?

First, the clubs enabled the development of administrative and leadership skills among the membership. [52] As women gathered to conduct meetings, plan events, and shape constitutions and by-laws, they acquired techniques that facilitated consensus around goals and purposes as well as democratic participation in decision making. As they honed their executive and managerial skills, they discovered that their *savoir faire* had applicability in other areas of life and that they could be effective catalysts for change and growth among widening segments of the population. As they deepened their convictions about the purposefulness and meaningfulness of their activities, they challenged those strictures that obstruct women's advancement toward the highest positions in areas of leadership and service. Accordingly, their productivity and satisfaction increased.

In addition to enabling the development of leadership skills, music clubs contributed to women's self development in other areas. The late nineteenth-century clubwoman functioned in a society in which the accessibility of higher education for women was in its initial phases. The nation's first institution of higher education for women, Vassar College, was not founded until 1865; not until a decade later, in 1875, were two more women's colleges founded, Wellesley College and Smith College. Even after more women's colleges appeared on the education horizon, for nineteenth-century women like Amy Fay, higher education was more the exception than the rule. Thus for women who desired an education in a subject such as music, the women's music clubs provided alternative educational opportunities:

---

[49] Quoted in Bessie L. Pierce, *A History of Chicago* (Chicago: University of Chicago Press, 1957), 484.

[50] *Sixth Triennial Report of the Class of 1869 of Harvard College*, 22.

[51] Adrienne Fried Block and Carol Neuls-Bates, *Women in American Music* (Westport, Conn.: Greenwood, 1979), xix.

[52] Ibid.

A whole series of meetings would be devoted to the study of a single composer's works, a single musical form, or a period of music history—subjects not universally taught in rural (or even urban) nineteenth-century America. Members were encouraged to perform and also to compose, and their compositions were performed. . . . America had several thousand women composers; in large part they were members of music clubs.[53]

Women's music clubs also afforded women opportunities for music-making outside the home. For those seeking an outlet from the confines of domesticity, the chance to perform with other competent musicians provided a wonderful incentive for club membership:

For those women who loved music but could not, for one reason or another, attempt a professional career, the club was a rewarding outlet. At the very least it fulfilled a social function. For music teachers and other professionals in small town and rural areas, the club provided performance opportunities and a chance to work with other musicians, amateur and professional. And clubs played a role in their communities, for not only did they present concerts by members but they raised money to buy instruments and import singers and instrumentalists (sometimes entire orchestras).[54]

Amy Fay provides a classic example of the nineteenth-century musical clubwoman. No sooner had she moved to Chicago than she helped found, in 1879, one of Chicago's most important music clubs for women, the Amateur Musical Club, which throughout its colorful history provided opportunities for amateurs and professionals to play for each other. In underscoring that only women would constitute this club, Amy noted that "no ungodly males were to be admitted, except to its public concerts, and by invitation only."[55] From an initial group of four members, one of whom was Amy's sister Rose, the club grew into an influential one comprising hundreds. In the beginning the members struggled to achieve organizational unity. As Amy recalled:

At first the club was desperately partisan in spirit, as it was chiefly composed of the best pupils of two leading teachers of the piano here: Mrs. Regina Watson and Mr. Emil Liebling. The pupils of these two teachers would group themselves on the several sides of the room and when a pupil of Mrs. Watson played well there would be loud applause, amid demonstrations of affection from the side of the "Watsonites," as they were called, and a corresponding dejection on the part of the "Lieblingites." When, however, a pupil of Mr. Liebling won the honors

---

[53] Ammer, 230.

[54] Ibid., 229-30.

[55] Amy Fay, "The Amateur Clubs," *Etude* 5, no. 12 (December 1887): 180.

of the day, the case would be reversed, and the applause would come from the opposition. Mrs. Watson and Mr. Liebling themselves were in no way affected by the violent sides taken by their pupils, and had the good sense to be only amused by it. They remained the best of friends while continuing to teach as hard as they could and turn out as many good scholars as possible. They reigned supreme over the club for a long time, but finally the pupils of other teachers in the city began to get in and the spirit of partisanship was broken up. The Watsonites and Lieblingites shook hands over their differences and both parties gave their suffrages to new-comers. These formed a sort of middle ground on which they could meet, though to this day the Watsonites have the settled conviction that *their* champion player is the best amateur in Chicago, while the Lieblingites would put forward with equal boldness the claims of *theirs*. [56]

As the club became stabilized, it produced annually three kinds of concerts: one for active members' meetings, one for all members and the general public, and the third an annual charity concert.

The feminization of the Amateur Musical Club extended beyond membership considerations to the very physical appearance of the club's meeting place. The members set out to replace masculine motives of power and efficiency with feminine appointments, which contributed to an atmosphere of collaboration rather than competition. Gradually they transformed the interior of the club room from a space which was highly utilitarian into one which was intimate, warm, and humane. On one particular occasion, when the members were preparing for a gala reception for the renowned prima donna Amalie Materna, who had been brought to the United States by Theodore Thomas to sing in his music festivals,

> The leading ladies of the club set their wits to work to make this reception a unique affair. They denuded their houses of rugs, hangings, pictures, marble busts, and what-not, to make the room attractive. . . . Masses of beautiful roses were put where they would be most effective—on pedestals, crowning the pictures, and in the hands of the ladies, or at their breasts. In short, the club rooms looked like a perfect power, and were completely transformed in a jiffy. (I could not help thinking how delightful our public halls would be if taken in charge by women. They would lose their comfortless look.) . . . [57]

When she arrived, Materna appreciated the effort of the women to provide an ambience worthy of their gender. The richly adorned prima donna was

> highly pleased at the compliment paid her. There was a general air of enchantment over everything which was due to the rosy light, the

---

[56] Ibid.

[57] Ibid.

flowers, and the elegant afternoon toilettes of the women present, and also to their delicate beauty. [58]

The Amateur Club became very popular, and, according to Amy,

> soon had a membership of four hundred subscribers. It hired expensive rooms, and began having occasional recitals from great artists travelling throughout the country, and ladies went to the club concerts without knowing each other, as they would go to any others. [59]

But after a while the membership resisted paying three thousand dollars a year just for the rental of their club rooms and decided to try another policy—namely, to give concerts only once a month in the small and intimate Apollo Hall. In addition, the active (performing) members inaugurated a series of afternoon teas for their own benefit in conjunction with which they would

> try and vote on new candidates for active membership. Every new member must play or sing on trial, before this august assemblage! The new members are then voted in or black-balled, according to their musical merit. In order to compensate the associate members for losing half of the concerts, they make the concerts that are given much finer, and have six "artists recitals" instead of only one or two, as formerly, in the course of the season. This they find a much better way, as it gives the large audiences something worth listening to at the public concerts, and, at the same time, the old sociability is restored in the meetings of the active members in private houses. [60]

Ironically, by deciding to vote in or refuse membership to applicants, the Amateur Musical Club adopted a very male strategy as it re-structured itself. Yet the use of rooms with a smaller range of occupancy provided the modicum of intimacy that the club membership considered important.

Amy's club activity in Chicago did not restrict itself to women's clubs. In 1884 she helped found yet another music club important to Chicago's musical life, one which included both men and women. This second club, the Artists' Concert Club, became a cooperative organization of singers and players dedicated to presenting concerts before associate members and immediate friends, in the hope of furthering art. Besides Amy, other charter members included such Chicago luminaries as Fannie Bloomfield (later, Zeisler), Clarence Eddy, Agnes Ingersoll, and Madame Rice—all names which appeared frequently in the musical columns of the press. Membership was highly selective—the by-laws called for "strict privacy" to be observed by the membership. As Amy explained:

---

[58] Ibid.

[59] Ibid.

[60] Ibid.

Congenial and trusted members were to be relied upon to write press criticism. The associate members were to pay five dollars for season tickets to the concerts. The net returns were to be prorated among twenty charter members of the organization, according to the number of associate memberships they secured. [61]

Despite such efforts to insure positive press coverage, Kenneth Rehage discovered that they were not always successful:

> The critic of the *Morning News* was not too friendly to this organization. When it had closed its first season with a concert at Weber Hall, it was said that a large proportion of the members were "aspiring amateurs" rather than artists. Nevertheless the club seems to have kept up its series of concerts for some time. In 1887, the total number of concerts given since its organization was well over thirty. [62]

Conducted along the same lines as the Amateur Club, and boasting both active and associated members (the latter being voted in by the former), members had the right to bring friends with them "on payment of fifty cents extra at the door." The first concert of the Artists' Concert Club took place on 30 December 1884, with Amy Fay performing in three of the six numbers on the program. She opened the concert with two movements from the Trio in E-flat major by Schubert; after a presentation of two vocal numbers by Charles Knorr, Amy performed three solo pieces: "Devotion" by W. C. E. Seeboeck, "The Nightingale" by Franz Liszt, and "A Midnight Barcarole" by Charles Jerome Hopkins. As her third offering for the initial concert of the newly founded club, Amy played the first movement from the D-minor Concerto by Rubinstein, with Seeboeck at the second piano. As founding members, Amy and Fannie Bloomfield appeared together on more than one occasion. At a concert on 9 November 1886, Amy accompanied Bloomfield (now Bloomfield-Zeisler) on the second piano for a performance of the Rubinstein Concerto in D minor. For a program presented on 28 February 1888, the duo performed a two-piano arrangement of Saint-Saëns's "Skeleton Dance" from the *Danse macabre*.

During the early years of its existence the Artists' Concert Club became a vital musical presence in Chicago. Despite the initial negative publicity in the *Morning News*, the contributions of the Artists' Concert Club to the musical life of Chicago did not go unnoticed by one of the city's major critics, W. S. B. Mathews, who observed that since its inception the organization had "exerted an important influence on the music of Chicago." [63]

Fourteen years after its founding, the Amateur Club would play a prominent part in the 1893 World Columbian Exhibition in Chicago. When organizers of the fair finally agreed that women should have an important role, a special women's building was built to house a year-long display of arts and handicrafts by women, and Amy Beach, the "dean

---

[61] Ibid.

[62] Rehage, 22.

[63] William S. B. Mathews, *A Hundred Years of Music in America* (Chicago: G. L. Howe, 1889), 141.

The Artists' Concert Club.

An association has been formed by twenty of the leading artists of Chicago, called

"THE ARTISTS' CONCERT CLUB,"

for the purpose of giving fortnightly concerts. The concerts will take place on alternate Tuesday afternoons, from four till half-past five o'clock, beginning on Tuesday afternoon, December 30, at the rooms of the Amateur Musical Club, Ayer Building, corner of State and Monroe Streets.

Should you desire to become an associate member of the club, you can do so by applying to any of the active members. The associate membership fee is five dollars for a season ticket. Associate members will have the right to bring friends with them to the concerts on payment of fifty cents each at the door. The names of the active members are as follows :

Announcement of founding of the Artists' Concert Club,

PIANISTS.

Miss Amy Fay,	Mme. De Roode Rice,
Miss Fannie Bloomfield,	Mrs. Regina Watson,
Miss Agnes Ingersoll,	Mr. W. C. E. Seeboeck,
Mr. C. W. Dodge,	Mr. N. Ledochowski.

ORGANIST.

Mr. Clarence Eddy.

VIOLINISTS.

Mr. Adolph Rosenbecker, Mr. Carl Becker,
Mr. Bernard Mollenhauer, Mr. Wm. Lewis.

'CELLIST.

Mr. Eichheim.

SINGERS.

Miss Jennie Dutton,	Miss Emma Romeldi,
Mrs. May Phœnix Cameron,	Mrs. O. K. Johnson,
Mr. Charles Knorr,	Mr. L. A. Phelps,
Mr. John McWade.	

EXECUTIVE COMMITTEE.

Miss Fannie Bloomfield, Miss Jennie Dutton,
Mr. C. W. Dodge.

SECRETARY.

Miss Amy Fay.

TREASURER.

Mrs. Regina Watson.

a prestigious Chicago musical club established in 1884.

The Artists' Concert Club.

⟶ First Programme. ⟵

1. **TRIO,** - - E flat major, (two movements), - - *Schubert.*

ALLEGRO. ANDANTE CON MOTO.

Miss FAY, Mr. BECKER and Mr. EICHHEIM.

2. **SONGS,** { *a.* EVER WITH THEE, - - - - - - *Raff.*
{ *b.* THINE EYES SO BLUE AND TENDER, - - - *Lassen.*

Mr. KNORR.

3. **PIANO SOLO,** { *a.* DEVOTION, (Song without words), - - - *Seeboeck.*
{ *b.* THE NIGHTINGALE, - - - - - *Liszt.*
{ *c.* A MIDNIGHT BARCAROLE, - - - - *Hopkins.*

Miss FAY.

4. **SONG,** - - - THE RUSSET LEAVES, - - - *Sponholtz.*

Mr. KNORR.

5. **CONCERTO,** - - D minor (first movement), - - *Rubinstein.*

Miss FAY, accompanied by Mr. SEEBOECK.

6. **DUETT,** - - - DAS VOGELEIN LIED, - - - *Rubinstein.*

(The Little Bird's Song).

Mrs. O. K. JOHNSON and Mrs. BUCKBEE.

The WEBER PIANOS for this occasion are kindly loaned by Messrs. CURTISS & MEYER, Weber Music Hall, corner of Wabash Avenue and Jackson Street.

Courtesy The Newberry Library.

First program of the Artists' Concert Club in which Amy Fay
performed as both soloist and ensemble player.

of American women composers," was commissioned to compose a piece, *Festival Jubilate*, op. 17, for soloists, chorus, and orchestra for the building's dedication.

Many of the nation's clubwomen, convinced that their presence at the fair would complement the material exhibits of women's progress organized for the Women's Building at the fair, were quick to ask Charles Bonney, president of the Congress Auxiliary, for approval to hold their meetings as part of the World's Congress. Bonney approved the request and assigned the first week after opening day to the Department of Women's Progress. Subsequently, over twenty separate women's groups were authorized to hold meetings of their national membership during the week. Among them were the YWCA, the D.A.R., the National Council of Women, the American Federation of Women's Clubs, and forty-two of the nation's music clubs, the latter being hosted by the Amateur Club of Chicago and its president, Rose Fay Thomas. By 1893 Rose had come into her own as a strong advocate of musical clubwomen in music. The element of sisterly strength she valued became a reality when over 150,000 people gathered to hear 330 prominent women read papers or address the World Congress on subjects ranging from women's position, history and potential in industry, government, and the arts to the dual themes of reform and women's solidarity.[64]

The visibility of the women's clubs at the 1893 Exhibition would demonstrate the importance of women's music clubs in America. In an opening address to the music club members, Rose Fay Thomas underscored the importance of music clubs like the Amateur Club, remarking that in them "musical art has its most valuable ally and its most beneficial friend."[65]

But four years later, at the June 1897 meeting of the Music Teachers National Association held in New York, musical activist and author Florence Sutro organized a women's department with one representative music club having fourteen sub-departments, one of which represented the music clubs, and the stage was set for a bitter rivalry to develop between Sutro and Rose Fay Thomas. During the convention, fifty-two delegates of the club convened to establish the National Federation of Music Clubs, naming Sutro as president of the initially temporary organization. The next year, at the meeting of the National Federation of Music Clubs in Chicago, the organization was chartered with Sutro as president. But Rose had contended that since Sutro was not president of the constituent clubs, she was an outsider. Some observers accused Rose of attempting to undermine the Federation's efforts to broaden its membership, and the rivalry between the two women became the subject of discussion in the musical press. Nevertheless, Rose had to sit by as Sutro was named as president, while she, in turn, was named first honorary president of the organization.

The clubs provided Amy and her professional colleagues in Chicago with yet another forum for their public performances. Yet Amy failed to include music by any of the women composers who had made or were beginning to make ripples in the musical world—composers like Jane Sloman (b. 1824), Augusta Browne (1821-82), and Faustina

[64] Reid Badger, *The Great American Fair: The World's Columbian Exposition and American Culture* (Chicago: Nelson Hall, 1979), 101-02.

[65] National Convention of Women's Amateur Clubs, *History in the Making* (Chicago: Stromberg, Allen & Co., 1983), 4-5.

Hodges (1822-95). Each of these women had composed keyboard music which could stand favorably beside the work of her uncle Charles Jerome Hopkins, which she did perform. Wasn't it to be expected that she would challenge the prevailing canon and perform works by the women who were beginning to achieve visibility on the musical scene?

Not in a musical climate shaped by George P. Upton, who was, after all, anxious to keep women in their proper sphere and who went to great pains to discourage them from being taken seriously as composers. In his book *Woman in Music* (1880), Upton suggested that a woman

> lacks the mastery of the theoretical intricacies, logical sequences, and the mathematical problems which are the foundation principles of music. She will always be the recipient and interpreter, but there is little hope she will be the creator. [66]

Upton's refrain did not go unchallenged. Occasional voices did cry out in opposition to Upton's pronouncements—and in 1900 Amy Fay would be among them—but even she realized that if she were to defy Upton's sensibilities by performing music by women, he would be ill-disposed to review her concerts favorably. Furthermore, her own book, *Music-Study in Germany*, had been published the very next year after Upton's, and its immediate popularity no doubt created the potential for a rivalry between the two authors. If Upton felt that his musical power base in Chicago was being threatened by Amy, she would be placed in the bind of having to remain on his good side by, among other things, avoiding programming music by women composers. Sensing that Upton surely would derail any efforts by her to promote music by women, no matter how well constructed the scores were, Amy determined not to put her career at risk by flaunting women's compositions before Upton's prejudiced ears and mind. If her decision seemed not to mesh with her self-proclaimed dedication to advancing the cause of women in music, she would try to compensate through the power of her pen and her affiliations. She would leave to other women with less to lose the challenge of evening the score by breaking the women's composition barrier in Chicago.

The Summer of 1885:
With Liszt Again

Meanwhile, her celebrity as the author of *Music-Study in Germany* had secured Amy's reputation as a member of Liszt's inner circle and, like so many of his scholars, she wanted to be among those who trekked to Weimar for a summer reunion with the maestro. She

---

[66] George P. Upton, *Woman in Music*, 4th ed. (Chicago: A. C. McClurg and Co., 1886), 31.

was aware that Liszt was aging and that if she were to fulfill her wish of seeing him one more time, she should lose no time doing so. Furthermore, there were other interests abroad; among the more fascinating was her friend and suitor from her student days in Germany, Camille Gurickx. Then too, in London there was George Grove, at the time a professor at the Royal College of Music; if she could interest him in her book he might write a preface for another edition.

Her travel itinerary included several stops on the continent as well as in London. In Brussels, her first stop, she was delighted to be in the city Liszt so admired, writing home:

> They are awfully knowing here in Brussels on art! I don't wonder Materna was so proud of her success here. Liszt said once that the order he had received here from King Leopold was one of the few he cared about as it was one which is rarely conferred. [67]

In addition to presenting a "Piano Conversation" assisted by Gurickx, [68] she attended the end-of-the-year student concert competitions at the Royal Conservatory, which seemed to her "one of the most complete and admirably managed in Europe." [69] She was particularly taken by the playing and singing of the female students, and was amazed when the first prize winner "gave a 'jump for joy'," while some of those who came off second best "went off in tears." [70] As Amy perceived it, "an American girl would neither have given a leap nor burst into tears before an audience." [71]

The reunion with Gurickx was charged with emotion as the still unattached bachelor once more pursued the possibility of marriage with the woman from Cambridge for whom he had been carrying the torch over the years. But some years earlier, Norman, not her father, had, for reasons unknown, put a stop to Amy's marriage plans, and Gurickx was forced to accede to this intrusive move on the part of his prospective brother-in-law. His emotional acceptance was slower in coming, however, for not until 1891, six years after his reunion with Amy in Brussels, did Gurickx finally marry another.

After making her farewell to Gurickx, Amy went to neighboring Antwerp, where she attended the Liszt musical celebration held in conjunction with the 1885 Universal Exhibition. Liszt, of course, was there. Following the June 7 concert conducted by François Servais, Amy, in company with several of Liszt's friends, gathered for revelry and music making with Liszt. As she describes it:

> All the artists, of which there were a good many in the room, stood round the piano while Liszt played, and then there was a general shout when he finished. "Je ne joue plus du piano, moi," he said to me

---

[67] S. Margaret William McCarthy, "Amy Fay's Reunions with Franz Liszt," *Journal of the American Liszt Society* 24 (July-December 1988): 30.

[68] Amy Fay, "The Royal Conservatory of Brussels." *Etude* 3, no. 8 (August 1885): 173.

[69] Ibid.

[70] Ibid.

[71] Ibid.

negligently. After that no one ventured to play a solo on the piano. . . .
I was rather sorry I did not get a chance to play myself as it was such
a distinguished company. The next day there was to be a celebration
of a mass by Liszt at the Church of St. Joseph at ten in the morning.
He wanted me to stay for it, though I was in a hurry to get back to
Brussels because I was expecting to give this Recital at the Fishes this
week, which fell through, as I said, owing to several complications.
He made such a point of it, however, that I said I would stay. He
said jokingly "et puis qu'il faut-être très précis avec vous, je vous
attendrai a la grande porte de l'eglise en sortant." I stayed over, of
course, and on going out I tried to get near him, but there was such
a crowd that the people fairly fought to get a look at him. He was
hurried into a carriage by Mehlig and her husband and wheeled off
to luncheon, and I saw him no more. I think he probably had intended
to take me with him. [72]

Next Amy went to London, where she made an unannounced call on Sir George
Grove. On learning of Amy's visit, Grove invited Amy to come by the following Monday
"to hear a lesson or two." [73] This contact with Grove afforded Amy that opportunity to
call *Music-Study in Germany* to his attention and to hint that Grove himself might like
to write a preface for the forthcoming edition. In October of that year Grove read the
book. Impressed, he successfully recommended it to Macmillan for publication and wrote
a preface a few days before the year's end. [74] Once again Amy's ability to tap into
effective networks had met with success. Furthermore, gaining Grove's endorsement
was a distinct accomplishment, given that previously he had refused Lina Ramann's
request to translate her "official" biography of Franz Liszt into English, on the grounds that

at present my opinion is that in order to be successful in England, it
will want a good deal of pruning. The taste of the English public with
regard to music is very different from that of the German public. We
like facts, but have a horror of anything like rhapsody or eloquence . . .
musical books do not sell in this country as well as they do in Germany
or France, and it is a remarkable fact that so very interesting and popular
a book as the translation of Mendelssohn's Letters has hardly done more
than pay its expenses. [75]

All the more of a coup for Amy that Grove found her book

---

[72] McCarthy, "Amy Fay's Reunions," 30.

[73] Letter from Sir George Grove to Amy Fay, 16 July 1885, courtesy the Theodore Thomas papers, Newberry
Library, Chicago.

[74] Percy Young, *George Grove: A Biography* (London: Macmillan, 1980), 33.

[75] Letter from Sir George Grove to Lina Ramann, 1 November 1880, Goethe-Schiller Archives, Weimar,
Germany.

thoroughly readable and amusing, which books on music too rarely are. The freshness and truth of the letters is not to be denied. We may laugh at the writer's enthusiasm . . . but no one can laugh at her indomitable determination, the artistic earnestness with which she makes the most of each of her opportunities, or the brightness and ease with which each successive person is placed before us in his habit as he lives. Such a gift is indeed a rare and precious one.[76]

Between August 12 and 20, Amy stayed in Weimar, where she had many visits with Liszt in the famous "Hoftgartnerei," the home where the maestro spent his summer months. By then Liszt had institutionalized the custom of holding summer reunions with his disciples on Monday, Wednesdays, and Fridays. On those days, at about four o'clock, some twenty disciples would gather round the piano of his salon, where they might be asked to play or sing. The atmosphere was one of warmth and conviviality as the master delighted his guests, often tossing off witty remarks that would keep his friends in continual laughter.

Amy—along with Arma Senkrah, August Gollerich, and her compatriot from New York, Albert Morris Bagby—was part of Liszt's charmed Weimar circle.[77] She played in the piano classes and spent recreational time with Liszt. On August 12 she played the Beethoven "Pastoral" Sonata at the afternoon session[78] and at a later select gathering she, together with Miss Senkrah, played a piece for piano and violin written by her uncle, Charles Jerome Hopkins.[79]

In the evenings she often played whist with Liszt and some of his other favorite students who were invited to stay after the lessons. These games were, in the words of Bagby, "the most enjoyable hours spent in Liszt's company."[80] Liszt spoke German and French during these games and, although he understood it, did not converse in English. One day, after Amy glanced distinctly at a card she led she said quietly, "I don't like that," before playing her hand. Liszt found this comment quite amusing and when at a disadvantage at future card games with Amy, Liszt would repeat in English, "I don't like that."[81]

By the time of her visit, Amy's book *Music-Study in Germany* had become a best seller among cultivated readers in America and England. Liszt must have enjoyed discussing the book in which he figured so prominently. Other subjects also entered their conversation, one of which Amy described several years later in an article she wrote for *Etude*:

---

[76] In the reprint of *MSG* (New York: Macmillan, 1922), 3.

[77] August Gollerich, *Franz Liszts Klavierunterricht von 1884-1886 argestellt an den Tagenbuch auf Zeiehnungen August Gollerich* (Regensburg: Gustav Bosse, 1975), 95.

[78] Ibid.

[79] *Indicator* 6, no. 39 (26 September 1885): 787.

[80] Albert M. Bagby, "A Summer with Liszt in Weimar," *Century Magazine*, September 1886, 664.

[81] Ibid.

I don't wonder that he manifested a sort of revolt against Beethoven the latter part of his life. The very last conversation I had with him, in 1885, when I returned for a short visit to Weimar, Liszt said, "I *respect* all that, but it no longer *interests* me," referring to Beethoven's works. [82]

While Amy's European sojourn was a highlight of 1885, the year had a downside for her. Zina moved to New York in order to continue her work of organizing women and of writing. Sensing that the publication in 1884 of her book, *Co-Operative Housekeeping: How Not to Do It and How to Do It*, would give her a new visibility and credibility, she took her causes to the city which had been the venue of her earlier efforts on behalf of women.

Wedding Bells in the Family

With Zina gone, Amy mingled more with Rose. In the summer of 1887 she had a memorable experience with her in St. Louis. At the invitation of conductor Theodore Thomas, by now a family friend, Rose and Amy went to St. Louis for a few days to hear the American Opera Company perform *Nero*. They were Thomas's guests in the hotel and accompanied him to the Opera House in the Exposition Building in St. Louis, where Amy recalled that Thomas

> had a private room facing upon the street in front of the Opera House, and it was quite a novel sensation to sit in it with the great conductor before the beginning of the performance and watch the people alight from their carriages and walk up the steps. [83]

Given that the first Mrs. Thomas was living at the time of the St. Louis trip, it is improbable that Thomas had any notion that following his wife's death two years later Rose would become his second wife. The end of the decade of the 1880s saw many changes in the life of the Fays. On 6 November 1888, Amy's father died of natural causes. A few months prior to his death Lily had begun keeping company with Charles Wilmerding, the general manager of the Chicago Arc and Light Company. After a suitable period of mourning following the senior Fay's death, Lily married Wilmerding on 12 June 1889, in an important social event of the season.

The following year an even more heightened social happening took place. In the twelve intervening years since Amy's Cambridge debut with the Thomas orchestra, the conductor had become an intimate friend of the Amy family, especially of Norman and Rose. In 1889 Thomas's first wife died. After the customary mourning period, the

---

[82] Amy Fay, "From Beethoven to Liszt," *Etude* 26, no. 7 (July 1908): 427.

[83] MLAF, 11.

renowned musician lost no time in courting the thirty-eight-year-old Rose, who yielded to his compelling magnetism and agreed to become his wife. Their wedding took place on May 5 at 8 o'clock in the evening in the Chapel of the Church of the Ascension and was *the* social event of Chicago's high society during the 1890 Chicago season. Rose's marriage to Thomas, though an affair of the heart, was also a marriage of convenience. As a conductor, Thomas had done as much as anyone to educate the musical taste of the American public. He made an enormous imprint on Chicago's musical life, coming there as a conductor of various orchestral programs from 1869 to 1890. Rose yearned to assist his cause. A marriage in the family would solidify his Chicago base and his musical aspirations. Rose acknowledged as much in a letter to her niece Kate Fay Stone, written fourteen years after Thomas' death:

> the reconstruction of Thomas' artistic career was brought about by my brother, C. Norman Fay. It was perhaps facilitated by our marriage which naturally brought the two men intimately together. [84]

Norman, too, recognized the importance of the union in terms of Thomas's career and Chicago's musical life. During an intimate meal with Thomas at Delmonico's Restaurant in New York, Norman suggested the idea of a permanent Chicago orchestra to his future brother-in-law. Norman recounts the event as follows:

> My thoughts went back to those ten years of Summer garden Concerts, and to some powerful and devoted friends of Mr. Thomas and his music at home, and I asked, "Would you come to Chicago if we could give you a permanent orchestra?" The answer, grim and sincere, and entirely destitute of intentional humor, came back like a flash: "I would go to hell if they gave me a permanent Orchestra." Well, Chicago has always resembled the west end of the next world in this, among other things, that it is wide open to good company. And then and there we roughed-out in talk the general principles of an agreement under which the Theodore Thomas Orchestra has lived, moved and had its being in that city for eighteen years." [85]

The couple settled in Norman's Bellevue Street home and enjoyed a marriage that was, according to Rose,

> . . . one of those rare and exquisite unions such as seldom occur in this imperfect world. As long as I had my husband with me I was absolutely happy. We never had a quarrel or an unkind word or inconsiderate act pass between us, and we were always each other's most cherished companions and were never separated a moment longer than we were obliged. [86]

---

[84] Rose Fay Thomas, *Memoirs of Rose Thomas* (New York: Moffat, Yard & Co., 1911), 35.

[85] Percy Otis, *The Chicago Symphony Orchestra* (Chicago: Clayton F. Summy Co., 1924), 26.

[86] Letter from Rose Fay Thomas to Pauline Jackson, 14 July 1905, private papers of Gregory Harris, FFP.

In Chicago the couple entertained world-famous composers, politicians, writers, and inventors. Such luminaries as Richard Strauss, Rudolph Ganz, Louise Homer, Edward Elgar, Alma Tadema, the Kneisel Quartet, Feruccio Busoni, Fannie Bloomfield-Zeisler, Horatio Parker, Mischa Elman, and Maude Powell were frequent visitors in their home. They welcomed into their home as well the children of Rose's sisters. One of them, Laura's daughter Madeline Smith, recalled being with them before and after the Saturday night concerts that Thomas conducted:

> . . . we drove down to the old Chicago Auditorium in a "hack," I on a little seat facing Aunt Rose and Uncle Theodore, and I shall never forget the expression on Aunt Rose's face, on the homecoming trip after the concert—perfect happiness was reflected there as we passed under the street lights. She adored her husband and was tremendously proud of him. Her first role in life was to make things run smoothly for him. . . . Later on, after the Saturday night concerts, she and Uncle Theodore used to give supper parties. As a young girl visiting them, I remember, among others, the famous historian John Fisk, who had a very large "bay window" and Dr. Moffit, the translator of various books of the Bible and at that time a professor at the University of Chicago. [87]

Rose offered her husband her loving devotion and emotional support. For fifteen years the couple lived together blissfully, dividing their time between Chicago and Thomas's home in New Hampshire. Theodore's death in 1905 devastated Rose. She wrote to her niece Pauline:

> . . . when he was taken from me I lost my all. I feel like an old woman now, and have done with life and the world. I only work because I do not wish to be useless and furthermore work is the only opiate for grief. [88]

The marriage did little to further Amy's career, however, and the aspiring concert artist regretted that her famous brother-in-law did not do more to create professional opportunities for his sister-in-law. Rightly or wrongly, Amy placed the blame for Thomas's indifference to Rose, whom she suspected of discouraging his taking an interest in her. The Thomas-Fay wedding brought out into the open the rivalry between Amy and Rose. Prior to that marriage, Amy was the family musician; now she had to concede that role to Theodore Thomas. She must have resented having to take a step down in her own familial setting. Amy wrote on the subject:

> I think that Rose has a jealous nature, and if she has a *man at all*, she *owns him*. It was so with Theodore Thomas, and I have always felt that

---

[87] Madeline Smith, "Portraits of My Aunts," 10-11, FFP.

[88] Ibid.

if she had *wanted* to, she could have got me the engagement to play with him that time. I am convinced that she did not care to have him take an interest in *me*. [89]

On the other hand, Kate viewed the situation differently, writing that Thomas would do nothing for Amy "because she was not a first class artist, and I don't think she ever got over it."[90]

The wedding precipitated another displacement of Fay family members in several ways. First, Norman gave the Bellevue Street home to the newlyweds. That gesture placed Amy at a new choice point in her life. She would have to find somewhere else to live. She chose New York City, where Zina had been since 1885. Was she ready for such a transition? It seemed so, judging from the professional strides she had made in Chicago.

While in Chicago she had earned the respect of colleagues, both at home and abroad, as a performer, teacher, and clubwoman. Her book *Music-Study in Germany* had retained its popularity and was in its sixteenth printing. She had overcome the nervousness that had plagued her for over nineteen years. She had made peace with the fact that she and Gurickx would never marry. Her circle of friends included Mrs. Clarence Eddy, Julie Rivé-King, Ignace Paderewski, and Fannie Bloomfield-Zeisler. Amy had once written in Bloomfield-Zeisler's autograph book the following ditty: "Curved is the line of beauty, Straight is the line of duty. Follow the last and thou shalt see, The other ever following thee!"[91] In New York Amy hoped to experience the truth of her own words. She looked forward to life in the hub of the musical universe.

---

[89] MLAF, 139.

[90] Letter of Kate Fay Stone, 13 October 1919, FFP.

[91] Fannie Bloomfield-Zeisler's autograph book, 3 July 1884, courtesy the Fannie Bloomfield-Zeisler papers, Newberry Library, Chicago.

PART 5

New York City

New York City

In 1890 Amy Fay, after twelve years in Chicago, relocated to New York City, a move that was timely for several reasons. For one thing, Norman's decision to deed the Bellevue Street home to Rose and Theodore Thomas necessitated a change of residence. For another, the flourishing of professional music schools in Chicago had diminished the pool of private students from which Amy could draw, and New York, which in 1890 enjoyed a reputation as the most musically influential city in the nation, held the promise of an even wider yield of private pupils. Lastly, since 1885 Zina had been living and working in New York, thus providing Amy with her most compelling reason to go there. For years Amy and Zina had been a team, and the prospect of once again living near her cherished and revered sister meant that Amy could not only pursue her own career, but also could assist Zina in her many activist causes.

What contrasts did Amy Fay find between Chicago and New York? Unlike Chicago, to which she moved in the late 1870s, the New York of the 1890s enjoyed a reputation as the nation's pre-eminent musical center, symbolizing all that was fresh, exciting, and new in music, as well as all that remained permanent, substantial, and hallowed by tradition.[1] No longer was it "the provincial town of two-story houses, where pigs ran through Broadway and ate the refuse," described by Fay's brother-in-law Theodore Thomas in his memoirs.[2] Rather, it was the capital of a new empire of bankers, merchants, ship-owners, speculators, and industrial magnates.[3] It had within its confines the largest number of performers and composers in the world, touted such institutions as the Metropolitan Opera Company, and was home to some of the most powerful members of the musical press. Its enlightened musical citizenry knew of Amy Fay's reputation as a pianist, clubwoman, teacher, and writer. Those credentials, in addition to her relationship by marriage to Theodore Thomas and her known personal friendships with such illustrious musical personalities as Ignace Paderewski, John Knowles Paine, Julie Rivé-King, and Fannie Bloomfield-Zeisler promised her ready acceptance into the city's social and artistic circles.

---

[1] Cecil Smith, *Worlds of Music* (Philadelphia and New York: J. B. Lippincott Co., 1952), 129.

[2] Rose Fay Thomas, *Memoirs of Theodore Thomas* (New York: Moffat, Yard & Co., 1911), 4.

[3] Ibid.

She was not content to rest on the laurels of her reputation, however, and from the outset of her arrival in New York she activated and expanded her already extensive affiliative network. She moved into a boarding house at 60 West 94th Street, a setting she found "admirably suited to her style and taste," and one conducive to her lifestyle. In keeping with the nineteenth-century tradition among cultivated women, she set aside a day once a week to remain at home to receive guests. During these weekly "at homes," she served tea and socialized with friends. She considered it a "very pleasant thing" to see her guests each Monday, claiming that "a cup of *tea* was an excellent medium for conversation."[4]

She advertised for students, and as New Yorkers became aware of her presence among them, they began to send their children to her studio for instruction in the Deppe method. In addition, she received numerous bookings for her "Piano Conversations," playing for children in public schools and for adults in club audiences. By her own accounts she was a great success on the school circuit and could tame the most unruly audiences, as on one occasion where she played for students at a school on the lower east side in which the principal forewarned her that its students were "lawless" and often chipped desks, stole pictures, and frequently had to be cleared out with clubs. Yet Amy was able to win over this challenging audience by her captivating manner, as she described in a letter to Zina:

> Do you know, they were as quiet as mice, all *through*, except when they were *laughing out* with amusement at my remarks! At the close, they applauded like everything, and then they crowded around me on stage, and begged to know "when I was going to play to them again?" . . . Well, it was lots of fun down there and I enjoyed myself like everything. It quite inspired me to talk to that audience, it was so responsive![5]

Adults, too, appreciated Amy's "Piano Conversations," as a letter to Zina following an appearance before the New York Iowa Club in 1914 demonstrates:

> You ask about my Piano Conversation before the "*Iowa New Yorkers' Club*," which I had forgotten all about! I am happy to say it was a *brilliant* success, and the *entire* audience came up to congratulate me afterwards and to express their pleasure! The president made a speech *full of feeling*, and said it was "the *most beautiful* afternoon the Club *ever* had enjoyed." What pleased *me* was her conclusion, in which she said that she found herself left "in the *loveliest frame of mind*, somehow," and that she did not think she would do anything *bad* for a long *while*![6]

While in many ways Amy's life patterns resembled those she had followed in Chicago, in reality the blend of teaching, performing, writing, and club work which characterized her New York days began to demonstrate a distinctly more "feminist" posture. Under the continuing influence of her older sister Zina, Amy's attention to the so-called "woman's question" affected her professional and personal involvements.

---

[4] MLAF, 154.

[5] MLAF, 17-18.

[6] MLAF, 151.

Women's Philharmonic Society of New York

Zina's causes were many. Since moving to New York in 1885, she had continued to give herself vigorously to activities aimed at improving the condition of women in America, while simultaneously earning her living by running a boarding house. By the time Amy arrived in New York, Zina already had helped organize the Street Cleaning Committee of the Ladies Health Protective Association, and the year after Amy's move she was busy doing "readings" throughout the city.

Amy admired her sister for striving to make things better for women in society, but occasionally she became alarmed at the large amount of time she gave to volunteerism. As she noted how caught up Zina became in such pursuits as advocacy on behalf of a New York women's movement for cheap summer-night concerts, membership on the Poe Cottage Preservation Committee, the Fraunces' Tavern Restoration Committee, and the Mary Washington Colonial Chapter of the D.A.R. she worried that perhaps Zina was doing too much to the detriment of her own personal projects, one of which was a novel-in-progress, *New York: A Symphonic Study*. Amy said as much in a letter to Rose written in 1895:

> She belongs to *several* associations, and you never saw anybody so giddy as she has become. First she is driving down to the Mayor's office about saving the Poe cottage; now she confers with Miss Fischer uptown about the Horne Hotel for aged and indigent workers, like myself. Between times she has interviews with Sam Franko and musical managers about summer night concerts. Then she pours tea at the receptions of the Authors' Club, in their rooms at Carnegie Hall. . . . I never know where to find her. . . . Occasionally she dabbles a little at her book, and corrects a proof or two. It is well in vain I harangue her on this subject and tell her her book ought to be the object of her life, and that she *must* get it done. She is too well entertained with her various projects to concentrate. It reminds me of your numerous kinds of fancy work at the Island.[7]

Despite Amy's misgivings about the multiplicity of Zina's projects, she did identify in a sympathetic way with one particular preoccupation of Zina's—namely, her consternation over the fact that New York's musical women did not have a Philharmonic Society of their own, despite the fact that in the midwest such groups had long been recognized as a power for good. As in the past, whenever Amy was ever eager to make Zina's desires her own, so now in this cause she rallied to her sister's side. In 1898, during the twentieth annual meeting of the Music Teachers National Association at the Waldorf Astoria, Amy's name headed the list of preliminary committee members gathered by Zina to address the need for such an organization. Throughout the next year she worked diligently with the committee, helping the members draw up a circular announcing the intention of

---

[7] MLAF, 15.

forming a women's musical society which would be dedicated to the support and encouragement of musical women in the performance, composition, theory, and history of music, and taking other necessary steps to inform the musical women of New York that they were eligible for membership in the organization.[8] On 29 September 1899, thanks in large part to Amy's support, Zina called the first meeting of the Women's Philharmonic Society and thereupon was elected its first president.

As the organization evolved, it came to comprise individual departments of voice, piano, organ, string instruments, sight singing, choral work, and sacred and patriotic song. These departments held regular bi-monthly meetings that usually included a short program on some musical subject. Through the Society and its efforts, young artists were given hearings without incurring great expenses, and scholarships were provided for talented people. The Society provided an opportune outlet for Amy's affiliative impulses and for other feminist leanings. Since her youthful days in Germany she had decided never to marry or even do housework if she could help it. She also declared her openness to seeing a woman on the stage conducting a symphony orchestra.[9] From the time of its inception the Women's Philharmonic Society of New York remained central to her New York years, and she retained an interest in every detail of its life, from the ambience of its meeting rooms to its governance and programs. Amy was an energetic member, spurring on the club in its efforts to give women a musical forum. From 1899 to 1902, during Zina's presidency, Amy chaired the Piano Department of the organization, and in 1903 she was elected president, a position which she held until 1914.

An incident very early on in the Society's history shows what a strong presence Amy could be. In 1902, the third year of its existence, some of the membership attempted to alter the club's original guidelines to accommodate the admission of male members and tried to have the name changed to the New York Musical League. This effort proved unsuccessful, but not before a degree of unrest and dissatisfaction had taken its toll on club spirit and morale, nearly threatening its survival. Amy and her cohorts prevailed, however, as she described in a spirited and authoritative account to Zina of the incident:

> I am delighted to be able to state that I have succeeded in changing
> the name of the Women's Philharmonic from the New York Musical
> League, back to its original title, which you gave it. I told the members
> about Mrs. Field's plan of rallying the disaffected charter members of
> which she had forty, and forming a new society under the old name
> and constitution, and inviting you to be Honorary President of it. I
> told the club that when you found you had made a big blunder, the
> best thing to do was to *acknowledge* it, and *retrace* your steps as quickly
> as possible. Mrs. Coe, pretty well frightened by the many resignations,
> and also by the inextricable confusion to our Club which Mrs. Field's
> enterprise would cause, was sensible enough to see that I was right
> and consented that we should return to the old name. Even Miss

---

[8] "The Women's Philharmonic Society of New York," *Musical Courier* 26 (April 1899): 12.

[9] MSG, 117.

Program of Women's Philharmonic Society of New York given around 1914
during Amy Fay's tenure as president of the organization.

Courtesy of Schlesinger Library at Radcliffe College.

CONCERT
OF THE
ORCHESTRA
OF THE
WOMEN'S PHILHARMONIC SOCIETY

MRS. MELUSINA FAY PIERCE, Founder
MISS AMY FAY, President
MADELINE HOBART EDDY, Conductor
LOIS HUNTINGTON, Concertmeister
assisted by
KARL FORMES, Baritone

PROGRAM
PART I

1.	Overture, Egmont	*Beethoven*
2.	Songs—(a) "Im Meiner Heimath"	*Hildach*
	(b) "Auf Wiedersehen"	*Liehe*
	(c) "Mein Madel Hat 'Nen Rosenmundt"	*Brahms*
	KARL FORMES	
3.	(a) Solvejg's Song	*Grieg*
	(b) To Spring	*Grieg*
4.	Piano Solos—(a) "On Quiet Woodland Path"	*Richard Strauss*
	(b) Impromptu, A flat major	*Chopin*
	MISS AMY FAY	
5.	String Orchestra—(a) Vision	*Rheinberger*
	(b) Tarantelle	*Madeline Eddy*

PART II

1.	Surprise Symphony, G Major	*Haydn*
	Adagio Cantabile: Vivace assai	
	Andante	
	Menuetto	
	Allegro di molto	
2.	Aria from Macbeth—Pieta Rispetto Onore	*Delibes*
	KARL FORMES	
3.	Meditation from Thais	*Massenet*
	(by request)	
	MISS HUNTINGTON and Orchestra	
4.	Piano Solos—(a) Ave Maria	*Liszt*
	(b) Die Loreley	*Liszt*
	MISS AMY FAY	
5.	(a) Cavatina	*Raff*
	(b) Barcarolle from Tales of Hoffmann	*Offenbach*

STEINWAY PIANO USED

Subscriptions are solicited for the support and enlarging of the orchestra

ORCHESTRA

VIOLINS
Cornelia Blaine
Leila Cannes
Laura Clark
Ada Heinemann
Idalian Van Heyer Hennen
Minnie Herzog
Lois Huntington
Margaret Krauss
Amy Robie
Elizabeth Ruddell
Martha Mayer Thompson

VIOLAS
Elsie Radler
Melinda Rockwood

CELLOS
Florence Brooks
Marie Eddy
Gertrude Wolf

BASS
Juliette Mousson

FLUTE
Gussie Blucher

CLARINET
Elsa DuBois

TRUMPET
Katharine Feman

DRUMS
Anna Fricke

PIANO
Frances Eddy

Collins was eager to retract, and the Club at large is attached to the old name on *your* account. So we are again the Women's Philharmonic Society, much to our *joy*. The astute Mrs. Courtney made the discovery that the change of name was not legal, to that of the New York Musical League, as thirty days notice ought to have been sent out, which was not done. Also it was not voted upon in the business meeting of the whole society, but only in the Council. It was all hurried through. [10]

As she had done with the Amateur Club in Chicago, Amy worked enthusiastically to transform the appearance of the Women's Philharmonic Society of New York from an organization reflecting a male bastion to a welcoming, home-like environment. Sometimes though, her efforts were in vain, as she described in a letter to Zina written 19 April 1902:

Early in the season the chairs were placed around the room as in a private drawing room, and the centre of the floor was cleared. This made a charming impression as you entered the room. Miss Hard, in her ambition to have large audiences, has the chairs in rows now, like any concert hall, and you are wedged into your seat all the afternoon. The members of the Council all agreed with me on this point, particularly Mrs. Boas, who was emphatic: I told Miss Hard afterwards what had been said, as she was absent from the meeting that day, and the members took advantage of it to express their opinions. I begged her to return to the former way of placing the chairs, and to have shorter programmes. It was to no avail! Today she had all the chairs in rows again, and two *more* numbers on the programme than usual! . . . I was quite provoked with Miss Hard, for even when I played on Saturday afternoon not long ago, and wrote her a special request to put the chairs around the room, she paid no attention to my request. [11]

Early in its history, on 2 March 1901, the Society featured a program of songs and instrumental music composed by women, at least one of whom—Laura Sedgwick Collins—was a club member. [12] Yet extant programs suggest that a more typical program included a mix of piano, voice, violin solos, and orchestral numbers by such composers as Bach, Handel, Scarlatti, Mozart, Beethoven, Schubert, Chopin, Raff, Grieg, and others. During Amy Fay's presidency (1903-14), however, such composers as Liza Lehman, Harriet Ware, Madeline Eddy, and Mrs. H. H. A. Beach periodically appeared on the Society's programs, indicating that Amy was more audacious in programming women's works than she had been in Chicago.

---

[10] MLAF, 25.

[11] MLAF, 33.

[12] Songs by Mrs. Stephen Bedell, Kate Stella Burr, Mary I. Chase, and Mrs. A. Hadley, as well as instrumental music by Caroline Maben and Helen C. Crane, were also included on the program described in an article, "New York Women's Philharmonic," *Musical Courier* 6 (March 1901): 34.

Amy valued her relationship to the Society, as she reveals in a letter to Zina dated 8 October 1907:

> My record for the [Women's] Philharmonic this week is as follows: Saturday morning I went down to Steinway's to select the piano; Monday I went down to the rooms of the Society to see them put in place on stage. The rooms were not ready, and so I went to Steinway's again to countermand them. Tuesday afternoon I went again to the rooms to meet the pianos. Stayed there till nearly five before they arrived. Rushed home and dressed and had dinner, and went back to the rooms for the meeting of the Piano Department. Evening *brilliant* success, large attendance, everybody delighted. Thursday evening went to the reunion of the Vocal Department. This morning (Friday) went to the Council at half past nine, and did not leave till two o'clock. Next Tuesday evening will be an adjourned meeting of the whole society, to decide about changing the name. Must be there. Next Friday morning Directors' meeting of the Piano Department, at ten! Besides all this, I have been running and writing incessantly for the last fortnight to get the programme arranged for Tuesday evening. I never saw such a Club in such a continued state of activity as this one, and there seems *no let-up* to it![13]

In addition to organizing events and showcasing other artists, Amy Fay herself was often featured on the Society's programs, as either lecturer or Piano Conversationalist. When she played on 27 February 1909, the New York Philharmonic Orchestra conductor Vassily Safonoff came to hear her perform her Bach pieces. The club members were most impressed that Amy could attract someone of such musical stature to her programs and were, in her own words, *taken down!*[14]

The leadership qualities that made Amy Fay so popular with the New York Women's Philharmonic made other clubs value her presence as well. For awhile she was a member of the New York Manuscript Society, but after about 1908 she began to cut back on her time with that group, declaring that she had "no mind to work for men . . . which is always a thankless task!"[15] Yet when the New York Fraternal Associations of Musicians, a prominent men's club, asked Amy to repeat a Piano Conversation on Liszt that she had given with great success at the New York Women's Philharmonic Society, she was only too happy to comply, writing to Zina:

> People always *love* the talk I give about the pieces and they *never get enough* of that. No matter *how much* I say, *they* invariably say I "don't talk *half enough.*" I gave a little talk on Liszt at the Women's Philharmonic

---

[13] MLAF, 76.

[14] MLAF, 83.

[15] MLAF, 81.

in celebration of his centennial, and now I am asked where I go to repeat the talk on Liszt. I played his *Ave Maria* and *Loreley*.[16]

Despite nodding involvements with other musical groups in New York, the Women's Philharmonic Society clearly gave the most zest to her life, as a letter to Zina demonstrates:

> As I said, I gave a recital on *Monday* evening; *Tuesday* evening I had a business meeting of the Council for the Women's Philharmonic. *Wednesday* evening I stayed at home, *Thursday* evening I went to the concert of the Philharmonic Orchestra, with its new conductor, Stransky. *Friday* evening I went to an exquisite piano recital of a Leschetizky pupil, Miss Monica Dailie, a new young lady pianist, and *Saturday* evening we had the *"Informal"* of the Women's Philharmonic at which Lucy Greenberg was the pianist, so I had to prepare *her* to play. You see I have been out every night but one this week![17]

While living in New York, Amy remained an avid and discriminating concert goer, attending concerts of the New York Philharmonic Orchestra and hearing such renowned performers as Josef Hoffman, Feruccio Busoni, William Backhaus, Teresa Carreño, Julie Rivé-King, Albert Spaulding, and her old friend Ignace Paderewski. She knew personally many of the artists she heard in concert and often was present at intimate social gatherings with them. Sometimes she was the hostess, at other times the guest. She enlivened many a party held in New York and elsewhere, and cherished time with family and friends. Yet she felt a growing disquietude about the difficulty of being a woman in a society controlled by men, and this concern became the subject of many of her writings.

Woman of Words

Whereas in Chicago her professional activities were undertaken during the years when Chicago critic George P. Upton was advising readers about the proper place of women in music, so in New York Amy's residency coincided with the reign of Henry T. Finck, critic of the *New York Evening Post* from 1881 to 1924. As one of the "Great Five" in the classical age of New York journalism, Finck played a leading role in the evolution of musical and art criticism in this country.[18] Like Upton, he had strong opinions about activities "proper" for women. Since 1880 Amy had been fuming inwardly over Upton's misguided claim that even though women had enjoyed equal advantages as men, only

---

[16] MLAF, 106.

[17] MLAF, 106-07.

[18] Editor's note in Henry T. Finck, *Golden Age of Music* (New York and London: Johnson Lane and Co., 1910), 123.

a few women during the last two centuries have created a few works, mostly unknown, and that no woman during that time has written either an opera, oratorio, symphony, or instrumental work of large dimensions that is in the modern repertory.[19]

Upton's conclusion that there was little hope of women ever contributing anything great to the repertory of music struck her as a stinging insult to women, who in fact had been denied equal opportunity in music composition. Her public response to such statements finally occurred in 1900 when she wrote an article for *Music* in which she pointed out that

if it has required 50,000 thousand years to produce a male Beethoven, surely one little century ought to be vouchsafed to create a female one![20]

Curiously, the very next year Finck wrote an article entitled "Employments Unsuitable for Women," in which he wrote:

. . . instead of being encouraged in the tendency to leave the refining atmosphere of home, girls should be taught that, except under the stress of poverty, it is selfish as well as suicidal on their part to go out and work. Selfish because they take away the work which poor women and men absolutely need for their daily bread; suicidal because by offering themselves so cheaply to employers, they either drive out the men, or by lowering their wages from the family standard, make it impossible for them to marry; wherefore, these same girls who had hoped, by thus going out to work to increase their marriage chances, are left to die as old maids, or "new women" as they now prefer to call themselves.[21]

As a well-read critic, Finck no doubt had seen Fay's 1900 article in *Music*; at the very least he certainly had heard about it, which was one of the principal reasons for leading him to articulate, as Upton had done before him in Chicago, his views on the "proper" occupations of women. In moving outside the musical circle to do so, Finck added his voice to that male chorus which typically created a societal backlash in the wake of bold public expressions by women like Amy Fay of their right to empowerment. Did Finck resent Amy's reminding the public that in the past women had been so much taken up by supporting the work of men that they neglected to place a value on their own talents? Did he feel threatened about the prospect of gifted women in the mainstream of life, even though he himself had married a talented musical woman? It seems so, even though he openly acknowledged in his memoirs that following his marriage to pianist Abbie Cushman in 1890 she cooperated with him in his critical career to the point of actually writing many of his columns.[22] Finck freely admitted that his articles often reflected

---

[19] George P. Upton, *Woman and Music* (1880), rev. ed. (Chicago: A. C. McClurg, 1886), 20.

[20] Amy Fay, "Women and Music," *Music* 18 no. 9 (October 1900): 506.

[21] Finck, "Employments Unsuitable for Women," *Independent*, 1 April 1901.

[22] Finck, *Golden Age of Music*, 272.

his wife's influence and that he frequently benefitted from her subtle observations. He explained how sometimes she jotted them down for him to use and at other times, especially in the case of a new opera, the couple divided the task, she writing about the costumes and scenery, he about the musicians and performance.[23]

Amy, however, was not about to be intimidated within a cultural climate shaped by men like Finck. In December 1901, eight months after the publication of Finck's article "Employments Unsuitable for Women," she contributed another article to *Music* in which, among other things, she pointed out the difficulties American women performers faced in the musical world, pointing out that in order to get ahead on the concert stage many even had to change their names and nationalities. She expressed outrage that Brooklyn-born violinist Mary Harkness, at the insistence of her manager, had to promote herself as coming from India, spell her last name backwards, and announce herself as "Arma Senkrah from India."[24]

"Senkrah"'s situation prompted Amy to muse on Harkness's unfortunate marriage to a dissipated lawyer in Weimar. As she wrote:

> She married him and settled down to matrimony and appeared no more in public, except twice. He vetoed that. The end was death by her own hand, at thirty-five. She must, indeed, have been madly in love, to put the pistol to her heart, through jealousy, ten years after her marriage, forgetful of her only child, a beautiful little boy, the image of herself, and adored by her.[25]

As Amy saw it:

> It was a pity she did not remain in her own country, and then she would not have shot herself through the heart from jealousy and despair over the faithlessness of her good-for-nothing German husband in Weimar. . . . She was a beautiful and fascinating young woman, and an artist of the first rank.[26]

As for women pianists, after hearing in one week Ernst von Dohnanyi, Ossip Gabrilowitsch, and Teresa Carreño—each playing with orchestra—she was happy to relate that

> Carreño swept everything before her. She and Gabrilowitsch had chosen the same concerto—Tschaikowsky's First in B flat minor, Op. 23. This concerto was introduced by von Bulow who played it in 1875 in this country. . . . Now it has suddenly leaped into popularity. Gabrilowitsch played it beautifully and musically, but Carreño was simply overwhelming in it, just as she was in Rubinstein's D minor concerto in her last trip.

---

[23] Ibid.

[24] Fay, "Music in New York," *Music* 18 (December 1900): 180.

[25] Ibid., 181.

[26] Ibid., 180.

I think this artist is at her best with orchestra, and it is the proper setting for the diamond. All of the critics lost their hearts to her, and their heads too, for that matter.[27]

Amy offered as proof a selection from the *Times* critic, who stated:

Carreño's was the performance of a mature artist, sure of her fame, sure of herself, and not afraid to hurl all delicacy and the hair-spinning of the raffine school to the winds, while she swept the keyboard with the rush of a whirlwind, set the "wild echoes flying" and the whole auditorium throbbing with the magnetic waves of her exuberant temperament. Power, majesty of conception, sonority of tone, and all the splendors of passion flamed through the performance of this gorgeous woman, who, at a period of maturity when most of her sex take to teaching or to charitable societies, is still able to reign over human hearts by the magic of the songs she sings through the keys of her chosen instrument.[28]

She even went on to quote the critic when he left the realm of music to praise Carreño as a sexual object, celebrating her physical presence rather than her playing, thus evoking how male critics typically treat "woman as spectacle," subjecting her to what feminist art historians call "the male gaze":

As a personality, she is the like, indeed, to the wondrous Cleopatra, for "age cannot wither her, nor custom stale her infinite variety." Carreño's dress was worth the price of admission to the concert. . . . She was attired in a royal gown of black velvet, richly trimmed with gold, in which she was beautiful as the day (or night, I should say)![29]

In 1902 Amy used her authoritative voice on behalf of women music teachers, writing an article for *Etude* in which she exposed the unfair working conditions created by a patriarchal system which denied them "equal pay for equal work." She pointed out that this injustice was made all the worse by the fact that women were not paid in advance as were men teachers, a situation which made it especially difficult in the case of missed lessons. In such cases the teacher would not get paid at all or, if the lesson were postponed, her payment would be deferred. Amy concluded that:

With a man, "business is business." Women do not dream of expecting anything else from the "lords of creation." With their own sex it is a very different matter, and I am sorry to say, they cut off corners in a most unblushing manner.[30]

---

[27] Ibid., 181.

[28] Ibid., 182.

[29] Ibid.

[30] Amy Fay, "The Woman Music Teacher in a Large City," *Etude* 22, no. 1 (9 January 1902): 14.

In other areas, too, Amy used her pen to raise consciousness about how women were held down in the field of music. In 1903, for example, she wrote to the editor of the *Musical Courier* to protest that, of seventy-two participants in the program of the annual convention of the Music Teachers National Association, only eight were women. In asking what was reserved for the women musicians of the whole country at large, she concluded:

> They may take part in the social gatherings of the association, and contribute to the running espenses of it by putting a card in the advertising organ of the M.T.N.A. As it would seem that the M.T.N.A. had become an association of men, it is the judgment of the writer that women would do well to turn their money into the National Federation of Women's Clubs, where they will have some show, or else found a Women Music Teachers' National Association for themselves and invite the men to contribute to the advertising. [31]

In New York, Amy's writing reveals her as a woman in charge of herself, as one experiencing a relative sense of empowerment, who, in Zina's absence, could continue to raise consciousness about the status of women in the world of music and, by extension, in the larger society.

Private Life

Amidst her activism on behalf of women, she made time to be with friends. Whether dining at Delmonico's Restaurant with the Paderewskis, or visiting friends in Europe, Amy continued to delight in her associations. Her *savoir faire* made her a charming hostess and guest. A letter to her niece Madeline describing a Thanksgiving dinner party hosted by Rose, at which the Fincks and the Paderewskis were present, gives a sense of Amy Fay as guest:

> Paderewski and I had a discussion about the comparative merits of *Beethoven and Wagner*, in which Mr. Finck took part! *Paddy* is the most *brilliant talker* and more *wholly spontaneous* than *any* I *ever* have talked with, but perhaps it is because I am sympathetic to him, as *Rose* says *she* has *nothing* in common with Paderewski, "and that they have nothing to say to each other." This is incomprehensible to *me*! I went down to see Rose beforehand, and told her to be *sure* to put Paderewski *next* to *me*, if she wanted him to *enjoy* himself! . . . On thinking it over I guess she concluded it would be good policy to follow my advice, so you will perceive that I was felicitously placed, round the corner to his right, at table! . . . It turned out to be a *beautifully* arranged dinner. After dinner Mme. Paderewski produced *her own* bundle of cigarettes, very long and delicate and presented them to the company. Paderewski lighted *mine* for me! [32]

---

[31] Amy Fay, "Women and the Music Teachers' Association," *Musical Courier*, 17 June 1903, 26.
[32] MLAF, 144.

Summers usually found her travelling or visiting with her siblings. In Cambridge she would stay with Kate and would have the opportunity to see old home-town friends again. Lucheons or friendly chats with Professor and Mrs. John Knowles Paine, Henry Wadsworth Longfellow, Emma Cary, and Henry and William James provided special moments of reconnecting with cherished friends and neighbors from the days of her youth.

On the occasions when she went to Woodstock, Vermont to stay with her sister Laura, the Chickering piano firm of Boston would send Amy a piano for her use. She reserved mornings for practice, while the afternoons and evenings were set aside for relaxation. During those summer visits Laura's daughter Madeline observed Amy at close range. She especially noted how fond her aunt Amy was of pretty clothes, commenting that she spent money freely and did look stunning in a Worth dress, the "Dior of her day!" Amy loved to give presents and often got herself in debt for overspending the allowance from her brother Norman. After contemplating her bills, she would ask her niece, "Now Madeline, would you pay one entire bill or give a little for each?"[33]

For several summers between 1890 and 1896, during a particularly prosperous period in her brother Norman's life, Amy became his hostess at his summer residence in Newport, that oceanside resort town labelled by some observers as "the nation's social capitol." Every summer prominent members of the literary, artistic, and scientific communities of Boston and Cambridge vacationed there: Henry Wadsworth Longfellow, Henry James, George Bancroft, and John Singer Sargent, to mention but a few. Amy enjoyed the glamor of such high society and delighted in her proximity to the "beau monde."

After the marriage of Rose and Theodore Thomas, Amy often spent three or four weeks each summer as their guest at Felsengarten, the Thomas summer home in New Hampshire, where she enjoyed the quiet beauty of that rustic setting in the White Mountains. Following Theodore Thomas's death in 1905, Amy assisted Rose while she wrote her famous biography of Thomas,[34] translating German for her as Rose went through Thomas's letters and papers.[35]

Like Amy, Rose too was clever. She had boundless self-confidence and, in the words of a grandniece, "thought she could do just about anything." She authored two books,[36] made her own clothes, and became an authority on gardening. At an older age Rose learned to drive and Amy, though she feared driving with her, would accompany her on her Sunday driving excursions, only to return to the house, flop in a chair, and exclaim "another escape from death!"[37]

Rose enjoyed celebrity status as Thomas's widow. When in 1910 President Taft presided over the dedication of a new statue in honor of Thomas at the Cincinnati Music Festival, Amy and Norman accompanied Rose to the celebration and experienced the benefits of being in Rose's entourage. Amy wrote of the occasion:

---

[33] Madeline Smith, "Portrait of My Aunts," Schlesinger Library, Radcliffe College.

[34] Ibid.

[35] Rose Fay Thomas, *Memoirs of Theodore Thomas* (New York: Moffat, Yard, and Co., 1911).

[36] Also *Our Mountain Garden* (New York: Macmillan, 1904).

[37] Conversation with Rose's grandniece Rosamond Jackson Ellis Chadwick, Weston, Massachusetts, 9 January 1987.

> I don't know *when* I have enjoyed anything as much as Rose and Norman
> and I had such pleasant little family meetings at our meals in the Grand
> Hotel. Rose was treated like a princess, and no doubt she told you how
> she was given the seat of honor between the president and the governor!
> The calm and tranquil way in which she walks over the heads of the
> swells everywhere fills me with admiration and mingled awe! But she
> was the same as a *child*, when she conquered Edith Longfellow, who
> was the swellest girl in *Cambridge*, you remember![38]

But frequently there were tensions between the sisters, and they seemed to tolerate one
another better in small doses. If the two were together for too long a time they grated
on one another, and Rose often became ill following Amy's visits.

Possibly latent sibling rivalry created strains between Rose and Amy. After all, in
Germany, Cambridge, and in Chicago Amy was special, but following the Fay-Thomas
wedding, she was no longer the primary musician in the family or the center of attention in
social gatherings where Rose was present. Furthermore, Amy harbored resentment that her
socially prominent sister did not use the Fay-Thomas connection to promote her professional
career as a concert pianist. These realities, combined with Amy's youthful observation
that the Fays were "a queer lot who got along just as well when they were separated
at the poles of the earth"[39] heightened the competitive spirit between Rose and Amy.

In the summers when Amy went abroad, Rose no doubt appreciated the reprieve from
the tensions brought on by Amy's vacation visits to New Hampshire. One such summer
was 1891, when Amy sailed for Europe in order to visit Paris, Bayreuth, and the Mozart
Festival in Salzburg.[40] Rose could enjoy Amy from afar through reading her three-part
series in the *Musical Courier*[41] in which, among other things, she extolled the beauty of
the Requiem that opened the Festival, and praised Annette Essipoff's playing of the Mozart
D-minor Piano Concerto.

As the years passed, Amy enjoyed other international excursions, which kept her
out of Rose's hair. Acting as surrogate mother for her sister Kate, who had to remain
at home in order to care for her ailing husband, in the fall of 1902 she journeyed to Lima
as a companion to Kate's daughter, Pauline Stone, for her wedding to Arthur Jackson,
owner of a rubber plantation in Bolivia. Her account of the wedding reveals how forward-
looking she was in her thinking about such matters as rituals and religious services. In
describing her niece's wedding service at the home of the American minister to Peru,
for example, she spoke of herself as the "best woman" for the occasion, *not* the maid of
honor. She was delighted that everything was done in style:

> When we reached the house the butler threw open the door, and a
> group of gentlemen came out from the drawing room to meet us. It
> was very swell. Mr. Dudley the American minister took in the bride

---

[38] MLAF, 90.

[39] Letter of Amy Fay to Zina, 1 March 1873, FFP.

[40] This was the predecessor of the present Salzburg Festival.

[41] "The Salzburg Festival," *Musical Courier* 11 November 1891, 549; 18 November 1891, 580; 25 November 1891,
615.

and the consul Mr. Crea followed me.   Arthur walked with Mr. Todd
and Mr. Davis took in Mrs. Todd.   The regular English clergyman was
absent, so we had to have the Methodist minister perform the ceremony.
He read our service, but was not very familir with it, but his name was
Pusey, and can trace his lineage way back to the year one thousand. . . .
I had expected to give away the bride, but the Methodist minister
omitted that sentence ("Who giveth this woman to be married to this
man?").   So I did not have to do it.   I was quite disappointed as I wanted
to give Pauline away. [42]

Her disappointment in not being able to give the bride away did not prevent her enjoying
to the fullest the elegant wedding reception, which Amy described in great detail in her
letter home:

When we got back to the hotel, Arthur ordered lots of champagne and
Pauline got out the wedding cake, which we had brought from Boston.
I played the Wedding March from "Lohengrin" and also the Mendelssohn
one on the piano in the hotel foyer. . . .   The whole wedding was a
great success from first to last and everybody had a good time including
the bride and groom. [43]

In the summer of 1903 Amy was a guest of her dear Chicago friend Mrs. Clarence
Eddy during a three-month visit to her summer home in Chatou, a suburb of Paris.   Mrs.
Eddy treated Amy royally, obtaining a Steinway piano for her use and driving her to Paris
three times a week for sightseeing purposes.   During her stay Amy had the opportunity
to meet old American friends like Charles Thayer and Mr. and Mrs. John Knowles Paine.
She also made the acquaintance of such distinguished musicians as the French organist
Alexandre Guilmant.   Most importantly, she got to see her beloved Camille Gurickx, who,
although he was by then married and awaiting the birth of his second child, had an
"emotional" reunion with Amy, as she described in her letter home:

Altogether it was a nice little episode to meet him again, and we mutually
avoided any reference to the past!   He *looked at me affectionately* though,
and as if he still had a *lot* of sentiment!   I was glad for him that he had
to go to Ghent the next day, when he could have a chance to think
things over, away from his wife.   I showed him a copy of my book and
he was delighted with the picture in it and exclaimed, "You must give
me a copy like that!"   So I gave him the book, and he gave me his
photograph, a very good one. [44]

---

[42] Letter of Amy Fay to Kate and Will Stone, 11 December 1902, private papers of Gregory Harris, a great
nephew of Amy Fay.

[43] Ibid.

[44] MLAF, 51.

Amy seemed never to get over Gurickx, and toward the end of her life, as she reflected on what "might have been" had she married him, she could acknowledge that:

> Gurickx did wisely to return to his own country, where he has a *fixed position* and for him New York would have been a poor exchange. His wife, too, suits him a great deal better than *I* would have done so it is all right. He was *stirred up* at seeing me again, though, and possibly had some regrets. [45]

During her visit, Mrs. Eddy extended Amy an "all expenses paid" invitation to attend the Wagner Festival held in Berlin in September and October of 1903. Amy was ecstatic at the opportunity to return to the city where she had spent her student years, and wrote home of her excitement:

> . . . it was a great pleasure for me to be in dear old Berlin once more, where I had spent six years of my youth. I picked up many old friends, and made some new ones. . . . I met Professor Paine and Mrs. Paine in Berlin at the Wagner Festival and you will be pleased to know that our Professor was treated with much honour there. He was the first to be called up to receive a medal and diploma, and his Overture to Oedipus was played and was much applauded. He had a triple recall from the audience. [46]

In 1911 Amy once again was eager to get to Europe in honor of the Liszt centennial year. But this time she could not look to her brother Norman for help in underwriting the trip, since he had suffered a series of financial reverses. Between 1909 and 1911 Norman had engaged in a series of business misadventures that caused him considerable losses. His investment in the Remington-Sholes Typewriter Company of Chicago caused him a heavy financial loss. That was followed by a financial misadventure with an auto manufacturing company. Next Norman entered into an unfortunate, though short-lived, connection with a large electric power company in the northwest, in which he accepted a vice-presidency offered by an old friend prominent in its councils, who immediately afterwards went insane.

Therefore the determined Amy looked to her sister Kate to help in underwriting her trip to Europe for the Liszt centennial celebration, writing her a letter hinting at how much she wanted to attend the festivities:

> I am just *crazy* to go abroad this summer, and I *ought* to be on hand for the grand celebration of Liszt's centenary, which will be at Heidelberg in August I believe. . . . Miss Read has engaged her passage on the

---

[45] MLAF, 52.

[46] MLAF, 70.

Venezia for July 1st and I would give anything to accompany her! I see no prospect of my being able to do so, however, and keep asking my brain how I could earn five hundred dollars the next two months! [47]

Kate's return letter from Seville offered to pay Amy's passage to and from Europe. The trip was a rich one for Amy, for not only did she attend the Liszt festival, but also visited Italy and Switzerland. Most importantly, she arranged to reunite for one final time with Gurickx. Her account of this meeting reveals that she still retained an intense feeling for him after so many years had passed since their romantic student days in Germany:

> I was so mad when I was in Brussels! Gurickx was most anxious to devote one day to me, but his wife was so jealous she would not permit him to carry out his scheme so all he could do was to invite me to dinner at the Hotel Royale, and I saw him only a little over two hours! They have been married *twenty years* and have a grown daughter, and I have seen him now for the *second* time only! I thought she was too *mean* for anything! But Gurickx was a fool to tell her anything about it that I was in town. He could have managed perfectly well if he had not been so frank and open. He is more charming than ever and is considered to have made a most successful career! His wife is young (compared with him) about forty-two and charming and rich, and the daughter of one of the most aristocratic families in Brussels. [48]

Even at age sixty-seven Amy had not lost her flirtatious manner nor her abiding affection for Gurickx. In April of the next year she was still reflecting on her reunion with Gurickx when she wrote to Zina:

> After all, one does not replace the old loves. When I saw Gurickx last fall I found him *more* attractive than ever! He is the quintessence of *elegance* now! He always *was so intelligent* in conversation! Gurickx is *all art!* I have had some lovely letters from him recently, *full* of affection and appreciation. He writes a *charming* letter, so caressing! [49]

In the spring of 1912, the year following her return from her last European sojourn, Amy hosted the annual family reunion of her mother's side of the family, the Hopkins. These family reunions were taken quite seriously by most of the family members and frequently led to publications in which the life of each member was brought up to date. Amy entertained the gathering and at the latter part of the celebration, after the family had returned to her room, she played a lot and evoked "shrieks of laughter" at her funny

---

[47] MLAF, 95.

[48] MLAF, 109.

[49] MLAF, 118.

stories illustrative of her pieces. Fittingly, at the close of the evening, the family sang "Like a Golden Thread, if Love" and "The Summer Doth Fade Away."[50]

TEACHING IN NEW YORK

Well into the second decade of the century Amy Fay remained prominent as a lecturer, performer, pedagogue, and clubwoman. As her reputation as teacher burgeoned, her students were often asked to perform for entertainments, schools, grand receptions, club concerts, and charity concerts, and she came to take great pride in many of them. She delighted in reporting on their progress in letters to Zina. Just as she considered Laura Sanford and John Alden Carpenter to have been her most gifted students in Chicago,[51] so she felt that Lucy Greenberg and Lemuel Goldstein were her outstanding students in New York. In 1910 she wrote to Zina that Lucy Greenberg "made a sensation" when she performed for the Women's Philharmonic Society and proved to be "a veritable virtuosa" when she performed Mozart's D-minor Concerto and Weber's "Perpetual Motion" at a party Amy gave for Rose.[52] Again, in 1912 wrote to Zina about her gifted students:

> My results from an *artistic* standpoint have been *brilliant* this season, and Lemuel Goldstein at fifteen has just played the first movement, with Hummel cadenza, of Beethoven's second concerto (B flat major) at the Morris High School, *with orchestra*, in a big concert, while Lucy Greenberg, in addition to *her own* concert, has rehearsed the difficult *Mozart* concerto in D minor with Volpé's orchestra, and came off with flying colors! . . . Volpé led the applause himself with repeated "Bravas," and Lucy was *surrounded* when she arose from the piano! . . . I wish you could have heard Lucy *roll off* the big cadenza, with her *impeccable technic!* It invoked the *shades of Deppe* while she was playing it! How *delighted* he would have been with the results of his method in America! . . . As for Lemuel Goldstein, he brought the house down the other night with the Beethoven, and I was taken by surprise myself at the exquisite quality of his tone in that big hall, for he is a fragile boy and has small hands. Every *note* was clear as a bell, and so musical![53]

Despite her artistic success with her students, she did not always experience financial success as a teacher, especially in her later years. Many of her students were drawn from the poorer classes, and they could not even afford the three-dollar fee she had been able to command in Chicago. Most often, therefore, she had to settle for two dollars per lesson, which meant in turn that she could not afford to advertise for more affluent students and still meet her expenses.

---

[50] MLAF, 122.

[51] "Amy Fay Celebrates Birthday," *Musical Courier*, 1 June 1916, 34.

[52] MLAF, 92.

[53] MLAF, 124-25.

After her students left her tutelage, she followed their careers with interest. If one or another of them met with disappointment, she was especially sympathetic, as a letter to Zina reveals:

> Poor Lucy Greenberg has had a hard time with her manager, and Mr. Aronson got her only one engagement, which was at Groaverson Hall, the home of the Duke of Westminster. Only the nobility of England were present, and Lucy made a great hit and was the only artist to receive an encore. Aronson then cooly informed Lucy that he had spent fifteen hundred dollars to give her this engagement, and that his money was at an end! She would either have to return to America or go to Berlin and continue her lessons with Scharwenka till next April or May, as the concert season was over in London! Lucy is now in Berlin again, and is bitterly repenting that she ever left *me*, but she is in for another year abroad. I only hope Aronson will keep his word and get her engagements in the spring but I very much *doubt it!* Her brothers are now sending her their savings to pay her board and that of her mother and little sister in Berlin! Isn't it a *shame!* She was already to *play* when she left me, and she is being managed just as Laura Sanford was, and all my work undone! She sees her mistake in leaving me but has the European bee in her bonnet! Scharwenka has fine pupils and is *well paid* for his lessons![54]

After twenty years in New York, she had savored fully the richness of that city's musical seasons, had relished three more European trips and one to South America, and had enjoyed several summers in Newport. The intellectual and artistic stimulation from those experiences can only be imagined. She came near to capturing her life situation in a letter to her sister Kate written in 1910:

> I have now lived in New York for twenty years and have such a nice circle of friends and acquaintances that I am in a whirl all the while, and experience the greatest difficulty in getting time to write or practice.[55]

In the fall of that same year the *Musical Observer* concurred with Amy's self-estimate in an article that stated:

> No club woman and no musician in New York is more universally beloved than is Miss Amy Fay, President of the Women's Philharmonic Society of New York. Miss Fay's following has always been large and her acquaintance with all the notable musicians both here and abroad has made her a charming leader of this prominent club, which has numbered among its members the very best musicians of the Metropolis.[56]

---

[54] MLAF, 152-53.

[55] MLAF, 90.

[56] "Miss Amy Fay," *Musical Observer* 4, no. 9 (September 1910): 18.

In 1914, she wrote to Zina about her fame as a teacher:

> My pupils are attracting a good deal of attention now, and I have a big
> reputation as a teacher here. A boy pupil of mine named Meyer Larkin
> played for the famous pianist, Harold Bauer, a week or two ago and
> when he had finished his piece, a difficult *Menuet* by St. Saëns, Bauer
> remarked to him "All Miss Fay's pupils will be *concert pianists*." . . . This
> same boy played for Rudolph Ganz last winter, and he was very much
> struck with the Deppe finger exercises. I am getting talked about in
> musical circles as a very wonderful teacher *at last!*[57]

As she approached retirement from professional life she continued to receive praise
from the musical press. In 1917 the *Musical Courier* stated that Amy Fay "as a pianist
of broad experience, originator of the 'Piano Conversation,' and one of the real Liszt
pupils, has established a name and fame which are unique among American instructors
of the piano."[58]

Between 1917 and 1918 Amy Fay experienced failing health and family members
became concerned that she was unable to manage on her own in New York. As they
noticed her decline, they began to press her to return to Cambridge to live with Norman
and Rose, who had returned there earlier. Finally, in 1919, at the insistence of Norman
and Rose, she joined them back in Cambridge, where she passed her time quietly. In
1923 Zina died in Chicago, thus depriving Amy of the family member she loved the most
and the one who was the recipient of most of her correspondence. After Zina's passing
her physical condition and her spirits declined even further, and eventually she had to
be placed in a nursing home at 53 Spruce Street, Watertown, Massachusetts, where, on
28 February 1928, Amy died of natural causes. After a funeral service at Christ Church
in Cambridge, she was laid to rest in Mount Auburn Cemetery beside her sister Zina
and close by the grave of Theodore Thomas. On the gravestone of Amy and Zina is
an epitaph composed by Norman which celebrates the special kinship between the two
sisters. It reads:

> They were lovely and pleasant in their lives.
> And in their death they were not divided.

Following Amy's death, Norman and Rose continued to make their home together in
Cambridge. Then in 1922, at the age of seventy-four, Norman married Lillian Hale, of an
old Newburyport family, and set up his home in Cambridge where the couple lived happily
together for twenty years.

After Amy's death, Norman memorialized her in the following poem:

---

[57] MLAF, 152.

[58] "Amy Fay at Work," *Musical Courier*, 8 November 1917, 7.

"Simplex Munditis!" Yes, she is dead. Thanks, old friend Horace-that
was well said. *In* the world, *not* of it. Why—that was she!
So let this our memorial be. Gone she is—visioner, dreamer of dreams!
As we look back at her, how oft she seems
Rapt in the infinite blue of the sky,
The laugh of the lake, the whisper or sigh
Of the old hemlocks—stately and tall,
Kings of the trees, overtopping them all—
There where the brown cliffs look to the west,
Where the red sun rolls down to its rest
Past purple mountains—there where she said
"Dear Old Rock Point!" And now she is dead.

Not many ecstacies, not many tears
Hers, as she wandered the world of the years.
Duty, and beauty, and always the dream
Of an art exquisite, single, supreme—

And its great masters. Ambitions? Yes, one—
To be a true artist! Jealousies? None.
Lovers? A plenty of lovers there were.
And she loved the loving—but, not so fair
The vision of love as the vision of art.
So in her dream-life she lingered, apart.
Artist in words too, to tip of her pen;
Camera-like, swift limner of men
"She could have struck," Fra Elbertus wrote,
"Thirteen in Literature," but for the note,
The rhythm, emotion, insistent refrain,
The master-musician that beat in her brain.
Humor, wit, sweetness she had; and her gold
Ripple-hair many a fairy-tale told.
Many a name illustrious lends
Glint to the galaxy of or her friends.
Painter, romance, ambassador, bard
Sculptor, philosopher, verily starred
Her wide horizon. Birds of a feather,
Genius and beauty flock away together.
Farewell, loved artist! memory goes a-roaming
Back to dim parlors and midsummer gloaming,
Whence unseen keys and shadowy fingers roll
Billows of melody over thirsty soul.
Ballade, Prelude, Fugue, Appasionata—
Of *all* the beautiful inamorata—
How is thy charm delicious to remember,
As a flame of youth burns down to old-age ember!
Though thou are past that ultimate dark portal,
Still dost thou leave us love and art, immortal!

Source: *Twenty-First Annual Report of the Hopkinsfolk Association*, 12 May 1928.

3.

Hasten, sinner, to return;

    Stay not for the morrow's sun;

Lest thy lamp should cease to burn,

    Ere salvation's work is done.

4.

Hasten, sinner, to be blest;

    Stay not for the morrow's sun;

Lest perdition thee arrest,

    Ere the morrow is begun.

Miss Amy Fay is an American, born in Bayou Goula, Miss., May 21st, 1844. Daughter of a musical family her childhood has been nourished with what is best in music. In the Germany of her time her musical nature found a proper atmosphere in which to breathe and grow, and under Tausig and Liszt it was not long before she came into prominence. Her art as a pianist and as an interpreter has been proclaimed by Liszt, Paderewski, Vincent d'Indy and others. She appeared in America under Theodore Thomas and her recitals in the form of "Piano Conversations" won the favor of the public all over this country.

Her book "Music Study in Germany" was a favorite one of the poet Longfellow. At the request of Sir George Grove it was published in London by MacMillan and at the request of Liszt it was translated into German. Vincent d'Indy, the celebrated French composer, wrote the preface to the French edition, recalling with gratitude Amy Fay's interpretation of Bach when he heard her in Germany.

The New Singing Society considers it a great privilege to present to its members and its friends the above hymn by Amy Fay. The circumstances under which it was composed are explained in the following letter:

New York, Jan. 16th, 1917.

Dear Mr. Camilleri:

One night last summer, while I was visiting in the country home of the late Theodore Thomas, in the White Mountains, I fell asleep, and in a dream I was singing, to my own melody, the old-fashioned hymn, "Hasten, sinner, to be wise;" etc. While composing the tune, I woke up, and not wishing to forget it, I wrote the melody down. Herewith I submit it to your friendly consideration, and in the hope that it will please you, I remain,

Yours very cordially,

68 West 91st Street, New York.   AMY FAY.

Miss Amy Fay is now in New York devoting her time to teaching and she delights her numerous friends with her bright and joyful disposition.   ✳ L. C.

The only known composition of Amy Fay,
the hymn "Hasten, Sinner, to Be Wise," written in the summer of 1916.

Conclusion

Did Amy Fay fulfill her promise as a musician? Certainly she never reached the professional performing heights toward which she aspired during her years as a music student in Germany. Although she was a good, solid pianist, the nervousness that plagued her during her student and early professional years prevented her from making the strong beginning in the concert hall that would have ensured a brilliant performing career. To be sure, the "Piano Conversation" she eventually developed enabled her to overcome her nervousness and affiliate with her audiences in new and important ways. But she came upon the concept too late in her career to compensate for the time lost earlier when she was a new, fresh face on the musical horizon. For all of that, her marked contributions to the musical life of the nation and of the world through her many involvements as a performer, lecturer, clubwoman, writer, and teacher, entitle her to her rightful designation as one of America's notable women.

As a woman whose career evolved in the context of late nineteenth-century American feminism and women's history, Amy Fay was an important presence in the musical life of the nation and of the world in the late nineteenth and early twentieth centuries. She was a "New Woman," not only in terms of the musical profession but also in light of the emergent life styles of social, political, and cultural life in the United States.

APPENDICES

Appendix 1

"How to Practice"
from *Etude* 2, nos. 11-12 (November, December 1884): 205-06, 213-14

The following two articles were originally a speech delivered to the Music Teachers' National Convention in Cleveland, Ohio. The articles reveal Amy's theory that there are two types of artists—those naturally gifted, and those who must work much harder to achieve the same results. She clearly viewed herself among those who must work hard, as can be seen in this analysis of her own methods of practice. Even more revealing is her final message in which she sums up the qualities of a great artist, "a special talent for technique, combined with the best training from childhood up." After returning from Germany, Amy has realized that she will never be a great artist, and she entreats her audience to "leave it to the privileged few to set the world on fire."

*   *   *   *   *

Artists may be divided into two classes: those who have a great natural gift for technique, and those who have to acquire it by hard study. The first class play "by the grace of God," as the Germans cleverly put it. The second have to work out their destiny slowly and painfully by the aid of man.

I have observed that those persons who have a gift for reading music rapidly, generally combine with facility of execution. They have an unerring instinct which tells them just where to put their fingers, and are obliged to analyze each note and its connection with the succeeding ones before they can play it. The latter requires a month to do what the former can accomplish in a few days, or even hours. The slow readers have some compensations. They are able to play by heart, and have strong memories. For the very reason that they are obliged to work harder to conquer mechanical difficulties, they are apt to be better interpreters, because they listen more closely. If they cannot read the printed pages with rapidity, once learned, they are independent of the manuscript. The greatest artists possess both gifts equally.

One would think that all artists of high rank ought to be able to impart to their pupils the principles of a fine technique. Having got over the hill difficulty themselves, they ought to be able to retrace the steps they have taken with a talented conscientious scholar.

Such, however, is not the case. Whether it is that they have forgotten how they have arrived at a given result, or whether it is laziness and indifference on their part, I cannot decide. I am inclined to think they have never systematized their ideas into a definite form of expression. They play more by instinct than by rule. Yes, rules are just as important in practicing as they are in everything else.

I have heard many artists play in the course of my life, but I have rarely met with one who could give me any practical hints about technique.

I went to Germany to study the piano with Tausig, than whom I suppose a greater virtuoso never lived. At the first lesson he said: "Play me the scale of F sharp Major." I played it. The only thing he said was, "Put the fifth finger on the top note of the scale, instead of turning the thumb under and ending on the second," which was what I had been doing. He also said, "Curve your fingers," and indeed, he made me curve them so much that it seemed to me I was playing upon my finger nails. Not a word more did I get out of him, who could play scales with a velvety smoothness and velocity which seemed like a zephyr blowing over the keys. I know very well by subsequent experience that I must have played that scale of F sharp Major with a stiff wrist, and there must have been wholly absent from it either smoothness or velocity. All that I did was to play the notes correctly, nothing more.

Now, why did not Tausig take that scale through with me, note by note, and show me how to practice it with one hand! Why did he not at least play the scale through before me as he practiced it himself? Then I could have got an idea. I knew nothing of the legato or wrist movement. All I knew that the scale ought to sound like a string of pearls, and that I couldn't do it. That was one of the things I had crossed the ocean to learn, and I had come to Tausig as the man who could teach me.

"You must practice the scales every day," he said, and he never heard me play another one, though I did practice them religiously every day. At the end of four years, having spent an immense amount of time over them, I had, of course, made some improvement, but I was still very far from being able to do what I now teach my own pupils to do in six months. My pupils practice one scale from ten minutes to half an hour per day, while I used to practice them all a whole hour per day. I remember that my brain used to feel benumbed when I had played the last one. But I show my pupils how to practice rightly, and ten minutes well spent is worth more than an hour wrongly.

After spending a year in Tausig's conservatory, working myself to death over scales and the Gradus ad Parnussum, I went to Kullak, with whom I studied three years and a half. The first year I took private lessons, and after that I was put into the highest class of his lady pupils.

Kullak had an immense reputation, both as artist and teacher. He was thought to have no superior in Germany, and even Liszt had the greatest respect for him as a teacher.

How well I remember my first lesson. It was in the evening, from seven to eight o'clock. I was shown into his large music room, wholly bare of any carpet or furniture except two grand pianos in the centre of it. A lamp stood on each one, making a circle of light upon the floor, while the distant corners of the room were quite in shadow. In a moment Kullak stood before me. His personality was extremely interesting and artistic. His deepset eyes looked penetratingly at me through his spectacles, and his strong and passionate mouth at once impressed me. I said to myself: "Here is an artist, and no mere pedagogue." Kullak did not ask me to play a scale, nor did he say anything about technique, whatever. He probably thought that as I had been in Tausig's conservatory a year I must know how to practice. He asked me what pieces I had been studying last. I said Tausig had just given me Liszt's "Au bord d'nue sonne [d'une source]." "Play it," said he, taking the music and setting it up on his own piano, at which he seated himself. I sat at the other one and played by heart, as I had no second copy. I had then been about six weeks without any lessons, and so I had a good chance to practice and learn it. Moreover, Tausig had condescended to play the last of it for me, so I got a conception of it.

Kullak gave me some additional beautiful ideas about the first half. "Those skipping notes in the left hand were stray drops of water sparkling through the air," he said, and certainly, as he played them, they were. I was inspired and helped by his playing, and I imitated him as well as I could. When I had finished he exclaimed, enthusiastically, "Fraulein, Sie sind eine geboren Kunstlerin!" ("You are a born artist!")

Now, this was not true. I wasn't a born artist, for if I had been I should have had that natural gift for technique of which I have already spoken, and which born artists always possess. It was evident later on that he did not think so himself, for one day in a tirade he gave me to know what an artist should be able to do, he turned short round on his stool and said, "What do you know about playing scales in double thirds and double sixths?" and then began playing them in most magnificent style himself. I meekly confessed that I knew nothing, though I did not add "thanks" to him, as I might have done. I then asked him to recommend me a work out of which to study them. He told me to get Kortski's technical exercises, which I did, and at once added the daily study of double thirds and double sixths to my scale practice. Kullak also told me to study his Octave School and Czerny's School of the Virtuoso. Many wearisome days I spent practicing this latter work, which is fatiguing to the mind to the last degree, and I would not condemn a scholar of mine to it, since, useful as it is, there are others which are equally so,. which are really delightful to study. The Stuttgart habit of playing Bach an hour per day is much better, for it improves the mind as well as the fingers.

Kullak's strong point as a teacher consisted in his constantly playing with his pupils. Scharwenka said one day, in speaking of him: "By playing with his pupils, Kullak trains their ear, so that they are insensibly led along. They learn their weak points by constant comparison with him." He always used two grand pianos in teaching, which stood side by side, he sitting at one and the pupil at the other. While it was a good plan in some respects, in others it was not, for it disaccustomed the pupils to play alone, and his touch was so powerful that it drowned them out completely. But we got a standard of how a piece ought to sound when played by a great artist, and that was a great thing, and was probably the secret of Kullak's success as a teacher.

And now I come to the man who taught me more about practicing than all my other teachers put together. I allude to Deppe, in Berlin. I owe the good fortune of making his acquaintance to Mr. Sherwood, who met him before I did, and who introduced me to him.

Whether Deppe's ideas are entirely original with himself I do not know. Sometimes I am inclined to think he may have got some of them from Wieck, as Wieck's method seemed to me identical with his in some respects. Certainly, Wieck was a great master, as his daughter Clara's playing showed, not to speak of the many other great artists who were trained by him.

Like Wieck, Deppe begins his instruction at the very beginning, that is, he first forms the hand by certain technical exercises, showing the pupil how to place it upon the keys and raise the fingers and let them fall separately. I maintain that not one person in a hundred can raise the finger and let it fall on a key without stiffening the wrist, unless their attention is particularly called to it. I have never had a pupil that I did not have to limber out their wrist, and show them they were unconsciously contracting the muscles and tightening them. In fact, the only way I could detect it myself was by holding one hand between the thumb and middle finger of the other while practicing the exercises, when the contraction is at once felt.

It is precisely the same difficulty that singers experience with the muscles of the throat. Now, if a singing master should say to his pupil, "don't contract the muscles of the throat when you sing," that is all very well as far as it goes, but if he can't show him how to avoid it it would not do much good. Probably very few teachers can do this, and that is why so many fine voices are ruined. Yet it must be a very simple thing if you know how; as Deppe often used to say in teaching, "It is the egg of Columbus."

Deppe's technical exercises are ten in number, and require twenty minutes to play through, ten minutes for each hand. Each one has a definite object, and I find I cannot omit one of them with my pupils without loss to them. They include raising the fingers and pressing them down on the keys without stiffening the wrist, the trill in slow movement, in single notes and then in double thirds, five notes of the scale, which is the foundation of the whole scale. Then follows the raising of the fore-arm and letting the fingers drop on the black keys from above, sinking with the wrist but holding the first joint of the finger very firm. This is a most important exercise, and is the foundation of chord playing, which is done on the same principle. We all remember the pictures in the instruction-books where the hand is represented thrown back at right angles from the wrist in striking chords and octaves. This would be diametrically opposite to Deppe's system, which would be to let the weight of the fore-arm rest upon the key, and to take up the chord from the arm, the hand hanging loosely from the wrist.

By following the instruction-book method the fingers are thrown suddenly back from the keys, and the arm is rigid. This produces the effect of shutting the mouth instantly at the conclusion of a phrase in singing. The sound is cut off instead of dying away. By adopting Deppe's method the arm and wrist rise from the keys before the fingers leave them, and this momentary clinging of the fingers to the keys prolongs the tone, and makes it aesthetically beautiful. The movement is also graceful to look at, and the arm is supple and free. It is the same in practicing octaves, and even in the staccato. The hand is never thrown back, but is always lifted by the arm.

Deppe's ideas in regard to the scale are also very important. He teaches the pupil not to tuck the thumb under, but to prepare for the thumb by turning a little on each finger, turning the wrist outward, and making the thumb a point of support on which to lift the hand over the next key, in fact, stretching from the thumb. Contracting the thumb is one of the stumbling-blocks in technique. It is a habit I have to break in every pupil. The thumb must be curved and free from the hand in order to work properly. The advantage of this is cearly seen by looking at the hand from the inside with the fingers curved. Pinch the thumb in or let the hand fall over it and motion is at once impeded. If the scale is practiced ten minutes per day according to Deppe's method, it is sufficient. In six months a beautiful scale can be acquired. I know it by actual experience in teaching.

A petition has lately been circulated in Berlin begging the police to regulate the hours of practice, and a regular war against pianists has been declared, because, it is said, that the numberless hours of scale practice and finger exercises indulged in by students is having a serious effect upon the mental and physical welfare of the people there. In Weimar practicing with the windows open is not allowed, and in a letter to Emil Liebling from his brother, Paul Liebling, who is now in Weimar, and which I read a day or two since, he says it is a difficult matter for Liszt's pupils to get a boarding place.

If people knew how to practice according to Deppe's method they would not meet with this difficulty, for instead of setting the nerves on edge it quiets them. I have sometimes been in the house with invalids and have practiced all day long, and they have enjoyed it and have been impatient to have me begin again the following day.

When I was in Goshen, Ind., last summer I was practicing very hard for recitals in Mr. Straub's Normal. The lady of the house was ill upstairs, and I had serious compunctions, but the practicing had to be done. After she was well enough to come down stairs she said: "Your playing was the greatest comfort to me while I was ill. It soothed me and seemed to be an accompaniment to my thoughts. After listening awhile I fell asleep." The same thing happened to me some years ago in Grand Isle, Vt. I was passing the summer in a farm-house. An old lady who was a great sufferer had the room next to that where my piano stood. Before my arrival the people in the house were afraid the old lady would not be able to endure my practicing, particularly as she had never been in the habit of listening to the piano. On the contrary, one morning as I seated myself before the instrument she came in and laid her trembling hand on my shoulder and said, "I can hardly wait till you begin to play, even your finger exercises are a pleasure to me. The moment I hear that little sound it seems to quiet my nerves all down, and I forget my ailments."

As to my own family it has often occurred that when I have practiced a great deal during the day they will say in the evening, quite with the air of proposing something new, "Oh, do sit down and play."

The reason they can bear it so well is because I practice a great deal with one hand alone slowly and without pedal. This obviates the noise element. One must practice with a musical tone and without excess of emotion. Practicing should be an entirely different thing from performance, except, indeed, when one is practicing concert effects previous to playing in public. My rule is as follows for daily study: Twenty minutes for finger exercises with each hand alone. Ten minutes for a scale. Half to three-quarters of an hour for Etudes, including ten octave studies. After that pieces *ad libitum*, which I play through three times slowly with each hand alone, and then repeatedly with both together.

There is one point I should like to discuss with the artists present, and that is, whether it is best to pick out the hard passages and study them by themselves, giving them particular attention and more time. This has been my method until quite lately, but I now begin to think perhaps it is better not to fix the mind on the hard places, but to play the piece right through with one hand from beginning to the end until they are mastered.

I was once learning Wagner's Spinning Song, and I had a great deal of trouble with the run on the first page. I practiced it immensely much, but still never felt sure of it. At last I said to myself one day, I will not practice this any more. I will play the piece through no matter how it goes. To my surprise, after playing it right through a number of times, I got it. I saw then it was a mental difficulty. My mind had stood still every time and trembled before that little run. My imagination had exaggerated the difficulty of it, and I could not get over it.

It is a nice point to decide when a passage is hard in itself and when it is so from what goes before. Take for example the broken octave passage for the right hand in Chopin's A flat Ballade, in my judgment one of the most difficult pieces written for the piano. Nine pianists out of ten are unequal to it. I should like to know for curiosity's sake how many hours I have spent at different times in my life over that passage. It requires at once immense strength and immense lightness and flexibility. I discovered after awhile that the passage by itself was not difficult, but as the culmination of the climax which precedes it for a page back, it is almost beyond human endurance. In a case like that it seems to me better to practice the whole piece straight through. The mind should not become fixed too strongly upon the difficulty of certain passages, as is done by constant repetition. Don't think about it, but do it, somehow or other.

I suppose that every artist at a certain point in his career is brought to a sense of his own limitations. He has gone a certain distance, he plays beautifully, and now he would like to be something extraordinary, he would like to be equal to the first, if not the first in his own line. Then comes the period of real work.

Paganini, who was probably the greatest apparition ever seen in the musical world, studied enormously until he was thirty, after which time he never played except at rehearsals and concerts. Between 1805 and 1812 he reached the acme of his power if not of fame. Haweis says of him: "He had for years been at work upon new effects and combinations, but at the very time when each new exploit was being greeted with frantic applause, he betook himself to an exhaustive study of the old masters. Something he seemed to be groping after—some clue he wished to find. In studying the ninth work of Locatelli, his brain was set suddenly to going in the peculiar direction of his own aspirations. Something in Locatelli's method inflamed Paganini with those conceptions of simultaneous notes struck in different parts of the instrument, the hitherto unknown management of the screws, in which the violin was tuned all sorts of ways to reach effects never heard before or since; the harmonics flying out at all points, the arpeggios and pizzicatos, these which were in after years brought to such perfection, were born out of infinite study and practice. His method is to be noted. For ten or twelve hours he would try passages over and over again in different ways and with such absorption and intensity that at night fall he would sink into utter prostration through excessive exhaustion and fatigue. There was a strong thoroughness about him—nothing which any previous musician knew or had done must be unknown or undone by him; there was to be no hitting him between the joints of his armor; no loop-hole of imperfection anywhere. He occupied himself solely with his instrument and with composition. At the age of thirty the great violinist had exhausted all the resources of his instrument. From this time, incredible as it may appear, Paganini seldom, if ever, played, except at concerts and rehearsals. If he ever practiced he always used a mute. Mr. Harris, who for twelve months acted as his secretary, and seldom left him, never saw him take his violin from its case. He used to say he had worked enough, and had earned his right to repose; yet without an effort he continued to overcome the superhuman difficulties he himself had created, with the same unerring facility, and even watched by the eager and envious eyes of critics and rivals. In vain! No false intonation, no note out of tune, no failure was ever perceptible. His hand was a geometrical compass which divided the finger-board with mathematical precision."

"When Liszt heard Paganini," continues Haweis, "it seemed to him the message for which he had been waiting. From him he doubtless received that passion for transcendant execution," that absolute perfection of technique, which enables him to create the modern piano-forte school, and win for Erard & Broadwood what Paganini won for Guarnerius & Stradivarius.

As Paganini had done before him, Liszt now suddenly retired from the concert-room. He was no longer heard in public; he seemed disinclined, except in the presence of his intimates, to exhibit his wondrous talent; but he retired to perfect himself, to work out the new impulses he had received from Paganini. His transcription of Paganini's studies, the *arpeggio*, the *floriture*, the prodigious attack and *elan* had took audiences by storm, the meeting of extremes which abolished the spaces on the piano-forte key-board by making the hands ubiquitous— these and other developments were doubtless inspired by the feats of Paganini.

Like Paganini and Liszt, Tausig, after his first successes in public, retired for three years, during which time he gave no concerts, but studied unceasingly. At the end of that period, feeling indignant at the opposition to Wagner in Germany, he came forward again and gave a grand concert, at which he played Wagner's compositions, and achieved a triumph.

Thalberg, who carried the *cantabile*, or singing touch, to such a point, studied this one thing alone for five years, as is proved by his great work, *l'Art du Chant* (the art of singing).

To Chopin belongs the credit of using dispersed chords in extension, which were formerly played in close harmony. When studying these chords in his youth, not being able to reach certain notes with his fourth and fifth fingers, he is said to have slept holding a cork between them, in order to widen his grasp. Intervals, which were considered impossible when he introduced them first into his compositions are now thought to be quite practicable. Chopin relates than when he first met Czerny in Vienna, Czerny looked at him and said, *"Na, fleizig studirt"* (Well, have you practiced faithfully?) a characteristic remark from the indefatigable Etude writer.

Our own Eddy, who has done such wonders on the organ, took my breath away by describing to me *his* manner of practice in Germany, where he thought nothing of ten hours per day.

I conclude, therefore, that in order to be one of these virtuosi, these tremendous luminaries, which fill a whole firmament, as it were, one must practice nearly every minute one is awake, and must have in addition a special talent for technique, combined with the best training from childhood up.

It is better for the majority of us not to consume our lives in the vain attempt to compass an impossible ambition. Let us practice four or five hours per day when we can get them; let us do our best to become fine musicians; let us teach our pupils not to practice with a stiff wrist; and, above all, let us leave it to the privileged few to set the world on fire.

Appendix 2

"The Deppe System Vindicated"
from *Etude* 3, no. 4 (April 1885): 79-80

This feisty letter to the editor constitutes a response to an anonymous attack on the Deppe method that Amy promoted with such enthusiasm and zeal. Despite apparent skepticism about the authenticity of Deppe's method in certain circles within the music establishment, Amy retains the courage of her convictions concerning her idol, maintaining that far from being too enthusiastic over the Deppe method, she never considered that she had done Deppe half-justice. She suggests that she knows very well who the anonymous author of the February article was,* and that rather than signing off cowardly as "Boston," the author at least should have signed "Chicago."

*   *   *   *   *

Editor of The Etude:

My attention has been called to an article in the February issue of your journal, in which an attack is made on me. I would state that I never answer anonymous attacks, but, on Deppe's account, I feel obliged to take some notice of the article. If a person has not sufficient courage of conviction to sign his own name, but calls himself *"Boston,"* and talks in a vague way about my ways with my pupils without giving any authority for his statements, it must be because he feels his case to be a very weak one. I left Boston seven years ago, and at the time of

---

* Possible "suspects" are Chicago musicians and critics W. S. B. Mathews, George P. Upton, and Frederick Gleason, with whom Amy occasionally sparred.

my departure I divided up my pupils between Mr. Sherwood and Mr. Warren Locke. Those are the only teachers who ever had any opportunity of teaching my pupils in Boston, and I can hardly think that since they obtained them from me, they would be likely to come out in an article against me. I shrewdly suspect, therefore, that the letter ought to be signed "*Chicago.*"

My antagonist, in his zeal for attacking the Deppe method, should not allow the facts to get away with him. He begins by saying that Deppe is an "obscure violinist." Now, will he please give his authority for this statement? Deppe is not a violinst, nor is he known in Germany as such. It is true that he began life with the study of the violin, as all orchestra conductors nearly do. He soon abandoned it for the baton, and has conducted ever since. It would be about as sensible to speak of Thomas and Damrosch as "violinists," because they formerly played that instrument.

Deppe was called from Hamburg to Berlin expressly to conduct Stern's orchestra there during the latter's absence in Italy, which was a fine and old established orchestra. While I was studying with him he received a splendid offer to go to Wiesbaden to take charge of the orchestra there, which he refused. He is in the habit of conducting oratorio and miscellaneous concerts in various parts of Germany, and recenty he conducted a musical festival in Schlesien. As a proof of my statements I will refer "*Boston*" to Kiel, the well-known composer in Berlin and teacher of composition in the *Hoch-Schule* there; to Professor Gustave Engel, the critic of the *Vossische Zeitung*, the leading daily in Berlin; to Joachim, the great violinist; or to Taubert, the former conductor of the royal orchestra concerts at Berlin; or, if he would like authority nearer home, to Joseffy, whose first concert with orchestra in Berlin Deppe conducted. I was present at the concert, though it was long before I knew Deppe personally.

I had a call a day or two since from Mr. P. C. Lutkin, of Chicago, who has just returned from a three years' stay in Germany and Paris, where he has been finishing his musical education. He said "Deppe has nearly given up teaching. He is highly thought of as conductor, composer, and musician in Germany. He is at present absorbed in conducting and in composition."

My own experience in teaching has wholly confirmed me in the opinion I express in my book, "Music Study in Germany," of the value of his method. Far from being too "enthusiastic" over it, I never considered that I had done him half justice!

My class has been largely composed of teachers from all over the West, who were eager to learn Deppe's method. In every case, after studying with me they have written to express their delight with the results both in their own playing and with that of their pupils. They say they have improved as they never had before. I can point with pride to Miss Alice Heald, the head of the musical department in Carleton College, at Northfield, Minn., a young lady of brilliant musical gifts; to Miss Ida MacLagen, the head of the musical department of the Iowa State Normal School; and to Mrs. J. J. Jelley, who is at the head of the musical department in the Ohio State Normal School, all of whom give lessons at the rate of sixty per week, and who use the Deppe method with the greatest success. Besides these I have many letters from others who are private teachers, and they say without exception that it has given them a command in teaching such as they never could have had without it.

I take no credit to myself in saying this, because I simply teach them as Deppe taught me, and transmit his ideas literally.

With regard to octave playing, I maintain that octaves must be practiced with a loose wrist. To practice them in any other way is highly dangerous. They can be played with high wrist or low wrist. There must be a certain contraction of the muscles in holding the notes, just as the muscles contract in catching firm hold of anything. That is not the point. It is in *letting go.* How must the wrist be in the brief space of time that elapses between letting go one octave and taking hold of the following one? It must be loose. The stiffness or firmness must be *in the ends of the fingers*, or in the first joint. The muscles of the arm must be supple, and rigidity avoided. It is because people practice octaves with stiff muscles of the arm that they often weaken and lame their wrists for life, and have to give up playing altogether. I teach my pupils, therefore, in the slow practice of octaves, to hold firmly with the fingers and to sink with the wrist between each octave, towards the fifth finger of each hand, so as to compel the fifth fingers to be curved upon the keys, and to make the stretch from the thumb, which is naturally the stronger finger. I tell them to *listen* to their fifth fingers, and then they do it right instinctively, in endeavoring to equalize the tones of the thumb and fifth fingers and to prevent the thumb from predominating in loudness. In raising the hands from the keys I tell them to loosen the wrists. If you sink with the wrist in taking hold of an octave, you can rise with it better in letting go, on the same principle as when you strike a rubber ball against the floor it will rebound from it. The more rapidly an octave passage is played, the more imperceptible becomes the sinking of the wrist, because there is not time for it. The wrist looks as if it were high, but there will be a slight depression between each octave, just enough to show that the limberness is there. The best octave player I know of in this country is Madame Teresa Carreno. I shall recommend "Boston" to hear her play the long octave passage in Gottschalk's arrangement of "Trovatore," if he wants to see elasticity of the wrist in octave playing.

In conclusion, I am obliged to "Boston" for finding my book "immensely interesting, all but the Deppe part:" but, as a matter of fact, my book has now been before the public for three years, and since then I have received a perfect broadside of letters from all parts *of* this country, and *all* of them inquiring about the Deppe method!

Please compare Mr. Sherwood's remarks, found in the last issue of THE ETUDE with the description of the Deppe method in my book, pages 288, 289, and 293. They will be found identical. The "low seat," the keeping the elbow "down and heavy." (Deppe said "your elbow must be lead, and your wrist a feather"), the various wrist movements, and the keeping the outer side of the hand or that part of it which would naturally slope away, *high*, all of these points are in Deppe's system, and all peculiar to him.

In speaking of the greatest artists and teachers of the world, I hope I shall always be "enthusiastic."

Yours very cordially,
AMY FAY.

Appendix 3

"The Royal Conservatory of Brussels"
from *Etude* 3, no. 8 (August 1885): 173

The following article, written for Etude *during Amy's European visit in the summer of 1885, describes the Royal Conservatory's very structured program and a most interesting account of the yearly public student concerts, which she attended during her stay. She devotes nearly all of her description to the playing and singing of the female students, apparently having been impressed with their performances. She comments on the strong emotions displayed by the girls, adding that "an American girl" would not have displayed either excessive joy or disappointment at such an event.*

*   *   *   *   *

MISS AMY FAY.

Since my arrival in Brussels I have been much interested in the Royal Conservatory, which seems to me one of the most complete and most admirably managed in Europe. I am surprised that there are so few American pupils in it, but it is because we do not know much about it. Brussels has long been celebrated for its magnificent violin school. The conservatory having had such great artists as De Beriot, Leonard, Vieuxtemps and Wieniawski for its professors, it is not to be wondered at that they have the traditions of good violin playing here, traditions which are admirably kept up by the present leading professor, Hubay, who is a most finished artist and thorough teacher. The conservatory existed as a school of music long before the year 1832, but it is since that time that it has gradually been organized upon its present basis, owing to the wise and energetic efforts of Fetis, its first director, and of his successor, Gevaert, both of them men of profound musical erudition and foresight. Gevaert is the present director, and he was appointed in April, 1871. He had been director of music of the opera in Paris before assuming this position, and is a most important man.

The faculty consists of nearly fifty professors of distinction.

The instruction of the conservatory includes the following branches:

1st. The solfège and the elementary theory of music.

2d. Vocalization and singing in unison for the pupils of both sexes.

3d. Part singing.

4th. The diction and declamation of the French and Netherland languages.

5th. The Italian Language.

6th. Lyric declamation and dramatic study.

7th. Wind instruments, stringed instruments, and the piano; instrumental ensemble, chamber and orchestral music.

8th. The analytic study of form.

In 1871 a class quartette in stringed instruments was created, and a class for mien and facial expression ("de maintien et de mimique") was added in 1875.

A library and a museum of rare musical instruments, interesting for the science and history of music, has been annexed to the conservatory since 1877.

Every year, immediately after Easter, there is an examination of all the pupils of the conservatory, and each professor sends in to the director a detailed report of the progress, the zeal, and the exactitude of each member of his class. From this report the candidates for the *concours publics*, or public concerts, at the end of the scholastic year, are chosen. A jury of from four to six members, is appointed, presided over by the director, M. Gevaert, to pronounce upon the merits of the candidates and to award the prizes.

The pupils who aspire to a *diploma of capacity* must be submitted to the following tests, of which three at least are obligatory.

[We omit for want of space the outline of the examinations for singers, for organists, for classes in declamation, for the orchestral instruments, and present only the one for pianist, which will give a fair idea of the requirements in the other departments.—*Editor.*]

For Pianists.

1st. The execution of a piece designated two weeks in advance.

2d. Reading at sight.

3d. Transposition at first sight, in a given key, of the accompaniment of a piece, vocal or instrumental.

4th. Reading of score at sight.

5th. Accompanying on a figured bass.

6th. The improvisation of an accompaniment for a given melody.

7th. The execution by heart of several pieces chosen by the jury from a *repertorie* of twenty compositions.

The "diploma of capacity" is accompanied with a gold medal, or, if the pupil prefers, with an instrument or musical works.

The course of solfège or harmony is obligatory for all the pupils in singing and in instrumental music. The course of counterpoint is obligatory for the advanced pupils on the organ.

I have been particular in stating what is required for a *diploma of capacity*, because we had such animated discussions last year at the meeting of the Music Teachers' National Association, at Cleveland, on this subject.

I shall not take time and space to give the names of all the professors, however eminent they may be, but will limit myself to those of a few which interest me as a pianist. The leading professors of the piano are August Dupont and Jules Zarembski. Madame Pleyel and Louis Brassin were formerly also professors of the piano in the conservatory. Franz Rummel, who is well-known as a pianist in America, was a pupil of Brassin and a native of Brussels, and his rival was Camille Guricky [Gurickx], a pupil of Dupont, and a pianist of decided genius, whom I hope we shall one day have the pleasure of hearing in our country also. The schools of Brassin and Dupont were great rivals for a long time, but now Brassin is dead and his place is taken by Zarembski, who was recommended for the place by Liszt, with whom he was studying when I was in Weimar ten years ago. August Dupont has been teaching here for thirty-two years, and has steadily maintained his supremacy all that time against all newcomers. He is a magnificent teacher, and I was greatly impressed with the playing of his class, which I had the pleasure of hearing the other day at one of the concerts. He is a fine artist and composer himself, and I would recommend to concert pianists his *Toccato* and *Staccato* as brilliant concert pieces. He has composed a concerto for piano and orchestra, but I have not had the pleasure of hearing it. He takes the most devoted interest in his pupils and expends himself for them, and their performance in public shows the fruits of his labors. He particularly excells in given [giving] to his pupils *concert style*, and that is what people, studying to play in public, want.

Zarembski is a talented composer and a fine pianist, especially technically. His playing is more remarkable for admirable mechanism than for beauty of conception. Zarembski is unfortunately in very delicate health, and has only one lung. I fear he will not live to be old.

The chief professor for the organ is Alphonse Mailly, a splendid artist. I heard him play Bach's Fugue in G Minor the other day in the most *stunning* manner. He took the tempo very fast, and yet it was as clear and crisp and steady as could be. Not a note out. It was one of the finest pieces of organ playing I ever heard.

The leading professor of the violoncello is Joseph Servais, who is a son of the great 'cellist Servais, and who is a fine concert artist also. The well-known 'cellist Adolph Fisher was a graduate of this conservatory.

The leading violin performer is Jenö Hubay, and the leading professor of singing is M. H. Warnots, who is especially fine as director of a chorus. The department of solo singing is the weakest in the conservatory.

I now come to the *concours publics* or public concerts given by the pupils at the end of their scholastic year. They are seventeen in number, and I have attended nearly all of them with great interest.

These concerts give the results of the work for the past year, and that all the gifted pupils have a chance to show what they can do before the public. There is a charming concert hall with boxes all round it in the conservatory, and it is here these concerts take place. The interest felt is very great by the citizens of Brussels, and many of the aristocracy attend. The Queen herself is sometimes present if the occasion is an unusual one. It gives a great opportunity to the talented and industrious pupils to bring themselves before the public and to obtain engagements after graduating. The most interesting concert of the course was that of the young girls in Dupont's class for the piano. They were five in number. The young ladies were led out in their white dresses, like so many little race horses, put to their mettle, and about to go on the track. While they *all* played well, three covered themselves with glory, Mlles. Helen Schmidt and Uhlmann were the best. The *morceau au concours* or test piece was Moscheles' difficult and brilliant concerto in G Minor. This they all had to play. Besides this each girl was required to play one or more preludes and fugues by Bach *by heart* (from a repertoire of four, chosen at the moment by the jury from the list given by her), and also a *morceau au choix*, or piece of her own choice.

Mlle. Uhlmann, who was the most remarkable of them all as a virtuoso, played first the concerto, then two preludes and fugues by heart of Bach's, and then a nocturne in E flat Major by Chopin and Liszt's "*Feux Follets*" as *morceaux aux choix*. After that she came out again and played against another young lady for the thousand franc prize three more pieces, "Elfenspiel," Op. 7, Carl Heymann, "Canzonetta," Dupont, Sonata A Major, Scarlatti.

This was nearly a whole recital practically that the little Uhlmann played in the most dazzling manner, and she is not over sixteen years of age. Nevertheless, after executing this difficult task so splendidly, the prize was carried off by the other young lady, Mlle. Dratz. She only played one piece, too, the "Carnival," by Schumann, but she was richer and more developed in style. She was a former pupil of Dupont's, and studied five years with him. Last year she had already had a first prize as his pupil. From where I sat she looked like a beautiful blonde, with a lovely little head. She played with great fire and musical feeling. Dupont's pupils are celebrated for their fire and for their definition. Their fugue playing is splendid, and nothing could be more clear and steady. Mlle. Helen Schmidt played the fugue in A Minor, No. 19, of the first book of the well-tempered "Clavichord" by Bach, which is so long and difficult, by heart, absolutely perfectly. She has a sister who is in Hubay's class in violin playing, who is also a beautiful musician. She is first violin in one of the quartetts, and it seemed very nice to see a young lady playing first violin accompanied by three young gentlemen. I heard her play Schubert's exquisite quartette in D Minor in this manner, and very artistically.

In Hubay's class the *morceau de concours* was Kreutzer's Concerto in D Minor. There were eighteen in his class, and they had to have two concerts the same day. In the morning they all played etudes by Kreutzer, and in the afternoon the concerto and a *morceau au choix*.

The largest audiences was [were] naturally present at the concerts for singers (young ladies). There were two of these also, the same day, as the class numbered eighteen. In the morning they sang the *morceaux de concours*. There were two of them, according as the singer had a dramatic or a flexible voice. They were "Air de Didon," *Ah prends pitie*, Piccini; "Air de la Faune Magie," *Comme un eclair*, Gretry. The latter was a beautiful air, and very effective.

In the afternoon each young lady sang a long and elaborate aria from some opera, in the grand and dramatic style, but in general they were not equal to what they undertook. An exception was Mlle. Fierens, who sang an air from "Don Carlos," by Verdi, "*Toi qui sus le neant des grandeurs de ce monde.*" She showed great talent, and may become a great singer. She won the first prize "with the greatest distinction" over the heads of three other young ladies, who had won a prize "with distinction" last year. Mlle. Fierens was tremendously applauded, by the public as the prize was accorded her by the jury. Just before leaving the stage she gave a "jump for joy" to the great amusement of everybody, while some of the other young ladies who came off second best went off in tears. It was quite tragic. I was surprised to see how unreservedly they showed their feelings. An American girl would neither have given a leap nor burst into tears before an audience.

Well, I think I have written you enough to show you that the conservatory of this most artistic city of Brussels is a remarkable institution. What I like about it is that the pupils are not left to their own devices, but a steady surveillance of their progress is maintained, and they are obliged to come up to the highest standard their talents admit of. Their musical education is many sided and complete, and they have distinguished artists for professors and models.

BRUSSELS, July, 1885.

Appendix 4

"Expression in Piano Playing"
from *Etude* 5, no. 8 (August 1887): 111-12

In this article Amy insists that performers must follow the expression marks written into the composition, as well as the actual notes. She gives examples of Beethoven and Chopin as great composers who demanded expression to be followed exactly as written. She also gives insight into the Chopin-Liszt relationship, citing a first incident where Chopin criticized Liszt for varying from the prescribed expression in a Chopin composition, and a second incident where Chopin was said to have remarked that perhaps Liszt's embellished interpretations of Chopin's works were justified, as Chopin played only "to hundreds," whereas Liszt played "to thousands." She also reveals that Liszt eventually tired of Beethoven's compositions and even found it hard to hear many of his own compositions during lessons. According to Amy, Liszt once remarked that when a student brought him the 14th Hungarian Rhapsody, for instance, he said to him "Sir, here is the window, and there is the door. Choose between them your manner of exit."

*   *   *   *   *

Read before National Teachers' Association.

What is expression? It is the art of playing in such a manner as to bring out the character of the piece and the intention of the composer. Expression is dependent upon many things. First of all upon the quality of the touch, and after that, upon the phrasing, tempo, accent, contrast in the use of *fortissimo* and *pianissimo*, and observance of all the expression marks placed by the composer to indicate his ideas, such as the *crescendo*, the *diminuendo*, the *retardando*, the moments of silence demanded by the rests and pauses, and many other signs too numerous to mention. To a person of the highest musical intelligence these signs would not be necessary to enable him to play with *expression*, though they might be, to enable him to play with exactly the expression intended by the composer. A composition can be interpreted in many different ways, and yet be beautifully expressed in either way. It is related to Chopin that he once rebuked Liszt by saying to him impatiently, "My dear Liszt, if you do me the honor to play my compositions, please play them as they are written." Who shall dare decide which was the greater artist in expression, Chopin or Liszt? "Circumstances alter cases," is a proverb which may be applied to the laws of expression as well as to any others, for on another occasion Chopin remarked to Lenz, who came to take lessons of him, and who added some embellishments to one of Chopin's compositions which Liszt had taught him, "You learned that from *him*, did you not?" "Yes," replied Lenz, "Liszt always *will* leave his mark on everything," and then with a sigh he added, "Well, perhaps he is right, for he plays to thousands where I play only to hundreds."

It is evident, therefore, that Chopin recognized the artistic necessity of playing with more effect, the bigger the place and the greater the number of people. What would sound well in a large concert hall, would be overpowering in a parlor, and *vice versa*, what would be delightful in a parlor, would disappear altogether in a hall. This is the reason why the playing of a talented amateur is often more enjoyed in a parlor than that of an artist firmness of which long practice gives the artist is too much for a contracted room, where everybody is close about him. I had a friend who played simple music very charmingly, and with a great deal of what is called "expression." It was a joke with her, that when she played at a particular house, the members of the family would exclaim, "We enjoy your playing more, a great deal more, than we do Rubinstein's." And they really did enjoy it more!

A sensitive artist would regulate his touch with reference to the place and to the company in which he is at the moment. The choice of the composition will often determine in the minds of his hearers whether "he plays with expression" or not.

A lady once asked me to select a piano for her. She had been the rounds of all the different makes, and was in the dazed frame of mind which that pilgrimage produces on the inexperienced purchaser. Each man had told her that *his* piano was the one and only piano, and that all others were frauds.

I advised her to buy a Chickering, and seating myself at one of the beautiful instruments of this firm I played a number of brilliant pieces to show off the piano. She stood there perfectly silent and unmoved. I thought I must be on the wrong tack, and changed to my tune to some soft and melodic compositions, such as Mendelssohn's *Duetto* and Jensen's *Canzonetta*. Her face at once lit up, and she exclaimed, "I always *did* like those soft, sweet things! Such *expressive* pieces would make *any* piano sound well."

This leads me back to the common idea of expression. It is apt to be considered a soft and sentimental way of playing, without any particular reference to the character of the piece.

The lady just mentioned did not know that a brilliant piece should be brilliantly expressed, just as a soft and tender one should bring out the opposite qualities and if I had not played pieces in which sentiment predominated, she would have thought I had no expression in my playing, simply because she could not follow brilliant and rapid execution.

Some musicians were once discussing Meyerbeer's merits as a composer with Mendelssohn, and were endeavoring to disparage him. One of them began to hum a certain air out of one of his operas, and exclaimed, "Was there ever anything more utterly frivolous than *this!*" "Well, gentlemen," replied Mendelssohn, "I don't know about that. The *words* are very frivolous, and Meyerbeer composed the music for the words. It seems to me that it fits them admirably, and, on the whole, I should not have been sorry to have written it myself!"

There is often about as much justice in the criticisms that artists receive from professional critics for not playing with expression, when the truth is, the critic does not understand the composition he is playing. The easiest way for him out of the dilemma is to say, "Mr. So-and-so has a very finished *technique*, but he is deficient in expression."

Chopin's *Nocturnes* are rightly regarded as the type of sentiment in expression, but they are often played in a manner which makes him the most passionate and affected of composers. It is a nice point for an artist to decide in playing these *Nocturnes*, where poetic warmth ceases and mawkishness begins. The *tempo* must not be strained too far, and unreasonable *ritardandos* and illogical *accellerandos* must be avoided. While Chopin frequently marks "*tempo rubato*," which is the nominal synonym for "go as you please," he himself most beautifully defines the use of it, and forbids the abuse of it. The "*tempo rubato*," said he, "must be like a tree. The branches may wave, and the leaves may flutter in the breeze, but the tree stands firm." The base of a composition he regarded as the stem of the tree, and kept it very steady.

Artists are divided into two classes, the objective and the subjective. The objective artists are those who endeavor to sink their own individuality in the thoughts and intention of the composer. The subjective artists are those who prefer to make a composition what *they* think it *ought* to be, and add something of their own. They wish to be original. There is much to be said in favor of both, but I believe the greater artist will be the objective rather than subjective. The subjective artist will make a more striking and immediate effect upon the public, but the objective artist will leave a more satisfactory impression on the mind.

Tausig went to both extremes. In his youth he was so violent and so intense in his playing, that he used to play his audience out of the hall, he told us. Later, he became so reserved, that he repressed his feelings too much, and was almost too reserved and restrained. He despised all effects which were not severe art. Deppe used to say of certain superficial pianists, "they play only *themselves*, and not the music." (*Sie spielen nur sich.*)

I was once talking to a very fine pianist, Mr. Camille Gurick[x], of Brussels, Belgium, Dupont's best pupil, about this matter of getting at the true expression of a piece. Said he, "I find it a good plan to take the piece and read it over *away* from the piano, just with reference to the expression marks. Note what and where they are. Then go to the piano and play the piece from the notes, putting them in just as they are written."

This is a safe way for those pianists who are afraid of the critics, for they can at once produce an authority for their interpretation, and can say, "I play the composition as it is written." Nobody can go back of that! I was very well disciplined in this regard by a pupil I had who was very literal and painstaking, but also very unimaginative and pedantic. I used to play her pieces over for her in order to give her an idea of how they should sound.

She always stood by my side and followed the music as I played. Sometimes, when not looking at the notes myself, or in a moment of distraction or inspiration, it would happen that I would not play according to the expression laid down in the piece. As I rose from the piano in the state of excitement that one is in when one has been playing according to the feeling of the moment and perhaps quite contrary to rule, I would suddenly be recalled to myself by hearing this pupil quietly ask, "Excuse me, Miss Fay, but did you play that note "*fortissimo?*" "Perhaps I did," said I. "I only wanted to know because it is marked *pianissimo*," continued she.

This kind of criticism was like a pail of cold water thrown over me, and my illusions vanished at once. I explained that she could play a thing in two opposite ways, and that both might make a good effect. She would appear to be satisfied, but the next time I made a deviation from the text, she would pin me down again. Finally, I limited myself to playing just as the expression marks in the piece indicated, when giving her an illustration, and it was a very good habit to get into! One can learn sometimes from one's own pupils.

The old masters, such as Bach and Haendel put no expression marks in their works but left the interpretation of them entirely to the players, taking it for granted that he would be musician enough to do them in the right spirit. Beethoven seems to have been the first to make a point of the expression marks. During the rehearsals of the opera of "Fidelio," preparatory to its first performance, he writes to a friend, "All *pp.*, *cresc.*, all *decresc.*, all *f.* and *ff.* may as well be struck out of my music, since not one of them is attended to. I lose all desire to write anything more, if my music is to be so played."

Comparatively careless as to the right notes being played, Beethoven was angry at once at any failure in the expression or shadowing of a piece; saying that the first might be an accident, but that the other showed want of knowledge, or feeling, or attention.

I think all teachers will agree with me, that Beethoven is harder for the average pupil to comprehend than all other composers, but the few who do comprehend him love him better than all the rest. As a little girl, whom I was teaching, said one day: "I don't know why it is, but I always like this man's pieces," meaning Beethoven, whose name stood at the head of the "Sonatina." She knew nothing about Beethoven, except that she liked his music! I could not help wishing that Beethoven were there to hear the unconscious testimony to his greatness. It reminded me of another compliment, which was paid to the genius of Shakespeare, by an equally unconscious book agent, who came to my office to sell me a copy of Moody's sermons. Failing in doing so, he took out another book, which was a copy of Shakespeare's plays. "If you don't want Moody," said he, "*here* is a book which seems a good bit read!"

Beethoven was right in being so severe with regard to the observance of the expression marks in his composition, because they are of a character that do not admit of liberties being taken with them. He always has a definite idea in his mind, which has to be brought out in a particular way. With the more modern composers, notably Schumann, who was often vague, this is not the case, and more latitude in the expression and *tempo* may be allowed. I understand that *von* Bülow has refused to teach out of his edition of Beethoven's Sonatas, which would seem to indicate that he feels some qualms in regard to his own suggestions and emendations.

I once heard Beethoven's "Moonlight Sonata" played in public by two different artists successively, within a few nights of each other. The first was a man whom I will call "*Monsieur*," and the second was a woman, whom I will call "*Madame*." (I take my illustration from Beethoven, because, as a German professor once said to me, who knew more about music than he did about the construction of the English language, "If I am to judge of an artist's playing, I must hear him play Beethoven. *That are ideas!*") Let us analyze how the above-mentioned artists played the "Moonlight Sonata." The first movement was given with very much the same conception by both, and was beautifully done. The second movement (which Liszt likened to "a flower growing between two abysses") was played so slowly and so sentimentally by Monsieur that it lost all interest. Madame, on the contrary, took it very fast, and with too heavy a touch. It was so ponderous that it lost its ideality and lightness. In the third movement, Monsieur, who was a bad imitation of Joseffy's style, ran flippantly down the opening passages in the right hand, with a *decrescendo* that made the two chords at the top (those chords which ought to stand out like an obstacle in the path of danger!) utterly inaudible. I confess that I was so irritated that I regretted that Beethoven was not there to box his ears! I am sure he would have done it!

Madame played the passage with faultless *technique* and with perfect distinctness, but the chords were given with such weight and overemphasis, that it made one feel uncomfortable. One could not help wondering if the piano would not go through the floor! With the exception of these chords, the playing of the Madame was superb, but as they recur frequently throughout the last movement, it was a blemish on the general effect. Still Madame was nearer right than Monsieur. He gave the impression that the two chords were of no consequence, and not particularly worth playing.

The last movement of the "Moonlight Sonata" is a whirl of passion hemmed in by self-restraint. Those *arpeggios*, which slip up the piano so lightly and so fast, each one a little different from the preceding one (like an insidious temptation which varies its form), and each one headed by its two sharp chords, reiterated again and again (like two barriers which stem the tide, until finally the chord of G sharp major lands one firmly on dry ground), seem to represent the two natures of man. The one makes him feel the fascination of giving way to evil. The other forces him to be good. The contest of passion with reason is kept up to the very end of the Sonata, when even the left hand abandons its post and rushes madly off in company with the right hand in the final attempt to get away. But the invisible law compels them to return and fences them firmly in with the two concluding chords. Good triumphs over evil, but the fight has been almost too severe, some regrets remain, and the chords are in the minor key. Like Lot's wife, one sometimes cannot help casting a regretful look backward, even when trying to go in the right direction. Let us congratulate ourselves that the immediate consequences of such relenting are not always so severe as they were in her case.

To return to the expression marks: I maintain that in playing Beethoven one must adhere rigidly to them, and that in freshening up a Sonata that one has played in public and half-forgotten again, it is essential to study it with the notes rather than from memory. I do not allude to the actual performance in public, which I think is always more inspired when one plays by heart, but to the slow and thorough practice which should precede a concert. Liszt gave his pupils a striking example in this respect. When teaching a Beethoven Sonata, he always opened the book and laid it on the top of his grand piano, where he could stand and refer to it. Now he knew Beethoven so thoroughly, and had heard him, that he so much would not enjoy him any more. In one of the last conversations I had with Liszt two years ago, he exclaimed, "No more *Sonatas Appasionata*, no more *Pathetiques*, no more Moonlight Sonatas for me! And as for the Symphony in B flat major, when *that* is played, I take my hat and leave! As for Chopin, I like to play a *few* things of his, *when I am in the vein*, but very few. Indeed, I can't hear many of my own compositions. If any one brings to me 14th Hungarian Rhapsody, for instance, I say to him, "Sir, here is the window, and there is the door. Choose between them your manner of exit."

As Liszt made these remarks he looked at me as if he felt he were uttering a musical heresy. I looked at him and thought to myself: "It is time for you to die, Master, for you have outlived yourself!"

Had Monsieur used the notes when studying up the "Moonlight Sonata," he could not have failed to notice the *sf* mark below the two chords, which he dismissed so frivolously. Had Madame also freshened her memory with them, she would not have overlooked the *staccatto* [sic] mark, which indicates a short, sharp accent, and not a heavy, bearing down touch.

There is a great responsibility involved in playing those Sonatas of Beethoven, whose poetic manners, as well as their beauty, have contributed to make them universally known, the *Moonlight*, the *Pathetique* and the Appassionata Sonatas. One never knows how many music pupils have come to hear one's interpretation, or how many teachers from the country are tucked away in different corners who have come from a distance to see whether *your* way of playing confirms *their* way of teaching. At a piano Recital that I gave last season in Pittsburg, a lady came up to shake hands with me after the concert. She was an experienced teacher of the piano, and she said, "Miss Fay, I am not in good health, but I made a journey of seventy miles to hear you play this evening."

My friends, when people feel interest enough to make an effort to hear us, ought we not to study in the most conscientious manner? Ought we not to give them something which makes it worth while for them to come? We should set up a standard in the Beethoven

Sonatas, as Theodore Thomas has done in the Beethoven Symphonies. Where is his equal? I must confess that I have yet to find it, although it seems to have become the fashion of late, to detract from his merits as much as possible.

There is one point to which I would like to call attention, which has a most important effect upon expression in playing, and that is, to the strict observance of the slurs. Piano teachers are very neglectful about this. I never had a scholar come to me who knew the meaning of the slurs, nor did I know it myself until I studied with Deppé [*sic*]. Indeed, I can remember vaguely looking at those lines and wondering what they were for? Phrasing correctly depends entirely upon the observance of the slurs, and pupils should be taught to lift the hand from the keyboard *both before and after* a slur. It gives a *definition* to playing that nothing else does, and makes the greatest difference in the *accent*. It requires the closest watchfulness on the part of a teacher to enforce this rule. I am constantly saying to my scholars "take up your hand," but they *will* slide out of it whenever they can, because they hate to take the trouble to mind the slurs, until I have made it second nature to them to do so.

Another point which affects the expression, is the way in which the hand is taken up from the keyboard. The hand should be lifted from the wrist, with the arm loose, and the fingers should cling to the key till the last instant, dropping the notes from the ends of them as it were. The movement is much the same as if one should plunge one's hand into a basin of water and then take it up and let the drops trinkle off from the ends of the fingers.

In the instruction books we often see in the frontispiece a picture of the hand thrown backward from the wrist with a stiff arm, as an illustration of how one ought to take up a chord. This is very bad, and is exactly wrong. Throwing the hand back from the wrist in this manner produces a short, choppy touch, and takes away all resonance. It has exactly the effect of shutting the mouth suddenly in singing. The reason of it is that the muscles of the arm are made tense and rigid, and the sudden movement of throwing back the hand raises the hammer to fall back too quickly from the string.

Another important point in expression on the piano, is the proper use of the soft pedal. I have been teaching constantly for eleven years, and I never had but one pupil who had used the soft pedal before coming to me. *That* pupil was a young girl from the country who had never heard good music, but she was a genius, and she felt instinctively that she ought to use it. Now there is no reason why even small children cannot be taught the value of the pedal in producing a velvety and melting touch. How is it possible to play a *Nocturne*, a Romance, or a Song Without Words, *without* the soft pedal and give it the right effect? The soft pedal imparts poetry, warmth and sentiment to the piano. It is the feminine element, as it were.

Deppé [*sic*] lays great stress upon not sitting too high at the piano. He says, "You may have the soul of angel, and if you sit too high your touch will not be musical." This is perhaps an exaggeration, since the true artist will manage to produce a musical touch no matter how he is seated, but I know, from personal experience, that it is infinitely more comfortable to sit so that the arm is on a level with the hand and wrist, and not above them. It gives the fingers a much better chance to move from the knuckles, and keeps the muscles of the arm looser. Moreover, the weight of the arm can be brought to bear better in chord playing. Sitting high obliges the pianist to bend over the keyboard, and that is the reason that most pianists have such ugly, round-shouldered backs. If they sat lower and threw out the chest, their position at the instrument would be much handsomer, and certainly much more healthful. I always feel uncomfortable when I see a pianist screw up the stool to the utmost, and then perch himself on it like an insect on the point of a pin! Men look particularly awkward seated in this way.

Ladies and gentlemen, these are only some of the mechanical means of expression, of which I have been speaking. The real source of expression is in the *soul* of the player. If he have a grand and beautiful soul and a passionate temperament, combined with the intellectual comprehension of music, he will express himself accordingly. But in music, as in everything else, it is a great thing to know how to go to work and to have the mechanical means at one's command.

The sculptor may have a conception of a statue in his mind, but how is he to make it a reality without the aid of the chisel?

We find that the most celebrated artists are those who are not only the most gifted, but who have also had the advantage of the best education, under the most celebrated teachers of their day, from their earliest childhood. The training of a great teacher alone can give the technical mastery of the instrument, which will make it possible to the player to interpret his ideas. Liszt received a long and severe training from Czerny. Rubinstein was sent to the Paris Conservatory when not six years old. Bülow and Tausig were pupils of Liszt. Joseffy was the pupil of Tausig, and so it goes! Great artists are but links in a chain, and each one transmits something of his gifts to those who come after him.

Expression is largely a matter of imitation, that the musical student should neglect no opportunity of hearing artists play, in order that he may compare their styles, and learn to discriminate between what is "*good*, BETTER, or BEST" in forming his own style.

Appendix 5

"The Amateur Musical Clubs"
from *Etude* 5, no. 12 (December 1887): 180

This article should be titled "The Amateur Musical Club," since it focuses on a capsule history of the early years of the "Amateur Musical Club," one of Chicago's important women's musical clubs. In its early years, the members of the club were drawn from the students of two leading Chicago music teachers, Regina Watson and Emil Liebling. Amy emphasizes that no "ungodly males" were admitted into the club, "except to its public concerts," and "by invitation." And after a reception given by the club to the great German singer Materna, Amy mused about "how delightful our public halls would be if taken in charge by women."

*   *   *   *   *

MR. EDITOR.—You ask me for a letter to your paper, and I think I cannot do better than give your readers an account of a very important musical society in Chicago called the "Amateur Musical Club." This club has been round at each others houses for the purpose of reading music together, arranged for eight hands. Gradually a singer or two was added, and then other amateur pianists crept in, with solos, until finally the club numbered thirty people. Its members then adjourned to a piano-house, where they could have more room and better pianos, and their lady friends began to find it pleasant to drop in of an afternoon and listen to the music. (I must state that women only constitute this club. No ungodly males are admitted, except to its public concerts, *by invitation*.) With the growth of the club came small expenses for music, doorkeeper, etc., and the ladies who performed for their friends hit on the brilliant idea of making these friends pay for the privilege of listening to their siren strains, in order to meet the expenses of the entertainment. This they were nothing loth to do. The first year only a small fee was required. The second year doubled it, and the third year was more than doubled again, making the admission come to five dollars per season for the listeners. This has since remained the fixed price of the Amateur Musical Club for the *Associate Members,* or listeners. The *Active Members* also pay a fee, but in consideration of their being the performers, it is only one-half as much as that paid by the Associate Members.

The doing of the club now began to assume a definite form. Regular concerts were given on a fixed afternoon, every fortnight. The programmes were printed and were arranged with care.

At first the club was desperately partisan in spirit, as it was chiefly composed of the best pupils of two leading teachers of the piano here, Mrs. Regina Watson and Mr. Emil Liebling. The pupils of these two teachers would group themselves on the several sides of the room, and when a pupil of Mrs. Watson's played well there would be loud applause, and demonstrations of affection from the side of the "Watsonites," as they were called, and a corresponding silence and dejection on the part of the "Lieblingites." When, however, a pupil of Mr. Liebling won the honors of the day, the case would be reversed, and the applause would come from the opposition.

Mrs. Watson and Mr. Liebling themselves were in no wise affected by the violent sides taken by their pupils, and had the good sense to be only amused at it. They remained the best of friends while continuing to teach as hard as they could and turn out as many good scholars as possible. They reigned supreme over the club for a long time, but finally the pupils of other able teachers in the city began to get in and the spirit of partisanship was broken up. The Watsonites and Lieblingites shook hands over their differences and both parties gave their suffrages to the new-comers. These formed a sort of middle ground on which they could meet, though to this day the Watsonites have the settled conviction that *their* champion player is the best amateur in Chicago, while the Lieblingites would put forward with equal boldness the claims of *theirs.*

The club became very popular, and without exerting itself in the least soon had a membership of four hundred subscribers. It hired expensive rooms, and began having occasional recitals from great artists travelling through the country, paying them handsomely out of a treasury that was always full. With the large membership dropped out the old sociability, as well as the old rivalry, and ladies went to the club concerts without knowing each other, as they would go to any others.

On one single occasion they determined to give a reception to the great German singer, Materna, who was brought over here by Theodore Thomas to sing in his musical festivals, of which he gave a chain stretching across the continent. The leading ladies of the club set their wits to work to make this reception a unique affair. They denuded their houses of rugs, hangings, pictures, marble busts, and what-not, to make the room attractive. A pink curtain was drawn over the skylight which lighted the rooms, in order to be becoming to the complexion of the guests. Masses of beautiful roses were put where they would be most effective—on pedistals [sic], crowning the pictures, and in the hands of the ladies, or at their breasts. In short, the club rooms looked like a perfect bower, and were completely transformed in a jiffy. (I could not help thinking how delightful our public halls would be if taken in charge by the women. They would soon lose their bare and comfortless look.)

Finally Materna arrived, very richly dressed, and seeming to fill everything with her glowing presence. She was received by a crowd of exquisite women, who handed her a magnificent bouquet, and they tried to talk to each other in broken English and broken German alternately. Fortunately some German-Americans were there to piece out the conversation, and prevent it from falling into utter dislocation. The pink curtain had a most beneficent effect, and everybody looked their best. It was certainly as pretty a gathering as one would wish to see, and the *prima donna* herself was highly pleased at the compliment paid her. There was a general air of enchantment over everything which was done to the rosy light, the flowers, and the elegant afternoon toilettes of the women present, and also to their own delicate beauty.

Last year the Amateur Club got tired of paying out a thousand dollars per year simply for the rent of its rooms, and finally decided to give them up and pursue a different policy. The concerts were given only once a month to the *entire* club, and then in Apollo Hall, instead of every fortnight in their own rooms, as formerly. The actave [active] (or performing) members of the club inaugurated a course of afternoon teas, which are also given in Apollo Hall, a small and cosey place. Here they have a little programme for their own benefit, and try and vote on new candidates for active membership. Every new member must play or sing on trial, before this august assemblage! The new members are then voted in or black-balled, according to their musical merit. In order to compensate the associate members for losing half of the concerts, they make the concerts that *are* given much finer, and have six *artists'* recitals, instead of only one or two, as formerly, in the course of the season. This they find a much better way, as it gives the large audiences something worth listening to at the public concerts, and, at the same time, the old sociability is restored in the meetings of the active members in private houses.

The artists greatly delight in playing before the Amateur Musical Club; and in my next I will tell you how this club reacts upon the artistic world.

Appendix 6

"Some Suggestions"
from *Etude* 12, no. 12 (December 1894): 262

In this article, Amy describes the playing of such artists as Paderewski, Carreño, Joseffy, and others. She also relates a moment of her visit to Liszt in Weimar in 1885. Her enthusiastic and passionate love for music come across clearly in her recollection of the "crushing brilliance" of Joseffy's playing. Amy's flair for prose becomes evident in her last paragraph, where she compares Gottschalk's playing to the "bursting of a rocket," that "breaks into a myriad of fiery balls."

*   *   *   *   *

It is a great pity that the study of chamber music does not, as a general rule, receive the attention it ought to do, in the education of young pianists. The reason for this lies doubtless in the fact that it is difficult to get a chance to practice with violinists and 'cellists, unless they are well paid for their services. I have all my life wished it might be my good fortune to board in the house with a good violinist, in order that I might have the opportunity of studying sonatas, etc., with him daily, instead of learning one occasionally and limiting myself to two or three paid rehearsals of the same, preparatory to playing it in public.   None of my masters ever had called my attention to chamber music before I came to Deppe, that wonderful "all-round" teacher, and never shall I forget the delight I took in this rich mine which he was the first to open up to me, and the great help it was to my technic, as well as to my musical knowledge. It was so soothing, and such a relief to the mind after a stiff tussle with "*Gradus ad Parnassum*," with concertos, and Chopin's *Ballades*, to sit quietly down and play an accompaniment of a Schubert or Mozart or Beethoven sonata.   It is a division of difficulty, and a doubling of pleasure, to take a flight with another artist, who plays on a stringed instrument, and then, what admirable practice it gives for *reading* music! If any pupil desires a recreation and a delight, let him take up the Beethoven's trios, for example.   There are twelve of them, and each is more beautiful than the other.   He will then get outside of the set of stock pieces which everybody has to learn and which are now a drug in the market.

I wish that for a while Liszt's Hungarian Fantasisie for Piano and Orchestra might disappear from our concert programmes, or at least, that nobody but Paderewski would play it! He did it so wonderfully, that it was, in a manner, born again, and we were forced back to the consideration of the beauty of the composition.   Everybody plays it well, for that matter, as it is the grand show piece for the modern virtuoso, and has taken the place in piano literature formerly occupied by the "*Battle of Prague.*" It is like the stereotyped Turkish rugs in the pictures of the French artists, upon the reproduction of which so much labor and care has been expended.   I have never seen a Turkish rug badly painted, nor heard the Hungarian Fantaisie badly played.

However, when Paderewski played the Fantaisie, he started right in, with the very first octave (that big one in the bass), with such overwhelming power and passion, with such grandeur and nobility of style, that one involuntarily exclaimed to one's self, "what a magnificent composition!" One paid tribute to *Liszt*, and not to the digital skill of the pianist.   That is what I should call truly *objective* playing, when one is carried back to the *composer* as the prominent figure; although, in another sense, it might be called the most *subjective* playing, too, to produce that effect.

As most people play the Hungarian Fantaisie, one thinks only, "how beautifully he did those runs! how clean and brilliant the trills are!" etc.   It is always technic, and technic, and technic, that attracts your attention, and not the musical contents of it.   I wish every body could have heard Paderewski play this hackneyed composition the first time he did it in this country, in Carnegie Music Hall.   O my stars!

Well, I won't say any more about it.   There are times when silence is more eloquent than speech.

We have had a long succession of great pianists, and it is interesting to look back and see what things they have done which stand out prëminently in the mind, and distinguish them from each other.   Each one has struck out some spark which flashed upon the inner consciousness of the listener, and left its image there forever.   It was not always the most difficult pieces that produced it, either.   Of Rubinstein I remember how he played the Erl-King, by Schubert, and Beethoven's Turkish March.   Could any one ever forget the frenzy of terror of the first, or the effect of the whole band in the second, dying away in the distance?

Von Bülow lives in my memory chiefly by his playing of the Moonlight Sonata, which is, in my humble opinion, the most beautiful work ever written for the piano.   If I had a choice I should say, "take away everything else, but leave me the Moonlight Sonata."   Not that there is any "moonlight" in it, as Rubinstein says.) I also remember of Bülow his wonderful interpretation of Chopin's Nocturne in B major, Op. 9, No. 8.   Was there ever anything so airy, so exquisitely graceful as that? I made up my mind never to learn it till after his death, and now I am studying it in memory of him, and how very hard I find the left hand in the middle part! And yet one had no thought of its being difficult under *Bülow's* fingers. It seemed like nothing at all.

Carreño first dazzled me by her octave playing in Gottschalk's arrangement of *Trovatore*, in the Boston Music Hall, when she was in her early twenties. What a tremendous concert effect she produced in it! The air was fairly atremble when she rose from the keyboard. And then, her performance of Rubinstein's *"Etude on false notes"*—*that* might be said to be "piling Pelion on Ossa." Her playing was always cumulative, rolling up as she proceeded, and carrying you away as under an avalanche. And then, her extemporization before every piece; there has never been any one to compare with her in that, always striking into the key of the artist who preceded her on the programme, and modulating into the one in which her solo was written. I have never known her to fail, so absolute is her sense of pitch.

De Pachmann we shall always recall by Chopin's Etude in thirds, a display of virtuosity which made one dizzy, although his rendering of the great Ballade in F major, of the Barcarole, and of many other things, was equally wonderful, but I speak now only of artistic *moments*.

Joseffy I think of, in what do you suppose, of all pieces? In the modest little *Berceuse*, by Chopin. Nobody can play that comparably with him. It is an absolute test of memory to play the bass *exactly* as it is written, and he is the only artist I have ever heard do it. The way he brought out certain notes of the melody, is quite indescribable. They shine out like stars across the years since I heard him do it. When it comes to crushing brilliancy, I remember him in Liszt's E flat Concerto and *Veneziae Napoli*, which he played at Mc Cormick's Hall in Chicago, on his very first tour in this country. The audience simply went crazy. When I told Liszt about it, in 1886 [1876 or 1885], in Weimar, I think the old man felt a little twinge of jealousy, for when I assured him that "nobody had ever played his compositions as Joseffy did," he repeated to himself musically and with a slight accent of pique, *"Personne?"* as if he might have added that *"he* had," if he chose.

However, he sent Joseffy his Concerto in A afterwards, the only one Liszt cared about, although I do not know if what I said had anything to do with it.

Mme. Bloomfield Zeisler, I like to think of in Rubinstein's D minor Concerto, particularly when I recall how she got up out of a sick bed, when she had not touched the piano for three days, and dashed it off like a mere bagatelle. The cadenza in the last movement, for instance, which everybody has come bang up against, the way she did *that*, was what the Germans would call, *"Haar-sträubend!"* Well, that was just fun to hear, but not to practice oneself. It was mere child's play to *her*, and made me think of a famous golf player I saw this summer. His ball was in a deep rut in the middle of a road, with two large stones on each side of it, and a big willow tree in front of it, between him and the hole he was making for. His adversaries were chuckling, thinking it would take several shots for him to get out, when lo! he measured the distance with his eye, and with his "lifter" scooped the ball right out of the rut, past the stones, and over the big willow, landing just where it could go neatly into the hole. The laugh was on the other side then; one of the champion's foes said to another, "He just *loves* willow trees." "Yes," growled the other, "he eats paving stones for breakfast, damn it!"

The most wonderful piece of chromatic scale playing I ever heard was from Slivinski, in Liszt's exquisite and subtle Étude in F minor. Slivinski, for some reason or other, was not appreciated in America as he ought to have been, but the way he rendered this composition was one of those unforgetable things which rarely happens to one. The limpidity of his tone, the smoothness and sweep of his execution, the artistic unity of effect, were simply amazing, and, combined as they were with the greatest velocity and with a poetic conception of the contents of the piece, were transporting.

Another thing that he did divinely was the "*Chant-Polonais*," No. 5, by Chopin and Liszt. This I heard twice from him, once with*out* and once *with* the cadenza, which he did not always care to play, but which he did in the most marvelous way! I shall never forgive myself for not attending all of Slivinski's recitals here; I feel that they were an irreparable loss. But, of course, I thought he was going on here indefinitely, as most of the great artists do. Probably the financial outcome of them was too meagre.

I might run on endlessly, so I will draw this article to a close with our own American pianist, Gottschalk. Does any one but myself remember his playing of his "*Murmures Eoliens?*" Never was there such a climax worked up in double trills, as he made in that. It was enough to draw an audience right up onto its feet. I used to feel my flesh creep when he began it, and hold my breath toward the close. "No, I can't bear it another instant," I would say to myself, and then that *iron* arm of his would keep on intensifying its *crescendo* and seeming to say relentlessly, "Yes, but you *must* bear it." And oh! the relief when, with a smile, he broke into that shower of pearls at the end! It was like the bursting of a rocket, which rushes skyward with you, almost parting your soul from your body, and, at an immense height breaks into a myriad of fiery balls.

Appendix 7

"Women and Music"
from *Music* 18, no. 10 (October 1900): 505–07

In this reply to a London article which highlighted the lack of female composers, Amy champions women in composition. She reminds her readers that if the record of women in composition is dismal, it is because women have for too long been handicapped by the lack of opportunities to study composition. Furthermore, for too long "women have been too much taken up with helping and encouraging men to place a proper value on their own talent." Amy quickly adds, however, that now "this is all changed," and that women, in time, will make substantial gains in composition. As Amy expresses it, "if it has required so long to produce a male Beethoven, surely one little century ought to be vouchsafed to create a female one."

*   *   *   *   *

An article, which takes women to task for not being great musical composers, has recently appeared under the above caption, in the London "Musical News," and is being largely quoted in our papers. (See Musical Courier for Aug. 1st.) Says the writer:

"It is impossible to find a single woman's name worthy to take rank with Beethoven, Handel, Mozart, Rossini, Brahms, Wagner, Schubert; we cannot even find one to place beside Balfe or Sir Arthur Sullivan. As a writer to the Musical Times remarked nearly twenty years since, 'A few gifted members of the sex have been more or less fortunate in their emulation of men, and that is all. Not a single great work can be traced to a feminine pen.' Nothing has been done since to lessen the truth of this remark. Year by year our great festivals produce new works; it is rare for even a minor production to be from the pen of a woman."

This is true, but when one reflects on the vast antiquity of the human race, which Professor John Fiske tells us in his "Discovery of America" may date back as far as 50,000 years, one is tempted to ask why the men have been so long about producing a Beethoven, a Schubert, or a Wagner? These great geniuses belong to the nineteenth century, and Beethoven's nine symphonies were composed during the first quarter of it, from 1802 to 1828, or thereabouts.

Music is the youngest of the arts, and is the most difficult of them all, since it creates something out of nothing. It has been developed within two hundred years, to its present height. Only towards the end of this century have women turned their attention to musical composition, and it is altogether premature to judge of what they may, and probably will, attain.

Women have been too much taken up with helping and encouraging men to place a proper value on their own talent, which they are too prone to underestimate and to think not worth making the most of. Their whole training, from time immemorial, has tended to make them take an intense interest in the work of men and to stimulate them to their best efforts. Ruskin was quite right when he so patronizingly said that "Woman's chief function is praise." She has praised and praised, and kept herself in abeyance.

But now, all this is changed. Women are beginning to realize that they, too, have brains, and even musical ones. They are, at last, studying composition seriously, and will, ere long, feel out a path for themselves, instead of being "mere imitators of men."

For the matter of that, men have been imitators of each other at first. We all know that Mozart began to write like Haydn, and Beethoven began to write like Mozart, before each developed his own originality of style, and as for Wagner, he has furnished inspiration and ideas for all the composers who have succeeded him. Why, then, should we expect of women what men could not do (although Minerva was said to have sprung fully armed from the brain of Jove)? If it has required 50,000 years to produce a male Beethoven, surely one little century ought to be vouchsafed to create a female one!

It is a very shallow way of looking at the matter to say that "women have not been handicapped in music, because more girls than boys have been taught to play the piano or the harpsichord." What does such teaching amount to? Really very little. To be a great creator in art, one must be trained to it from one's earliest years by a gifted parent or teacher. Mozart and Beethoven had fathers who fully realized the capacity of their sons, and they made them study early and late, "every day i' the hour," as Shakespeare says. No doubt, an hour of such work as these composers did in their youth, would be worth many days of the kind of musical preparation demanded of girls of this or any other period.

Edgar Poe, in his wonderful essay on the "Philosophy of Composition," in which he analyzes how he composed his own poem, "The Raven," makes the following remarkable statement:

"My first object (as usual) was originality. The extent to which this has been neglected, in versification, is one of the most unaccountable things in the world. Admitting that there is little possibility of variety in mere rhythm, it is still clear that the possible variety of metre and stanza are absolutely infinite; and yet, for centuries, no man, in verse, has ever done, or even seemed to think of doing, an original thing. The fact is, that orginality (unless in minds of very unusual force) is by no means a matter, as some suppose, of impulse or intuition. In general, to be found, it must be elaborately sought, and although a positive merit of the highest class, demands in its attainment less of invention than negation."

When we read this marvellous analysis of Edgar Poe, we realize that he must have made the same exhaustive study of the art of poetry, that Beethoven did of the art of music, in order to be able to produce that masterpiece, "The Raven." This is the kind of mind training to which women have never been subjected, and it is idle to talk about their achieving great results in musical composition without it. To play the piano or the harpsichord is but one rung on the ladder which mounts to world-wide fame.

Yonkers, N.Y.

Appendix 8

"Music in New York"
from *Music* 18, no. 12 (December 1900): 179-82

In this lively article, Amy describes various concerts of the New York music season. Not surprisingly, Amy has chosen to review concerts given by women. After an account of a concert by the violinist Leonora Jackson, of Chicago, Amy digresses to give a fascinating account of the multi-talented American violinist Arma Senkrah, with whom she performed at Liszt's home in Weimar in 1885 during a reunion with her beloved teacher Liszt. Amy concludes with a description of pianist Teresa Carreño's concert, and, in her true style, includes a description of Carreño's black velvet concert dress.

*   *   *   *   *

The season in New York has opened with a rush and there are so many things to hear and see that one is puzzled what to choose or whither to turn one's steps. Like the Athenians of old, we are always running after "some new thing," and if St. Paul were living here he would have the same reason to chide us as that furnished him by the gadding of the Athenians in his time. They were the most cultivated people on earth, however, so it must be a good thing to keep one's ears and eyes open to what is going on. St. Paul himself shows a tendency that way when he prides himself on having "sat at the feet of Gamaliel." We don't know anything about Gamaliel, but if a St. Paul "sat at his feet," this one circumstance shows that Gamaliel must have been "worth while," and that St. Paul was not wasting his time.

The first concert this year was given by our own little Leonora Jackson, violinist, formerly of Chicago, assisted by Madame Schumann-Heink, or rather it was a joint recital by these two, at Carnegie Hall. It was a long jump from Leonora Jackson's first public appearance, as a child of ten, or thereabouts, in the Kimball Piano Hall in Chicago, to a concert of her own, as a full-fledged artist, in Carnegie Hall, New York; yet she was as equal to the one as to the other. I can remember her first appearance as a little girl perfectly, and how steadily and well she played the little pieces she was then studying with Carl Becker. Her mother told me then that "Leonora loved her violin and enjoyed practicing," and I thought it was the best omen for her future. Many people have great talent and learn to play beautifully, but only those who play from love for music reach the topmost heights.

Leonora Jackson is now a most remarkable artist, and she has all the touches which are the result of long training under the greatest masters. I must say I listened to her with the keenest pleasure. Her technical perfection and purity of intonation are great, and her feeling[,] accentuation, phrasing and *nuances* are simply exquisite. It is charming to watch her play, as her youthful figure is slight and graceful and her pose is modest and girlish. She conquers Herculean difficulties with hardly a turn of an eyelash, and shows such ease of execution that people are tempted to think her cold. This is not so; she has plenty of heart, but also wonderful finish.

That the West has turned out two such artists as Maud Powell and Leonora Jackson is certainly cause for congratulation. Maud Powell was from Aurora, Ill., and began her studies also in Chicago, under Mr. Wm. Lewis. Her European tour during the last four years has been one succession of triumphs, and she has made a sensation wherever she has appeared. Times are changed since 1885, when that other gifted violinist, Arma Senkrah, of Brooklyn, L. I., was obliged to allow herself to be given out as coming from India! The celebrated manager in Berlin, Wolff, simply would not hear of her appearing as "Mary Harkness, from America," but made her spell her name backwards, and announce herself as "Arma Senkrah, from India."

People can say boldly that they come from America, now, especially since the wars with Spaniards and the Chinese. We have gained some battles in the world of art also. As for Arma Senkrah, it was a pity she did not remain in her own country, and then she would not have shot herself through the heart from jealousy and despair over the faithlessness of her good-for-nothing German husband in Weimar, on Sept. 4. She was a beautiful and fascinating young woman, and an artist of the first rank. There was a very interesting account of her, with portrait of her and Liszt, in the Musical Courier, Oct. 17, by Arthur Abell. I met her and her mother frequently in Weimar during the summer of 1885, at the time this photograph was taken, when Arma was twenty, and heard her play with Liszt, who was constantly sending for her to come and play with him. One time I had the honor of playing with Arma Senkrah myself, in Liszt's parlors, a composition by Jerome Hopkins. The piece was a transcription of his own song, "Oh, That We Two Were Maying," for violin and piano. Never shall I forget how beautifully she played it and how exquisite it sounded!

Arma Senkrah fascinated everybody, the great musicians as well as the rest. Her poor bereaved mother, who is living in New York, gave the most extraordinary account of her career the other day, and the success she had was phenomenal. Said Mrs. Senkrah: "Baby always played like a man, she drew such a bow! Once she was playing for Brahms, and she ripped out the music with such tremendous fire and dash that the master called out, 'Save the pieces, little one!' in German."

Arma Senkrah made her debut in Paris when she was sixteen. A young singer, aged eighteen, assisted her, and the next day one of the critics called the singer "Lilies and Roses," and the violinist "Peaches and Cream." He said he found it hard to choose between "Lilies and Roses" and "Peaches and Cream," but, on the whole, he thought that "Peaches and Cream" went to the spot better than "Lilies and Roses."

Mrs. Senkrah said Arma objected, and she exclaimed, "I don't want to be 'Peaches and Cream,' mamma, and be all eaten up!"

From this first Parisian success Arma Senkrah was speedily engaged for a tour, and everywhere she went she had an ovation. She received two thousand rubles for playing in a concert in Moscow. I think it was here Mrs. Senkrah said they let fly pigeons over her as a mark of enthusiasm. In St. Petersburg she had an enormous bouquet thrown at her, which they could hardly get into the carriage door afterwards. This bouquet, with its long satin ribbons, with an inscription on them, Mrs. Senkrah has kept and has yet in her possession. At Stockholm twenty-one bouquets were thrown on the stage. They were thrown by "experts," and went flying through the air like comets, with their long white ribbons floating behind. At another place the students wanted to carry Arma on their shoulders, after the concert, but she would not allow it. One time she was to play at a place called Hirschberg and the train was buried in a snow storm and delayed for many hours. Mrs. Senkrah luckily had had the forethought to put up a luncheon and bring along a bottle of wine. When Arma got up in the sleeping car, early in the morning, it was quite dark, and she found the snow heaped up above the windows of the car. The deer followed the train in the woods for food, and the passengers threw out pieces of bread to them to eat. Arma arrived just in time to go upon the stage in her traveling dress and play at the concert. The audience was transported with delight, as her coming had been despaired of in the storm. She was greeted with overwhelming enthusiasm when she came out in her traveling dress, and had a triumph.

At twenty-five years of age, when in the zenith of her career, Arma Senkrah had the misfortune to fall in love with a dissipated German lawyer in Weimar. She married him and settled down to matrimony, and appeared no more in public, except twice. He vetoed all that. The end was death by her own hand, at thirty-five. She must, indeed, have been madly in love, to put the pistol to her heart, through jealousy, ten years after her marriage, forgetful of her only child, a beautiful little boy, the image of herself, and adored by her; Mrs. Senkrah insists that Arma was "hypnotized by her husband." (Somebody ought to go over and get the boy.)

Well, I have run on so about violinists that I fear I have but little space to say much about music in New York. Last week was the week for pianists, and we had three of them— Dohnanyi, in his own concerto, with the Boston Symphony Orchestra: Gabrilovitch, in a concert of his own, with orchestra, and Teresa Carreno, with the Philharmonic Society. I am happy to relate that America came out first, and that Carreno swept everything before her. She and Gabrilovitch had chosen the same concerto—Tschaikowsky's First in B flat minor, Op. 23. This concerto was introduced by von Bulow, who played it in 1875 in this country. Three years later Franz Rummel played it, and then it went to sleep for a long time, till Sieveking revived it. Now it has suddenly leaped into popularity. Gabrilovitch played it beautifully and musically, but Carreno was simply overwhelming in it, just as she was in Rubinstein's D minor concerto in her last trip. I think this artist is at her best with orchestra, and it is the proper setting for the diamond. All of the critics lost their hearts to her, and their heads, too, for that matter. As a proof of it I will subjoin the following from the Times, whose critic is famous for remorselessly chopping off the heads of artists, and who does not even take the trouble to toss them into the basket usually: "Carreno's was the performance of a mature artist, sure of her fame, sure of herself, and not afraid to hurl all delicacy and the hair-spinning of the raffine school to the winds, while she swept the keyboard with the rush of a whirlwind, 'set the wild echoes flying' and the whole auditorium throbbing with the magnetic waves of her exuberant temperament. Power, majesty of conception, sonority of tone, and all the splendors of passion flamed through the performance of this gorgeous woman, who, at a period of maturity when most of her sex take to teaching or to charitable societies, is still able to reign over human hearts by the magic of the songs she sings through the keys of her chosen instrument. As a personality, she is like, indeed, to the wondrous Cleopatra, for 'age cannot wither her, nor custom stale her infinite variety.'"

Carreno's dress was worth the price of admission to the concert to see. She was attired in a royal gown of black velvet, richly trimmed with gold, in which she was beautiful as the day (or night, I should say)!

Dohnanyi's concerto was very interesting, and was superbly played by him, of course. He is a very wonderful artist, but not of the sentimental school. Since Paderewski, we all adore sentiment, combined with intellect. One never touches bottom in Paderewski's feelings. He is the only one who goes down to the deepest deep, and yet touches the stars.

Appendix 9

"The Woman Music Teacher in a Large City"
from *Etude* 22, no. 1 (January 1902): 14

Amy writes that being a woman music teacher in New York City has held back her teaching career. She believes that women have difficulty attracting students because young girls, who comprise the bulk of piano students, find it more interesting to study with men. Amy discusses other hardships that women teaching music in large cities must face, such as delayed payments for missed lessons. As Amy sees it, "so long as one sex monopolizes the musical culture of the world, just so long will women music teachers find it hard to make a living."

*   *   *   *   *

We all know the old adage: "Before you cook your hare, first catch him." No doubt, if women music-teachers could get plenty of pupils, they would be able to teach them; but here is precisely the difficulty. The woman teacher usually begins her career as an ambitious girl in a small town. She has some talent, and perhaps is the organist of one of the churches in the place of her abode. Her friends and acquaintances think her something remarkable, and she gradually gets a good class of pupils, at very small prices, say, ten dollars per quarter.

When I began to teach, we used to have to give twenty lessons for ten dollars, and even then I thought myself favored, because formerly the quarter numbered twenty four lessons. Still, in one way, the country teachers are more fortunate than the city ones, for the pupils have no distractions or amusements, are interested in their music, and do not mind their lessons. Moreover, they take lessons summer and winter, and one time of the year is the same to them as another.

Difficulties

Now, how is it in the city? Here, in New York, prices are very high for the best teachers of music. Five dollars is not considered an extravagant price to pay per lesson, although it really is more than people can afford. On the other hand, city pupils begin their terms late in October, and begin to drop off in April. By the first of June every body who can goes out of town, to avoid the heat, and the music-teacher is left high and dry, "alone in her glory." She has the privilege of living on her income through the summer, and of spending all she has accumulated during the winter months. She returns to the city after her own vacation rested but short of money.

Now is the time, however, when she ought to have plenty of money to advertise, send out circulars, and call upon her friends in order to impress upon the public that she is there and wants pupils. Otherwise, she will go along with very slim classes until the middle of the winter, when she will have worked into her rut again.

Sex

A woman is at a disadvantage on account of her sex, and the reason of this is that, as a rule, boys and young men do not study music. Young girls find it more interesting to take of a man teacher, and this would be all right if the young men would return the compliment. They would enjoy taking lessons of a woman if she were competent to teach them, and for the same reason, that it is more interesting to study with a teacher of the opposite sex. I have had several excellent men pupils, but, unfortunately, they were all too few and far between.

I was returning to the city last year when a woman of my acquaintance got on the car and took a seat next to me. Said she, "Will you please tell me of some good man teacher in New York? My niece is going to take lessons in music this winter, and she declares she won't take of a woman." I meekly names several man teachers, and did not once suggest that in my own misguided opinion I could teach the young girl as well as any of them. I knew it would be of no use, for a man she would have!

This preference for men is so well known that it is almost impossible for a woman to get a good many positions in the private fashionable schools in the city. They want a "professor," and the parents feel better satisfied when their daughters have lessons from a "gentleman teacher." If women teach in schools, it is usually as under-teacher, poorly paid. If they do not teach in schools or conservatories, they must depend upon their own magnetic qualities to attract pupils. It is a precarious means of support, and I often wonder what becomes of the old music teachers! One never sees them. The elderly teachers must be shelved, and how in the world do they save enough to live on?

Women should urge upon parents to have their boys learn music, as well as their girls, and then there would be plenty of pupils to go round. So long as one sex monopolizes the musical culture of the world, just so long will women music-teachers find it hard to make a living.

Missed Lesson

The problem of missed lessons is a hard one for a woman. Parents realize that when they are dealing with men teachers they must pay in advance, and that, if their children do not take their lessons, they must expect to lose them. With a man, "business is business." Women do not dream of expecting anything else from the "lords of creation." With their own sex it is a very different matter, and, I am sorry to say, they cut off corners in the most unblushing manner.

Says a mother to me: "Mary has not been very well, and she has not practiced much this week, so she wants to be excused from her lesson." The probable state of the case is that Mary's mother has been too lazy to attend to her daughter's practicing, and the shrewd idea is in the back of her head that she will economize.

I have it in my power to charge for the lesson, but the fee will be grudgingly paid. For my part, I prefer to be cheated out of my money to having an unpleasant argument with a pupil.

Some will compound with their consciences by sending word beforehand that they cannot take the lesson. They reason then that "you have your time for something else," and that is so, but it may be something which does not bring in any money.

Some teachers try to equalize matters by saying that they will make up the lost lessons within the quarter, but most charge for it. This will do, if your pupils live in town. But, if they are some distance out, they will not take the trouble to make the extra trip. If you make it, the loss of time and railroad fare will make your profit extremely small. Fix it how you will, the woman teacher usually comes out at the small end of the horn, and after she has made up the missed lessons, lost those which come on holidays, like Christmas and New Year's, Good Friday and Thanksgiving Day, and finally triumphantly sends in her bill, pater familias delays and dallies about paying it until at least four weeks more have elapsed, and the next quarter is well along.

Appendix 10

"Women and the Music Teachers' [National] Association"
from *Musical Courier* 46, no. 24 (17 June 1903): 30

The following letter to the editor, written during her New York years, reveals Amy Fay's increased sense of outrage at the biases toward women in the music profession. She complaints that of the 72 musicians listed on the advance program of the MTNA, only 8 were women, a condition she finds unacceptable. Her letter, though brief, demonstrates Amy's dismay at the lack of respect shown by musical men toward their musical women colleagues. Her words remain timely and relevant.

*   *   *   *   *

To *The Musical Courier*:

A perusal of the advance program of the Music Teachers' National Association will afford food for reflection to feminine professional musicians of the United States, and will plainly demonstrate to them the artistic standing which they have in the eyes of the men who are brother workers with them in the noble art of music. Let us glance over the pages of this circular.

On the front page we see the list of officers, the program and executive committees and the educational board. These four committees are made up as follows:

> Officers—Four men.
> Program Committee—Three men.
> Executive Committee—Three men.
> Educational Board—Five men.

On page 2 we have a list of the artists who take part in the programs:

Pianists—Eleven men.
Vocalists—Three men and three women.
Violinists—Two men.
Organist—One man.

On page 3 is the Round Table Conference—fifteen men.

Special features are an analytical recital on the piano by a man, papers by two other men, and the public school music section, in charge of a man.

Page 4 gives the list of State vice presidents. Of these there are twenty-nine men and five women.

Adding up the number of men who take part in the programs we find there are thirty-five. As against these, there are three women, all singers, but not one instrumentalist! Alas!

Turning to the list of vice presidents we find twenty-nine men to five women. Total of all those on the circular—sixty-four men and eight women.

What, then, is reserved for the women musicians of the whole country at large? They may take part in the social gatherings of the association, and contribute to the running expenses of it by putting a card in the advertising organ of the M.T.N.A.

As it would seem that the M.T.N.A. has become an association of men, it is the judgment of the writer that women would do well to turn their money into the National Federation of Women's Clubs, where they will have some show, or else found a Women's Music Teachers' National Association for themselves and invite the men to contribute to the advertising.

AMY FAY,
President of the Women's Philharmonic Society of New York City.

Appendix 11

"From Beethoven to Liszt"
from *Etude* 16, no. 7 (July 1908): 426-27

In this lengthy article, Amy recounts the only meeting between Liszt and Beethoven in 1823 when Liszt, a twelve-year-old child prodigy, gave his second public concert in Vienna and was repeatedly and enthusiastically kissed by Beethoven after the performance. She lists this concert as the start of Liszt's brilliant career. She then gives some thought to the influences seen in Liszt's music, such as its wildness, drawn from exposure to gypsy music as a child, and the effects of Paganini, the great violin virtuoso, and Chopin, master of the polonaise.

*   *   *   *   *

[The following article by a well-known American pianist and teacher is doubly interesting in view of the fact that Miss Fay's work, "Music Study in Germany," which has been published in America, Germany and England with very great success, is just about to be brought out in France. Vincent d'Indy has written the introduction to the French edition. Miss Fay was born in Louisiana of parents of New England birth and education. She studied with Tausig, Kullak, Liszt and Deppe. She preserved her musical experiences in the form of musical letters to her American home, and the poet Longfellow, who read these letters, became so much interested in them that he suggested their publication. This was the origin of one of the most successful musical books known. Miss Fay will contribute additional articles for ETUDE readers.— THE EDITOR.]

"Music is never stationary; successive forms are only like so many resting places, like tents pitched and taken down again on the road to the idea."

LISZT.

Ever restless and reaching out for newer and greater things in art, the above is characteristic of Liszt's all-comprehensive mind, and well he realized that *his* innovations in music, startling and brilliant though they are, would be followed by those of future geniuses, and perhaps supplanted by them. And, in fact, after hearing Paderewski play his last two piano compositions, Variations and Fugue, Op. 23, and Sonata, highly interesting and important works, Liszt's Hungarian Rhapsodies begin to sound a little antiquated, and one perceives that another style is being evolved by the master pianist of today.

In the year 1822, when scarcely eleven years of age, Liszt gave his first concert in Vienna, and on the occasion of his second concert the great event of his life happened to him, for he received the kiss of Beethoven (then 53) at the close of the performance. To play before *Beethoven!* What could ever equal that? Notwithstanding his tender years, Liszt fully realized the extraordinary honor and was proud of this kiss from the gigantic genius, which seemed to consecrate him wholly to art.

Beethoven had become interested in the little Liszt by his devoted friend and companion, Schindler, who persuaded him to go and hear him, on learning that the boy had played Hummel's B minor concerto at his first concert, and had united, and, as it were, kneaded into one whole, the andante of Beethoven's A major symphony with an aria of Rossini's, who was at that time the popular idol of Vienna. This feat was probably an improvisation, for when Liszt was sixty-three the writer heard him weave into a musical web the finale of one piece which he had just played with the beginning of another he was about to play. This sort of thing he did with delicious cleverness, a little smile, full of meaning, illuminating his countenance the while.

Although Beethoven and Liszt both lived in Vienna at one period, for eighteen months, and Liszt was taking lessons on the piano of Karl Czerny (the indefatigable composer of finger exercises and etudes, and pupil of Beethoven), this seems to have been their only meeting, and this solemn kiss the only link between them. Liszt had begged Beethoven, by letter, to write him a theme upon which he could extemporize at his second concert, but no theme was forthcoming.

Beethoven, whose time was now entirely devoted to composition, was inaccessible; his door was inflexibly closed to strangers, whether provided with letters of introduction or not. Until Anton Schindler mentioned Franz's name to the maestro, the latter had no idea of the existence of one who was to enable the world to grasp the wonderful genius hidden in his own mighty works. Several times Franz, accompanied by his father, had endeavored to gain admittance to the master's presence, but without success. The perseverance of the boy seems, however, to have specially won the notice of the sympathetic Schindler, who urged his master to be present at the little Liszt's concert, and to encourage the boy by so doing.

A Famous Concert.

The second concert was given in the "Redoute" on the 13th of April, 1823, and was overcrowded. When Franz stepped before the public, which was expectantly looking up to him, he perceived Beethoven seated near the platform, and noticed the master's eye meditatively fixed upon him. Far from being abashed by so great an honor as Beethoven's presence, Franz was overjoyed by it. Among other pieces he played Hummel's concerto in B flat, and, as usual, concluded his performance by a "free fantasia," but not from a theme by *Beethoven*, much to the boy's disappointment. We are told that his playing became glowing and fiery, and his whole being seemed elevated and kindled by an invisible power. His success was electric, and the public gave vent to its enthusiasm without restraint. Beethoven, himself, could not restrain his admiration, and ascending the platform, he repeatedly kissed the glorious boy, amid the frantic cheers of the assembled multitude.

We do not read that Beethoven and Liszt ever met again. Beethoven disliked child prodigies, and seems to have taken no further interest in the little Liszt. Each went his separate way after the concert, which, however, had important results and was the starting point of Liszt's phenomenally brilliant artist career. It first awakened for him the attention of the press, and, ere long, the scene of his triumphs was transferred to Paris, whither his father, Adam Liszt, conducted him, and where "le petit Litz," as he was called, speedily became the rage in the salons of the French aristocracy.

Liszt in Paris.

It was in Paris five years later that Liszt was the first to play Beethoven's "Emperor Concerto," the great E flat, when he had just become seventeen years of age. At that time Beethoven's music was caviare to the French, and not in the least understood. Von Lenz gives an amusing account of the impression it made upon him when, a stranger in Paris, he read in gigantic letters on the bright green playbill the announcement of an extra concert to be given by Franz Liszt at the Conservatoire Royal de Musique, and at which he would play the concerto in E flat. Lenz regarded this as such a feat of courage to play *Beethoven* before a *French* audience that he drove immediately to Liszt's house and arranged to take lessons of him instead of Kal[k]brenner, who was his first choice as teacher.

Liszt's Strong Hungarian Tendencies.

Strange to say that although Liszt was an "inimitable interpreter" of Beethoven, as Wagner plainly asserted, he was not influenced by him as a composer, but branched out into a style of his own, or rather of his country, in the wild and untamable music of Hungary. It was the gypsy music which he heard as a child which became, as it were, Liszt's very blood, and which he has reproduced so wonderfully in his Hungarian Rhapsodies. So intimately has Liszt merged himself in these, and so much are they played by all the piano virtuosi of our day, that the moment we read Liszt's name, the "Hungarian Rhapsody" is called up to our minds. This, in spite of the great works Liszt has composed for orchestra, symphonies, overtures, not to speak of his oratorios, masses, cantatas, etc.

Next to the fifteen Hungarian Rhapsodies, his two concertos for piano and orchestra are the best known, and of these the brilliant one in E flat has been made familiar by the pianists in the concert room, although the one in A (played by Joseffy) is the more beautiful of the two. The E flat is so overpowering in its cumulative brilliancy, however, that its effect is unerring on an audience. Liszt understands better than *any* how to "pile up the agony," and build up a climax to the point of delirium. In this he is unique.

Of his orchestral works, "Les Preludes" is the only one which is really familiar, although the ["]Mazeppa["] is occasionally heard, also the "festklänge," "Hunnenschlacht," "Prometheus," etc. Once a year, perhaps, one hears the "Faust" or the "Dante" symphonies but not often enough to follow them as one does the Beethoven symphonies, in the mind. I do not recall of Liszt's two oratorios, "Christus" and "St. Elizabeth," that the *first* has ever been given in this country, although "Christus" made a deep impression on my mind on the single occasion when I heard it, under the composer's baton, in Weimar. I should like to hear the cantata, "The Bells of Strasbourg," but never have had an opportunity.

Liszt's Operatic Transcriptions.

Liszt's big operatic transcriptions give the best idea of his enormous virtuosity as a pianist, but of thirty-two such, only a few are played to-day. These are the "Don Giovanni," "Rigoletto," "Lonhengrin," "Tannhäuser," "Fliegende Hollander," "Tristan und Isolde."

The Tannhäuser overture transcription is one of Liszt's most wonderful and is fairly *staggering* (as well as beautiful), in the humble opinion of the writer. He makes of the piano keyboard a whole orchestra. Paderewski did good work in playing Liszt's sonata during the past season, but it is a pity it could be heard but once from *him*, in each city. Like the concerto in A, the sonata has almost a divine melody in it, a theme of almost unearthly beauty and distinction of style. The etherealness of Liszt's nature is revealed in these two works, as well as his imposing grandeur.

The Influence of Paganini.

Paganini influenced Liszt powerfully, and in Liszt's "Grandes Etudes de Paganini" he reveals what he can do in the style of that master. The "Campanella," for instance, originally written for the violin by Paganini, is converted into a still more dazzling concert piece for the piano, with its showers of trills and brilliant runs. Paganini was the one virtuoso in whom Liszt found his match. Fascinated and enthrilled by the wizard of the violin, Liszt followed him from city to city, determined to wrest from him his secret. Nor was Liszt satisfied till he had achieved this, and transmitted Paganini's art to the piano. Chopin, Berlioz and Wagner were powerful factors in Liszt's career.

Chopin and Liszt.

Chopin, he once told me, was his "best friend." When about to play one of his own polonaises to his pupils, Liszt was wont to murmur, in a shamefaced way, "After Chopin one should compose no more polonaises," showing that he felt himself inferior to Chopin in these, notwithstanding the popularity of Liszt's Polonaise in E major with the public. (Franz Hummel used to play this polonaise splendidly on his first tour in this country, and Wm. H. Sherwood also excels in it.) Liszt is perhaps as much loved for his exquisite transcriptions of songs as for anything. Those of Schubert appear most to fascinate him, and he has arranged fifty-seven of them for piano. Among these stand out the "Erl-King" and the "Lark." How often have we shivered under the first, and sung, in our hearts, with the second! Of Schumann he arranged fourteen songs; of Franz thirteen, of Mendelssohn nine, besides six of Beethoven, six of Chopin, Three of Dessauer, two of Weber and two of Lassen.

Liszt's Inventiveness.

Liszt once told the writer that he had invented many new effects, as, for instance, the chromatic roll of octaves, to represent a storm on the piano, or the transposition of a melody to the lower part of the keyboard so as to make it sound as if sung by a baritone or tenor, as in the song "Du bist die Ruh" by Schubert, or Wagner's "Isolde's Liebes Tod." Formerly the melody was always written in the treble of the piano, and accompaniment in the bass. He sometimes reversed this.

Liszt declared towards the end of his life that only sacred music was "*worth while*," and that he was more interested in church music than any other. "Christus," oratorio, was Liszt's greatest church work, finished in 1866. I heard it performed under his direction in Weimar in the summer of 1873, and Wagner was present, as well as many other distinguished guests.

Nohl says of "Christus," that "it was not an oratorio in the ordinary sense, but that the composer retained the name because it denominates a general style of music. It is in fact, a pure epic poem, which an oratorio must be, as distinguished from dramatic music. It consists of a series of choral scenes which connect and embody the details of the subject. We behold a great world event arising and passing before us. All the gloss of action is avoided."

My impression of the oratorio of "Christus" from the one hearing I had of it is that it is the music of the Roman Catholic Church. It is mediæval, grand and imposing in style, but it has not the universality of Handel's "Messiah," or the convincing quality and depth of Bach's Passion music. I recall the quaint and primitive march of the "Three Wise Men," or Kings, when they went to behold the Saviour in the manger. But it is only a hazy memory in my mind, as I heard it so long ago. I did not keep the libretto, unfortunately.

Liszt, of course, wished to be known and judged by his large choral and orchestral works, and the way in which they were put aside and undervalued during his lifetime was a bitter grief to him, notwithstanding the apparent philosophy with which he used to remark, "*I can wait.*" But even at the present time we do not know Liszt as we should do, as a composer, although he is rising from the neglect of his contemporaries. A new and complete edition of his works is soon to be issued by the Liszt Society abroad.

It is to be hoped that this will do for Liszt what the same thing did for Bach, one hundred years after Bach's death, when his friends collected and edited his works.

The most surprising thing Liszt ever did, it seems to me, was to arrange a piano score of Beethoven's Septet and nine Symphonies. How he ever had the patience to do *that* passes *my* comprehension, and I don't wonder that he manifested a sort of revolt against Beethoven the latter part of his life. The very last conversation I had with him, in 1885, when I returned for a short visit to Weimar, Liszt said, "I *respect* all that, but it no longer *interests* me," referring to Beethoven's works. Besides his compositions, Liszt did a good deal of literary work, and left eight books or essays of various kinds which are still read, prominent among which is his life of Chopin, "Music of the Gypsies," "Robert Franz," etc. When we take into consideration the time Liszt devoted to teaching gratuitously, and the demands of society upon him, we are doubly amazed at his creative energy, and we must realize the greatness of the *artist* and the unselfishness and the utter lack of egotism in the *man*. Liszt never failed to be interested in the talent of others and to do all in his power to aid its fruition. He was the universal friend of the composers and artists of his day. Hardly one of them but received some kindness or encouragement from *him*, the sun to whom they all turned for light. Equally could Liszt present to the notice of a world the operas of a Wagner, or he could bend over some humble conservatory pupil and bring his lofty intellect to bear upon her piano playing.

Appendix 12

"Extracts from a Biographical Sketch"
from the Twenty-first Annual Report of the Hopkinsfolk Association,
12 May 1928
Courtesy Vermont Historical Society, Montpelier, Vermont

Miss Amy Fay was born at Bayon Goula, May 21st, 1844, on a plantation on the Mississippi River, eighty miles from New Orleans, La. Her parents were the Rev. Dr. Charles Fay and Emily Hopkins, a daughter of Bishop John Henry Hopkins.

The families were musical on both sides, but Cousin Amy describes her mother as "a veritable musical genius"—"she extemporized on any given theme in a remarkable way. Her ear was so perfect that when her husband put his finger on any key of the piano within range of her voice, without pressing it down, and asked her to sing that tone, she would do it immediately, and then when the key was struck, the pitch was identical with the tone sung." Amy was the third daughter of a family of seven children (six girls and one boy) all of whom were gifted musically, and all of whom played and sang. While they were not forced at all, they thus imbibed music as easily as they learned their letters, and the oldest girl, Melusina, called "Zina," played the melodeon and started the tunes in her father's church in New Orleans when she was only nine years old. Amy was made to learn Greek, Latin, German and French, as a child, reciting to her father daily. From her mother she learned music, drawing, and to write compositions.

Her father, Dr. Fay, was a man of unusual scholastic attainments, having graduated at Harvard University second in the class of 1829, a class which was unusually brilliant, and which enrolled the names of Professor Peirce, Oliver Wendell Holmes, and other noted men. When she was twelve years old her mother died, and after the marriage of her older sister, Zina, to Charles Peirce, a son of Professor Peirce, at nineteen years of age, she went to live with her in Cambridge, Mass.

It was in Boston that she first began to study music, but made her first great start under Mr. Pychowski, a Pole, when she was seventeen. Amy did not go to Europe to study music as a profession until she was twenty-five years old. She was attracted to Berlin by the fame of Karl Tausig, her teacher having remarked one day, "There is a young man in Berlin who played the piano like forty-thousand devils! His name is Karl Tausig. This remark was intended to be complimentary, and so excited Amy's imagination that to Tausig she was bound to go!"

After one year in Tausig's conservatory, he gave it up, and she continued her studies with Dr. Kullak, with whom she remained three years, going to Weimar in the summer of 1873 to put herself under Liszt's instruction. In the fall of 1873 she returned to Berlin and again studied under Kullak for several months. She was preparing to make her debut in concert in Berlin when she met Herr Deppe, a remarkable teacher, and she became so interested in his ideas on a first interview that she decided to take some lessons from him, which she did for a year and a half.

She then returned to Weimar for a few weeks more of Liszt before returning to America in October, 1875, after six years' absence. She made her debut in a concert of the Mendelssohn Glee Club in New York City. Her first piano recital was given in Cambridge, her old home town, and was attended by the poet Longfellow, a number of the most distinguished professors at Harvard, and by Mr. Dwight, the editor of the first musical paper in this country. Amy now played in many concerts, with Theodore Thomas' orchestra and at the Worcester Musical Festival.

She was the first pianist to introduce piano concertos with orchestra at these festivals. In 1878 she joined her brother, Charles Norman Fay, in Chicago, and remained there until 1890, dividing her time equally between teaching and playing throughout the Western towns and cities.

Her book, "Music Study in Germany," was published in Chicago in 1881, and was edited by her sister, Melusina Peirce, to whom the letters from Germany, which form its contents, were originally written. At the request of Liszt it was translated into German. It has passed through several editions in England and has also been translated into French. The book has gone through over twenty-five editions in America, and is now published by Macmillan in New York.

Appendix 13

Printing History of *Music-Study in Germany*

According to William C. Parsons (reference librarian, Library of Congress, in a letter of 6 January 1995), the "earliest edition . . . was submitted to the copyright office for registration of claim to copyright. The date of copyright by Jansen, McClurg & Company is 1880 on the recto of the title-page, while the date on the title-page is 1881. The receipt stamp of the copyright office is 1880. The register books—kept by the copyright office—contain an entry for the work indicating a date of deposit of 7 December 1880 and record the title-page material with the date of 1881. At the foot of the entry is recorded that two copies were received on 10 January 1881."

The difference of the 2nd edition is the addition of the entry signed Pyrmont, September 4, 1874, to the end of chapter 27 (this information kindly supplied by James R. Heintze). One should note that these various "editions" are actually reprints, since all of them derive from the original typesetting. This list is compiled from the *National Union Catalog Pre-1956*, and OCLC. The Macmillan publication cities of "London and New York," "New York and London," "New York," and "London" appear here according to the library records.

—jbc

Music-Study in Germany. From the Home Correspondence of Amy Fay. Edited by the Author of "Co-Operative Housekeeping." Chicago: Jansen, McClurg & Co., 1881, ©1880. 348pp.

Same, with "Second Edition, revised and enlarged" added to the title-page, 1881. 352pp. (See illustration on p. 81.)

Same, 3rd ed., 1882.

Same, 5th ed., 1883.

Same, 7th ed., 1885.

Same, 8th ed., 1885.

Chicago: A. C. McClurg & Co., 9th ed., 1886.

Same, 10th ed., 1887.

Same, 11th ed., 1888.

Same, 13th ed., 1891.

Same, 14th ed., 1892.

Same, 15th ed., 1894.

London and New York: Macmillan and Co., 1886. Preface to the English edition signed by George Grove. "First edition printed 1885."

Same, 16th ed., 1896.

Same, 17th ed., 1897.

Same, 18th ed., 1896 [*sic*].

Same, no. ed. cited, 1900.

Same, 18th ed., 1903.

Same, 1905.

Same, 1909.

Same, no. ed. cited, 1911.

London: Macmillan and Co., 1887.

Same, 1st ed. with corrections, 1897.

Same, 1904.

Same, no. ed. cited, 1911.

Same, 1926.

New York and London: Macmillan Co., 16th ed., 1896.

Same, 17th ed., 1897.

Same, 18th ed., 1905.

Same, 1909.

Same, 1913.

New York: Macmillan Co., 1900.

Same, 18th ed., 1903.

Same, 1904.

Same, 1908.

Same, 1909.

Same, no ed. cited, 1911.

Same, 16th ed., 1911.

Same, no ed. cited, 1922. Reprint of 1896 ed. Prefatory note by O. G. Sonneck. Portrait and autograph facsimile.

Philadelphia: Theo. Presser Co., [1896].

New York: Dover 1965. Introduction by Frances Dillon.

Same, 1991.

New York: Da Capo, 1979. Introduction by Edward O. D. Downes, index by Roy Chernus.

Musikstudien in Deutschland: Aus Briefen in die Heimath. Mit Erlaubniss der Verfasserin in's Deutsch übertragen. Berlin: R. Oppenheim, 1882.

Lettres intimes d'une musicienne américaine. Traduit de l'anglais par Mme. B. Sourdillon. Première traduction française après plus de 30 éditions à l'étranger. Préface de M. Vincent d'Indy. Paris: Dujarric et Cie., 1907.

BIBLIOGRAPHY

Bibliography

Ammer, Christine. *Unsung: A History of Women in American Music*. Westport, Conn.: Greenwood Press, 1980.

Andres, Robert. "Cherubim-Doctrine, *Harmonie-Piano*, and Other Innovations of Frederic Horace Clark." D.M.A. diss., piano, University of Kansas, 1993.

————. "Frederic Horace Clark: A Forgotten Innovator." M.M. thesis, musicology, University of Kansas, 1992.

Badger, Reid. *The Great American Fair: The World's Columbian Exposition and American Culture*. Chicago: Nelson Hall, 1979.

Bagby, Albert Morris. "A Summer with Liszt in Weimar." *Century Magazine*, September 1886, 654-69.

Baker's *Biographical Dictionary of Musicians*. 8th ed. Ed. Nicolas Slonimsky. New York: Schirmer Books, 1992.

Blair, Karen. *The Clubwoman as Feminist*. New York: Holmes and Meir, 1980.

Block, Adrienne Fried, and Carol Neuls-Bates. *Women in American Music: A Bibliography of Music and Literature*. Westport, Conn.: Greenwood Press, 1979.

Bloomfield-Zeisler, Fannie. Autograph Book. Entry of 3 July 1884. Courtesy Fannie Bloomfield Zeisler Papers, Newberry Library, Chicago.

Bomberger, E. Douglas. "American Music Students in Germany, 1850-1900: An Overview." Paper delivered at the annual meeting of the American Musicological Society, Chicago, 7 November 1991. Typescript kindly provided by the author.

Bowers, Jane, and Judith Tick. *Women Making Music*. Urbana: University of Illinois Press, 1986.

Chmaj, Betty. "Fry versus Dwight: American Music's Debate over Nationality." *American Music* 3, no. 1 (spring 1985): 63-84.

Eliot, George (pseud. for Mary Ann Evans). *Selections from George Eliot's Letters.* Ed. G. S. Haight. New Haven: Yale University Press, 1985.

Fay, Amy. "The Amateur Musical Clubs." *Etude* 5, no. 12 (December 1887): 180.

————. "The Deppe System Vindicated." *Etude* 3, no. 4 (April 1885): 79-80.

————. "Expression in Piano-Playing." *Etude* 5, no. 8 (August 1887): 111-12.

————. "From Beethoven to Liszt." *Etude* 26, no. 7 (July 1908): 426-27.

————. "How to Practice" (essay delivered at the Music Teachers' National Convention, Cleveland, 2-4 July 1884). *Indicator* 5, nos. 13-14 (25 October, 1 November 1884): 13-14, 1. Also printed in *Etude* 2, nos. 11-12 (November, December 1884): 205-06, 213-14.

————. Letter to Henry Wadsworth Longfellow, 1876. Ms. Am 1340.2(1925), by permission of the Houghton Library, Harvard University.

————. Letter to John Sullivan Dwight, 3 March 1876. Boston Public Library.

————. *More Letters of Amy Fay: The American Years, 1879-1916.* Ed. S. Margaret William McCarthy. Detroit: Information Coordinators, 1986.

————. "Music in New York." *Music* 18, no. 12 (December 1900): 179-82.

————. *Music-Study in Germany.* Chicago: Jansen, McClurg & Co., 1881.

————. "The Royal Conservatory of Brussels." *Etude* 3, no. 8 (August 1885): 173.

————. "Some Suggestions." *Etude* 12, no. 12 (December 1894): 262.

————. "The Woman Music Teacher in a Large City." *Etude* 22, no. 1 (January 1902): 14.

————. "Women and Music." *Music* 18, no. 10 (October 1900): 505-07.

————. "Women and the Music Teachers' [National] Association." *Musical Courier* 46, no. 24 (17 June 1903): 30.

————, ed. and preface. *The Deppe Finger Exercises for Rapidly Developing an Artist's Touch in Piano Forte Playing.* Chicago: S. W. Straub Co., 1880.

Fay, C. Norman. "Memoirs of Rose Fay Thomas." Unpublished paper in Library of Congress, Washington, D.C.

Fay Family Papers. Schlesinger Library, Radcliffe College.

Finck, Henry T. *Golden Age of Music.* New York and London: Johnson Lane and Co., 1910.

————. "Employments Unsuitable for Women." *Independent,* 1 April 1901.

Gerig, Reginald. *Famous Pianists and Their Technique.* New York: Robert B. Luce, 1974.

Gleason, Frederic Grant. Diary. Courtesy of Frederic Grant Gleason Papers, Newberry Library, Chicago.

Gollerich, August. *Franz Liszts Klavierunterricht von 1884-1886 dargestellt an den Tagenbuch auf Zeiehnungen August Gollerich.* Regensburg: Gustav Bosse, 1975.

Graf, Max. *Composer and Critic.* New York: Norton, 1946.

Grove, George. Letter to Amy Fay, 16 July 1885. Courtesy of the Theodore Thomas Papers, Newberry Library, Chicago.

Harvard College Class of 1869 50th Anniversary, 11th Report. Cambridge: Riverside Press, 1919.

Higginson, Thomas W. *Old Cambridge.* New York: Macmillan, 1900.

Hitchcock, H. Wiley. *Music in the United States: A Historical Introduction.* 3rd ed. Englewood Cliffs, N.J.: Prentice Hall, 1988.

Hopkins, Charles Jerome. Diary, entry of 4 February 1866. Ms. Am 1993(20), by permission of the Houghton Library, Harvard University.

Hopkins, John H. *Autobiography in Verse, Dedicated to My Children.* Cambridge: Riverside Press, 1866.

James, William. Letter to Henry James, 12 December 1875. Ms. Am 1092.9(2596), by permission of the Houghton Library, Harvard University.

Johnson, George H. *One Branch of the Family Tree.* Columbus, Ohio: Champlin Press, 1913.

Kelly, Joan. *Women, History, and Theory.* Chicago: University of Chicago Press, 1984.

Lachmund, Carl. *Living with Liszt: From the Diary of Carl Lachmund, an American Pupil of Liszt, 1882-1884.* Ed. Alan Walker. Franz Liszt Studies Series, 4. Stuyvesant, N.Y.: Pendragon, 1995.

La Mara (pseud. for Ida Maria Lipsius). *Briefe hervorragender Zeitengnosses an Franz Liszt.* Leipzig: Breitkopf & Härtel, 1940.

Legbany, Dezsno. "Liszt's and Erkel's Relations and Students." *Studia musicologica academiae scientiarum hungaricae* 18 (1976): 19-50.

Letter from Charles Sanders Peirce to James Peirce, 10 December 1875. Peirce Family Papers, Ms. CSP (L 339), by permission of the Houghton Library, Harvard University.

Longfellow, Henry Wadsworth. Letters to Amy Fay, 28 February 1877, Ms. Am 1340.1(2361), and 8 February 1880, Ms. Am 1340.1(2575), by permission of the Houghton Library, Harvard University.

Loesser, Arthur. *Men, Women and Pianos.* New York: Simon and Schuster, 1954.

Mayhew-Simonds, Anna. "Letter from Germany." *Folio* 19, no. 10 (October 1880): 377.

Mathews, William S. B. *A Hundred Years of Music in America.* Chicago: G. L. Howe, 1889.

Max Fisch Papers. Courtesy of Peirce Edition Project, Indiana University-Purdue University at Indianapolis.

McCarthy, S. Margaret William. "Amy Fay: The American Years." *American Music* 3, no. 1 (spring 1985): 52-62.

————. "Amy Fay's Reunions with Franz Liszt." *Journal of the American Liszt Society* 24 (July-December 1988): 23-32.

————. "Feminist Theory in Practice in the Life of Amy Fay." *International League of Women Composers Journal*, December 1991, 9-12.

McCoy, Guy. *Portraits of the World's Best Women Musicians.* Philadelphia: Theodore Presser, 1946.

Miller, Jean Baker. "Toward a New Psychology of Women." In *Women's Spirituality: Resources for Christian Development*, ed. Joann Wolski Conn, 107-27. New York: Paulist Press, 1986.

Morin, Raymond. *The Worcester Music Festival: Its Background and History, 1858-1946.* Worcester, Mass.: County Musical Association, 1946.

Moses, John, and Joseph Kirkland. *History of Chicago.* Chicago: Munsel and Co., 1895.

Murphy, Lucy E. "Business Ladies: Midwestern Women and Enterprise, 1850-1880." *Journal of Women's History* 3, no. 1 (spring 1991): 65-89.

National Convention of Women's Amateur Clubs. *History in the Making.* Chicago: Stromberg, Allen & Co., 1983.

The New Grove Dictionary of American Music. 4 vols. London: Macmillan, 1986.

Nohl, Louis. *Life of Liszt.* Transl. from the German by George P. Upton. Chicago: Jansen, McClurg Co., 1884.

Notable American Women: A Biographical Dictionary. Ed. Edward and Janice James and Paul Boyers. Cambridge: Belknap Press of Harvard University Press, 1971.

Otis, Percy. *The Chicago Symphony Orchestra.* Chicago: Clayton F. Summy Co., 1924.

Peirce Family Papers, Ms. CSP (L 339), by permission of the Houghton Library, Harvard University.

Peirce, Melusina Fay. *Co-Operative Housekeeping: How to Do It and How Not to Do It.* Boston: James R. Osgood and Co., 1884.

———— (pseud., Zero). *The Democratic Party: A Political Study by a Political Zero.* Cambridge: John Wilson & Sons, 1875.

_____. *The Landmark of Fraunces' Tavern: A Retrospect.* New York: Women's Auxiliary, American Scenic and Historic Preservation Society, 1901.

_____. "Musical Hours in Weimar with the Pianists of the Future." *Boston Daily Advertiser*, 3 and 20 June 1876.

_____. "The Pianists of the Future and His Disciples: Musical Hours in Weimar." *Boston Daily Advertiser*, 28 April 1876.

_____. *New York: A Symphonic Study.* New York: Neale Publishing Co., 1918.

Pierce, Bessie L. *A History of Chicago.* Chicago: University of Chicago Press, 1957.

Randall, Richard R. "Boston, Dwight, and Pianists of Nineteenth Century America: The European Connection." D.M.A. diss., University of Colorado, 1984.

Rehage, Kenneth J. "Music in Chicago, 1871-1893." M.A. thesis, University of Chicago, 1935.

Rice, Franklin P. *The Worcester Book: A Diary of Noteworthy Events in Worcester, Massachusetts from 1657-1883.* Worcester: Putnam, Davis and Co., 1884.

Ritter, Fanny Raymond. *Woman as a Musician.* New York: Edward Shuberth & Co., 1876.

Rogers, Clara Kathleen. *Memoirs of a Musical Career.* Boston: Little, Brown & Co., 1919.

Russell, Charles Edward. *The American Orchestra and Theodore Thomas.* Garden City, N.Y.: Doubleday, Page and Co., 1927.

Ryan, Thomas. *Recollections of an Old Musician.* New York: E. P. Dutton and Co., 1899.

Schabas, Ezra. *Theodore Thomas: America's Conductor and Builder of Orchestras, 1835-1905.* Urbana: University of Illinois Press, 1989.

Schonberg, Harold C. "Amy Fay and the Abbé Liszt." *American Music Lover* 7, no. 1 (September 1940): 7-10.

_____. *The Great Pianists.* 2nd ed. New York: Simon and Schuster, 1987.

Shenker, Israel. "A Thinker's Thinker Is Honored Belatedly." *New York Times*, 12 October 1976, 37.

Sixth Triennial Report of the Secretary of the Class of 1869 of Harvard College. Boston: Rockwell and Churchill, 1888.

Smith, Cecil. *Worlds of Music.* Philadelphia: J. B. Lippincott, 1952.

Smith-Rosenberg, Carroll. *Disorderly Conduct.* New York: Oxford University Press, 1985.

Solomon, Barbara. *In the Company of Educated Women*. New Haven: Yale University Press, 1985.

Spalding, Walter R. *Music at Harvard: A Historical Review of Men and Events*. New York: Coward-McCann, 1935; reprint, New York: Da Capo, 1977.

Stevenson, Robert. "Liszt's Favorite California Pupil, Hugo Mansfeldt (1844-1932)." *Inter-American Review* 7, no. 2 (spring-summer 1986): 33-78.

Strouse, Jean. *Alice James: A Biography*. Boston: Houghton Mifflin Co., 1980.

Sutro, Florence C. *Women in Music and Law*. New York: Author's Publishing Co., 1895.

Thomas, Rose Fay. "History in the Making." Paper given at the first session of the National Convention of Women's Amateur Clubs held in Recital Hall-Music Building, World's Columbian Exposition, Wednesday, 21 June 1893. In *National Convention of Women's Amateur Clubs*. Chicago: Stromberg, Allen & Co., 1883.

_____. *Memoirs of Rose Thomas*. New York: Moffat, Yard & Co., 1911.

_____. *Our Country Garden*. New York: Macmillan, 1904.

Tracy, James. "Personal Recollections of Liszt" (part 1 of 2-part article). *Folio* 4, no. 3 (February 1871): 31.

Upton, George P. *Woman in Music*. 1880. Rev. ed. Chicago: A. C. McClurg and Co., 1886.

Woloch, Nancy. *Women and the American Experience*. New York: Alfred A. Knopf, 1984.

Wood, Elizabeth. "Women in Music: A Review Essay." *Signs* 6, no. 2 (winter 1980): 283-97.

Young, Percy. *George Grove: A Biography*. London: Macmillan, 1980.

INDEX

Index

About the Author

MARGARET WILLIAM MCCARTHY, C.S.J., *is professor of music at Regis College in Weston, Massachusetts. She has earned degrees from Manhattanville College (New York), Pius XII Institute (Florence, Italy), and holds the D.M.A. in piano from Boston University. She is a member of the Sonneck Society for American Music, the American Liszt Society, the International Alliance for Women in Music, and the American Musicological Society. Her writings appear in* American Music, Black Perspective in Music, Clavier, College Music Symposium, Journal of the American Liszt Society, *and the* New Grove Dictionary of American Music. *In 1986 her book* More Letters of Amy Fay: The American Years, 1879-1916, *was published by Information Coordinators (now Harmonie Park Press). She has contributed several entries on musical personalities (including Amy Fay) to the forthcoming* American National Biography, *to be published by Oxford University Press under the auspices of the American Council of Learned Societies. Since 1954 she has been a member of the Sisters of St. Joseph of Boston.*